The world does not need another "how to" book, with ten easy steps to make your marriage work. (If the marriage relationship functioned that way, surely the spate of such books in recent years would have solved all our problems.) What we could use, though, is a book of wisdom, compassion, and piercing honesty, and that is precisely what Walter Wangerin has given us. He and his wife dare to use themselves as examples throughout. The bits of wisdom they have gleaned from their own pilgrimage, and from years in the pastorate, always come wrapped in a story, told with the fine narrative style that has become Wangerin's trademark.

Philip Yancey
Author of *Where Is God When It Hurts?*
and *Fearfully and Wonderfully Made*

Walter Wangerin is, quite possibly, the best writer of Christian literature we have, easily the equal of C. S. Lewis. In the words of his high school English teacher, "Wangerin can write the eyes out of a turkey at fifty paces"—and he does so with such astonishing Holy-Spiritedness that even a turkey must be brought to his knees.

These thoughts on marriage, like all his other work, sparkle with a unique blend of compassionate wisdom, energy, gentle faith, and startling originality.

Mike Mason
Author of *The Mystery of Marriage*

Walter Wangerin has written a book that is easy to read, yet powerful in its content. His book should be read by couples contemplating marriage, as well as by those who have been married for a number of years.

Wangerin speaks from experience, and his sharing with the reader the experiences that have shaped his own life provides valuable tools that can be used by those who marry and those who counsel them.

This is a book to be read and to be shared by those who take the permanency of the marriage contract seriously.

Rev. Theodore M. Hesburgh, C.S.C.
President, University of Notre Dame

Walter Wangerin writes redemptively and with an intensely personal touch. His insights about marriage are fresh, yet orthodox, loving, yet realistic.

Harold Myra
President, Christianity Today, Inc.

As For Me And My House

Other Books by Walter Wangerin, Jr.

Walter Wangerin, Jr.

AS FOR ME AND MY HOUSE

Crafting your marriage to last

Thomas Nelson Publishers
Nashville • Camden • Kansas City

Published in Nashville, Tennessee, by Thomas Nelson, Inc., and
distributed in Canada by Lawson Falle, Ltd., Cambridge, Ontario.

Printed in the United States of America.

Scripture quotations are from the Revised Standard Version of the
Bible, copyrighted 1946, 1952, © 1971, 1973 by the Division of
Christian Education of the National Council of the Churches of
Christ in the U.S.A. and used by permission.

ISBN 0-8407-5475-2

4   5   6—91   90   89   88

Library of Congress Cataloging-in-Publication Data

Wangerin, Walter.
    As for me and my house.

    1. Marriage—Religious aspects—Christianity.
2. Wangerin, Walter. 3. Wangerin, Thanne. I. Title.
BV835.W36   1987   248.4   87-5724
ISBN 0-8407-5475-2

Whenever I write, dear Thanne, whatever I write,
I write for you.

CONTENTS

·ONE·

WHEN DOES MARRIAGE BEGIN?

Introducing Marriage, Thanne, and Mortal Fears

*B*y Christmas, 1967, I not only did, but I also knew that I did, love Thanne. On New Year's Eve, then, 1967, such knowledge and such loving pitched me headlong into a crisis wherein I suffered a blindness, from which I arose—married.

Do you suppose the experience is a common one?

I had been courting Thanne Bohlmann in the old-fashionedest way for a full year, myself in perfect control of the progress of our relationship, congratulating myself for cool control. On May 2, 1967, I had written in my diary: "I have found the woman I intend to marry. Nothing has been said to her, nor shall anything be said until the time is right. She'll know before I speak, however, because I intend consciously to court the woman. No. As yet I don't love her with a marrying love—but I will. I'll be courting both Thanne and my love . . ."

Thus wrote a young man of supernal self-confidence, absolutely ignorant of the crisis he was preparing for himself and the anguish to come at New Year's Eve, the end of that same year. So I wrote my perfectly emotionless strategem in perfectly chiseled sentences in my diary—and so I began.

I sent a stream of letters from my university in Oxford, Ohio, to Thanne's in Milwaukee, Wisconsin, seeking to dazzle her with sunlight on my liquid language. This was my tool, that I could write. I philosophized, poeticized, postured, theologized, and generally drew a favorable portrait of myself in my own words. I spent the summer at my parents' house in Chicago, writing my master's thesis and junketing northward to Milwaukee in a beaten VW bug, there to visit Thanne, to talk with her, to watch her slantwise when she didn't know that I was watching, to assess our progress and to be, for her, a significant person. Oh, I withheld myself from her those days in a holy decorum—for three reasons. First, Thanne still suffered from an earlier rejection and was acutely suspicious of the motives of men. I could handle that. Second, I was myself waiting to feel a "marrying" (as I said) love for her—and I could handle the wait until I did. And third, I was in control of the situation. I was handling *everything*. Therefore, by the end of the summer I had done this: I had taken her hand as we walked on the shores of Lake Michigan; and I had drawn her portrait with soft pencils on expensive paper; and I had kissed her—once.

I wrote in my diary, "I will love her. I will." And I wrote, "God help me in my courting and her in her understanding. Amen."

My VW was a yellow convertible which I called Hadrian for the vast, triumphal traveling that it did. In October Hadrian and I drove to the farm in Illinois where Thanne grew up—again, there to meet her for a weekend.

The farmer's daughter. It was a wonder how easily Thanne fit to a country landscape, how familiar she and the black earth were, one with the other. Her spirit *was* the autumn air, and her forehead as smooth as the sky.

She had a younger sister named Dorothy who would live forever with their parents, who chose not to talk, and who got away with that because she had Down's syndrome. Whether or not anyone else in the family knew that I was courting Thanne, Dorothy knew—and she was not sure she approved. Dorothy, soft as dough; Dorothy, broad in the buttocks, no taller than she was wide; Dorothy, whose face was as unreadable as an empty plate; Dorothy, whose eyes slanted at the corners, made her doubts known, nonetheless, by her actions.

After supper Saturday night Thanne and I retired to the back porch, to the evening breezes and a chill October snap, to a fine old creaking hanging swing from which to watch the sunset together—a perfect place for courting. Do you know how close two people can feel when the round horizon seems so distant and burns so beautiful? They imagine they are an outpost, and they want to protect each other in the universe. So Thanne and I sat side by side, preparing to gaze across the fields now harvested, stiff and stubbled like animal fur. I had just begun to consider some nonsense we might murmur—

—when the screen door spronged open, hung fire a moment, then banged shut; and there stood little-large, retarded Dorothy directly in front, blocking the view, and staring at us. No, staring at *me*. Silent as a plate. All the nonsense fled my mind, and something of the romantic possibilities drained from the situation. Tenderness feels foolish in front of an audience which is not smiling.

I smiled. Dorothy did not. I nodded. Dorothy did not. The sun sank a little. The wild blew. Leaves flew out of a tree like birds.

And when I did not remove my body from Thanne's, Dorothy seemed to be seized by an inspiration. She turned to face the fields, presenting us with the continent of her bottom; then she herself sat down, presumably to share the sunset. But since there was no space between us, she wriggled and bumped her big hips left and right—all in a perfectly serene silence—and made the space we hadn't given her, dividing her sister from the man who, if he wished to court, would have to do it over Dorothy's peremptory body.

It was then that I heard Thanne laugh.

Dear God, how sudden, sweet, and free was that laughter! It took me by surprise, like an epiphany, and my control slipped in the instant. I looked at the laughing Thanne, whose eyes were damp and closed. I gaped across the Buddha between us, and lost my breath in awe. *Oh, Ruthanne, how you do laugh!*

But I took charge of things again, almost immediately. I suggested that Thanne and I go riding sisterless in Hadrian. Thanne agreed, and Dorothy had the swing to herself.

In the dusk we drove along the one-lane roads of Iroquois County, farmhouses shining an orange light from their windows as though all were warm contentment within. Ragged snatches of fog lay low in the fields. I kept the car top down because I love the feel and the smell of the crushed October air, the promissory cold; but Thanne sat with her knees drawn up to her chin, her legs covered by a great sweater, her arms wrapped around her shins. I began to notice, above the thick knit and the collar of the sweater, her mouth. There was something precious about it. When she smiled, she had a mouth like—

Suddenly, "There!" she said, gazing straight ahead.

"What?"

"There. Do you see it? Switch off the lights," she said. "Do you see it?"

I stopped Hadrian and turned off the lights, and the earth was dark, and the sky deep grey.

Thanne whispered with a holiness in her voice, "There. There is the Lantern, wandering—wandering and looking. Doesn't he make you sad?"

The moment made me something, not so much sad as filled with a sweet sense of mystery, sharpened by the fact that Thanne and I were alone and together and whispering like children or like spies.

"Do you see it?" she whispered.

Floating in the gloom ahead of us was a pale, nearly shapeless light, a luminescence, a cold-burning globe shoulder-high above the road. I saw it.

"Will-o'-the-wisp," I whispered.

But Thanne said softly, "No. No." She was considering the thing that hung in front of us. "No, it's the Lantern. He carried it out when he was lost. He's carrying it still"—her eyes gazing, full of a rural faith and sorrow. "Drive forward."

Slowly I let the car creep forward toward the luminous shadow.

"He was a farmer," Thanne whispered, "caught in the barn when a thunderstorm hit the land. He waited, but the thunder kept crashing and the rain never stopped. Finally he dashed for the house, so they say. It was pitch-black night. He found that all his children were missing. All of them. So he took a lantern—"

As we rolled forward, the light seemed to recede and bashfully to grow uncertain.

"He went out into that wild night," Thanne whispered, "crying for his children. He never came home again. Everything was just as it was, except that the Lantern was gone."

Gone, indeed! Just before we reached it, the floating light vanished, and the night seemed very empty.

"Wait, wait!" said Thanne. "Keep driving." And she sang softly on one note, "Here-comes-a-candle-to-light-you-to-bed." In a moment she turned fully round in the car seat and whispered, "See?"

I turned too, and there behind us hung the glimmering Lantern—perpetually sad, forever lonely, never to be found nor ever to find his children again. I was moved. Yes, yes—sad.

But then Thanne sang in a sing-song voice, this time looking straight at me, "Here-comes-a-chopper-to-chop-off-your-head."

Thanne? She was smiling. It was an imp's smile. And laughter bubbled just behind it. Thanne? For the second time in a single night I felt a rush of surprise for this woman who was revealing tricks and mysteries in her being that I had not even suspected. Such a tiny, innocent mouth; but when she smiled one tooth peeped through, and it looked like a chipmunk's mouth, the mouth of some canny, natural creature, quick and burrowing. Thanne? In a kind of helplessness I reached and touched her cheek, as cool as October—but my touch was no surprise to her at all. She hardly blinked. She put her hand on mine.

I did not, that autumn evening, record it in my diary, because I didn't recognize it then, though it was true from that night on: I loved Thanne. In spite of all my plans and strategems, the woman had called love out of me, and I loved her.

Yet, when I took account of the progress of things, when I sat in my Oxford apartment in meditations, surrounded by my books, I smiled a smile of self-satisfaction. Ask me: who was in control? Who was directing this relationship with a wise and watchful understanding? Smug, young Walter! In those days I would have answered, modestly, "Me."

Here was a boy, on the one hand ignorant, on the other hand all unprepared for the crisis still to come. This boy went forth prepared to be a hero.

Once more Thanne and I met that fall. We shared a picnic in a park, and then went walking. She wore an autumn jacket and the quizzical smile that had begun to fascinate me, two lines descending from her nose to the small corners of her mouth. Beside me, the woman was short. I liked that. Her shoes were tiny, swishing leaves—and her hair lifted so meekly to the wind that I felt myself swell with importance, her "protector." I felt that it was my fine office to protect her against the cruel or evil agents of this world. I strolled gladly beside her, then strongly in front of her. So able was I, in those days!

Deep in the park there appeared a hollow stump ahead of us. Now, with Thanne nearby my senses were so keen that I observed everything, every little detail of our universe. Therefore, I glanced inside the rot-cavity of that stump.

Immediately, I felt a flood of anger for some nameless vagrant. I took very personally what he had done in that tree stump—precisely because Thanne was here and might see it.

"Thanne," I commanded. "Don't look in there."

I was protecting her.

How could anyone be so indecent as to offend both society and Thanne's delicacy by leaving his singularly long feces in a public stump? I imagined the nighttime squatting of that bum, and I hated him whom I imagined, for Thanne's sake. But then I comforted myself with the thought that I had seen his vile excretion first and had saved her eyes the assault. I walked on. No, I strutted on triumphantly—

—until I heard behind me a perfectly helpless burst of laughter.

I whirled around. "Thanne?"

She was standing by the stump, holding her stomach and laughing till the tears ran down her cheeks. "Ohhh! Ohhh!" she gasped. "Saving me, were you? From what?" All at once she bent down and horrified me by running her hand inside the stump.

"Thanne!"

What she drew forth was a long, brown, curving pine cone. And she laughed.

If you had asked me, in those days, who was in control, who was managing the progress of our relationship, I think I still would have found evidence to support the lingering conviction that it was I. I think I would have referred to the letter Thanne wrote me several weeks after that last meeting. But now I think that this was a failing conviction within me, for that letter produced a confusion of feelings, some good, some frightened, and some so deep I could not name them. Loving, it began to appear, isn't simple after all, but dreadfully complicated.

"I am angry," Thanne wrote. "And I'm scared." These are her own words. "You told me once you'd be careful with me, Wally. I hope to God you have been, because it's too late for me to say 'I won't.' It's too late."

She went on to describe the date she had had with another man. She said he had been kind, interesting, and intelligent. She should have enjoyed the evening, but she could think of no one but me. She declared this to be unfair to her friend—and I felt accused. How curiously Thanne presented the thing, the marvelous thing, I'd planned for since last May.

"I don't know if I want to love you," she wrote. "I know I don't ever want to hurt again the way I did before. I hate the weakness. I do *not* like to be vulnerable. But I love you, and there it is. What are you going to do about it?"

There it was.

All my feelings—all of them, however contradictory they were—shot to heat intensity. *Satisfaction;* I had done it! A purely childlike *joy* in this, that I was loved, that Thanne loved me. But *fear,* because I didn't understand the strength or the nature of her passion; and again *fear,* because I hadn't done it at all. No, not at all, but some force greater than mine had been loosed between us, and where would that take us in the end? Woven through all these feelings, on account of them all, was *bewilderment;* and I was a boy again indeed.

Thanne surely had a capacity to surprise.

What, she asked, was I going to do about it? I didn't know. Not truly. Yet I did know that there was now an urgency about my loving her. No, you smug, young Walter, it never was, not even from the beginning, a light, inconsequential game that you were playing. It has always been a drama of the gravest consequence—emotional, physical, spiritual consequence. Walk carefully, carefully.

After her letter I confided a prayer to my diary. "But I *have* courted her," I wrote. "Not so fervently as I might have, nor yet so blandly as to ask nothing (though closer to the latter). Only, she was more responsive than my own heart." And I prayed, "Dear Lord, in my coolness I said she would be right to marry. Now let me say so in my ardor."

Loving wasn't simple at all. And even when one had predicted it accurately, one hadn't predicted it truly.

But what was I going to do about it? Well, this much I knew—that we would spend Christmas together at my parents' house in Chicago. And then—

But then in Chicago, this is what happened: while we shared those holidays together, the thought that had, till then, existed in my diary now took up a persistent dwelling in my mind. Like a physical sensation it needled my heart: *I could marry Thanne.* How strange! It felt, each time it seized me, like a perfectly new proposition, never truly considered before. Whenever I smelled her flesh, or felt the minimal degree of warmth that enveloped her, or glanced at her: *I could marry this one.* Compulsive thought.

Thanne has a chipmunk's grin. She dips her head (bright eyes! bright eyes!) and allows just the flashing edge of that front tooth its epiphany between her lips. The mouth is small, the chin so small she seems always to be tucking it into her neck, making her spine erect and her posture royal. She giggles high inside her throat. It is as if the punch line of some celestial joke were ever kept a private thing inside of her, for her sole pleasure alone. And then she laughs, and that is a wonder.

It snowed that Christmas. We walked through the snowfall. She giggled. She grinned like a chipmunk. I glanced at her and thought, *I should marry Thanne.*

But how well did I know this woman?

Thanne cries—except under the heaviest grief—silently. She cried that Christmas, once. In the naked wood along the Des Plaines River, standing lost in a gauze of falling snow, watching black water, she began to cry. There are golden carp in that river, three times the size of goldfish. They shadow just beneath the surface in slow schools. Do golden carp make women cry? I don't know. I shall never know why, silently, the tears began to roll down Thanne's cheeks; for all my asking I earned not a word from her. She stood on a snow bank, on a river bank, not looking at me, touching cold tears from her cheeks, hidden in some secret sorrow. But I thought, as I watched her, *I should marry this one.*

Thanne had knit a bulky green sweater herself, then given it to me for Christmas. I wore her sweater three days straight, delighting in the very intimacy of the gift. I had the exquisite sense that the fingers which had looped and stitched each knot of the sweater were brushing my skin, stroking me from my neck to the small of my back. Ah, Thanne! And look: totally unaware of her gift, I had bought Thanne a sweater, too, pure white and warm! Oh, it seemed to me an auspicious conjunction of our minds. *I truly ought,* I thought, *to marry Thanne.* Two sweaters on the selfsame Christmas! It was an absolutely convincing argument for marriage.

But then, the last days of the holiday, just before I was to return to Oxford, the crisis came down on me like a deadfall. The odd thing was that it was not sudden. I should have seen it coming, since it was caused by our selves, by our native limitations, and had been hanging over each detail of our relationship from the beginning. But crises come of things not seen. It dropped, dropping me—and I suffered a blindness not unlike Paul's on the route to Damascus.

When does the marriage begin?

The most important question is, "What is marriage?" But if you want to know what a person truly considers marriage to be, ask him first when he thinks it begins, for then he will answer you in concrete terms and not vague platitudes. Find the point of its true beginning (when everything which defines it is in place and working), and you have found its definition.

So, when does a marriage begin?

Not when two people fall in love with one another. Love (though it may be an overwhelming inducement, finally, to marry) does not make a marriage. At that point each may feel an intense commitment to the other, but that commitment is not independent of feelings. Rather, it's founded on nothing *but* feelings—and feelings are as unstable as water, while marriage is the establishment of stability itself in a relationship. Feelings come and go. Marriage is meant to endure *in spite of* them.

Neither does marriage begin when two people first "make love" to one another. Either the sexual act is the sweet physical completion of their joining; or else (in this sadly sinful world) it is an act that satisfies goals and desires more immediate than enduring. Sex blesses—but it does not make—a marriage.

Then when does marriage begin?

Surely, not at the engagement. We no longer make as much of the betrothal as the culture did in Christ's time, when it was a legal but unconsummated binding, or as people did in matches made by parents, when the practical decisions of guardians were more important than the heart's choice. Today, engagements are promises to make a promise and are not especially binding. The period is precontractual, a testing-time when partners plan, keep themselves from other involvements, and put on their best faces for their fiancés.

Nor (this we argue with vigor) does marriage begin when two people set up housekeeping together—"move in" together. If that occurs before a public wedding, it's like starting a job without a contract: there are no secure assurances, and one might be fired on a whim, at a change in the economy, for spite, or for expedience. One is compelled to trust in the sheer goodness of the other; but the world is sinful, and the entire judicial system is based upon the principle that people are not good. Too often, his "good" is your evil; what's "good" for her exhausts you; or "goodness" for one depends entirely upon the fulfillment of his own desires—failing that, you're fired.

So when does the marriage begin? Was it "made in heaven" even before the couple met and smiled on one another? Did God do it, fating them to live together and to love, and they but helpless leaves before the winds of his almighty purposes? Was it, then, their destiny?

That sounds romantic and devout. And couples are pleased, sometimes, to speak in such celestial terms: it seems to assure the course of their marriage forever (how *right* it must be, if God created it!); or it lays to rest any arguments that others might bring against their relationship. (How can mother, father, friends, or the bride's own soul then defy the purposes of Almighty God?)

But it also ignores the couple's own responsibility, both for their present relationship and for their future lives; and such thinking is, therefore, fatal, allowing emotions, now sanctified, to take over where wise and responsible and self-sacrificial judgment should rule. No, not God, but the two people marrying themselves make their marriage, consciously, freely, independently.

When, then? When, after all, does the marriage begin?

Can we be precise about a thing so spiritual? Can we be specific about a relationship so complicated that much of it happens unconsciously?

Can we fix that moment and say, "There! There is the clear beginning of this marriage"? Yes, we can—because that moment is *meant* to be historical (as well as spiritual) and is to be remembered for the rest of the couple's lives; because it *must* be accomplished consciously, in full knowledge of the implications that follow upon it; and because its very purpose is to *change* the relationship from one of accidental growth to one of careful conviction and responsible stability and trustworthy promises.

Marriage Begins with the Vow

Listen: marriage begins when two people make the clear, unqualified promise to be faithful, each to the other, until the end of their days. That spoken promise makes the difference. A new relationship is initiated. Marriage begins when each vows to commit herself, himself, unto the other and to no other human in this world: "I promise you my faithfulness, until death parts us." That vow, once spoken, once heard, permits a new, enduring trust: each one may trust the vow of the other one. And that vow forms the foundation of the relationship to be built upon it hereafter.

A promise made, a promise witnessed, a promise heard, remembered, and trusted—this is the groundwork of marriage. Not emotions. No, not even love. Not physical desires or personal needs or sexuality. Not the practical fact of living together. Not even the piercing foresight or some peculiar miracle of All-seeing God. Rather, a promise, a vow, makes the marriage.

"I promise you my faithfulness, until death parts us."

Here is a marvelous work, performed by those who are made in the image of God—for we create, in this promise, a new thing, a changeless stability in an ever-changing world. We do the thing that God does, establishing a covenant with another human being: we ask faith in our faithfulness *to* that covenant. We transfigure the relationship thereafter, transfiguring ourselves, for we shape our behaviors by the covenant. A new ethic has begun for each of us. We have called forth a spiritual house in which each of us may dwell securely. Whether we know it or not, it is a divine thing we do, and it is holy.

After Christmas I drove Thanne to the La Grange train depot. Hadrian got a speeding ticket on the way. I promised to see her once more before returning to Oxford, on New Year's Day, then gave her a good farewell and watched her board for Milwaukee. I drove home slowly, and sank into such a brooding meditation that my family feared for me.

Five days. I had five days. Five days were hardly enough. What do you think: can someone decide a whole life in five days?

Four days. I fried eggs I did not eat. I watched shadows on the television screen. I walked to the Des Plaines River, saw golden carp in muddy water, and wondered what Thanne's tears signified. Thick and murky was the Des Plaines; fish four inches deep were hidden altogether; God only knew what dwelt in the depths, and civilized people never even considered reaching in, or wading in, or jumping in to find out. But I was seriously considering the question of whether to marry Thanne—whose tears were like the golden carp.

Three days. Two days—and this is the truth: I grew so nervous that I could not smile. I had an urgent question. I had a question of tremendous consequences. But my question had no answer.

On New Year's Eve Day I looked plain sick. I prowled the house in solitude, received no friends, resisted parties, called no one, settled nowhere, not even in front of the TV. By midnight I was pacing the living room, thinking, thinking, rushing back and forth and thinking. I put Beethoven's Seventh Symphony on the stereo and played it at the level of sonic boom. The music matched my mood, rising from still meditations to explosive exaltations—while I hurtled the length of the living room, wringing my hands, blowing sighs, and thinking: *Should I marry Thanne? Should I? But what if—?*

I neither went to bed nor slept that night. And I received no answers. The God who remembered Gideon with signs, who revealed Rebekah by means of a sign, who relieved the uncertainty of Joseph in a dream—that God had forgotten me.

At dawn, then, haunted like some fated Greek, I haunched into Hadrian, bade my parents farewell, and drove through a light snowfall to my destiny. My parents waved and waved behind me, though I hadn't breathed a word of what I meant to do (not knowing myself what I meant to do). They waved solemnly until they were swallowed by the snow. I think they thought I was riding to war, so grimly did I go.

That snow—it would snow all day and all night long. The snow of the New Year, 1968, is memorable in three states. But that morning I was hardly aware of it while driving Hadrian to the north, raising clouds behind me. I hardly noticed that the weather was a perfect paradigm of my own mental state: for the snows white out the distances, and I was blind to the future, and that was my crisis. If I asked Thanne to marry me, if Thanne accepted, then we were binding ourselves together for life. Life! All choices were canceled by that act. *Dear God, what sort of life was this to be?* Such predestinating decisions shouldn't be made without some preknowledge, should they? Was this wise or dangerous, good or bad? To make a proper decision I ought to know that. But to know that I needed some vision of the future, and the future was lost in snows of ignorance.

Yet I loved Thanne. We'd given each other sweaters for Christmas gifts. That was significant, wasn't it?

The woman met me at the door of her apartment. She was wearing her woolen sweater, small-boned, smooth, and beautiful within the knit. Oh, Thanne!—comfortably, casually, effortlessly perfect, and at peace! Where did she get the grace, when I had to work so hard at things?

For her sake I painted a smile on my face. "Hel-lo, Thanne." I stalked past her, grinning below ghastly eyes, haggard and happy at once, my hands thrust into my pockets.

"Hello," she said, so perfectly. She had no idea what was in my head.

I did, you know. I loved Thanne.

The nail of her forefinger, her slender right hand, had a tiny corrugation in its center, a row of ridges that made my thumbnail buzz when I ran its tip across them. I knew Thanne so well. I didn't know Thanne at all.

Now the snow that was my veil became my timekeeper, too. As long as it kept falling, it shortened the time I had in Milwaukee—because I had to be in Oxford the following day. *Go, go, hurry up, speak and go,* it whispered at the windows. Speak! But what was I to say?

Thanne and I sat side by side on the sofa, she with her legs caught up beneath a green skirt, I with my feet planted wide apart, my elbows on my knees, my jaw in my hands, staring forward. Perhaps she was waiting for me to say something. I, for my part, was praying. I was pleading God for some picture, some guarantee. I was staring as hard as I could into 1968, 1969. This is the truth. I wanted to see the Thanne of two years hence, to see the person she *would be,* because that was the one I would be living with, not the one beside me—with her bright and laughing eyes! I was praying so hard that I sweat. I was asking to know the person I *would be,* and whether the Walt-to-come would be treacherous to these bright eyes, this chipmunk's grin, or good and nourishing for her. *Oh, please, dear Lord—show me the future!*

I was scared.

And this is the truth: I saw nothing whatsoever of the future. God might have smiled then; but God was keeping his own counsel. Walt stood on the black edge of a precipice, about to take one step forward, totally ignorant of the terrain, whether he would walk into an Eden, or else pitch headlong to his death.

Like an infuriating cat's paw the snowflakes brushed the windowpane.

And then it came as a shock to both of us that my mouth betrayed my common sense, not even consulting good reason whether it should speak or not. "Well, for heaven's sake, Thanne," I blurted, "do you think that you should marry me?"

We approach the wedding with fear. Is this right or common?

Why, most common (though perhaps the picture I've drawn is somewhat exaggerated by the hyperbolical quality of my own character)—made common both by the nature of the contract and by the nature of the world. Knowing the totality of this commitment to a spouse as well as that it is irrevocable, but knowing little or nothing of the future in which the commitment is to be lived out, men and women may righteously tremble at the wedding. It's normal to be afraid. The fear is caused by the nature of the contract we make with one another: "I will be faithful to you unto death."

The Four Characteristics of the Marriage Contract

This promise has two characteristics unique among human contracts; and it *ought* to have two more which the spouses bring spiritually to its making.

1. It is one's *total* commitment unto another. It is comprehensive, and that's why its language seems vague in comparison to other contracts: I promise my whole self to you; all that I am or shall be is now bound to you—and because I promise "all," there is neither need nor ability to list the multitudinous details of my self. "I promise you my faithfulness" is not vague after all, but grandly inclusive.

2. It is one's *timeless* commitment unto another. Time does not affect the contract. Time should neither change nor conclude it. In fact, the covenant's very purpose is to establish a surety, a bank, a wall, a dike against the dizzy, destructive batterings and evolvements of time. "Until death parts us" declares that though all other things shall change (*because* all things else do change, causing dreadful uncertainty in this world) this one thing shall persist to comfort you; this shall be a trustworthy stay against confusion, this marriage of ours, this covenant of mine.

As soon as conditions are introduced into the promise, it ceases to be timeless. It allows for an ending. As soon as someone says, "I will be faithful to you *so long as*—" What? "So long as it is expedient for me—"? Or "you remain faithful to me—"? Or "I haven't found a better relationship elsewhere—"? Or "We continue satisfied together—"? then the unique value of this contract is absolutely lost. It is no longer a special harbor in high seas, no longer a promise worth consecrating, but a contract like all others of human society and of no peculiar comfort. "Until death parts us" has the faithfulness of the divine. It makes a home for the vulnerable, besieged, and worried heart. But a qualification like "so long as it is good for us" invites all the fears of impermanence. Who will decide what "goodness" means? According to what principles? This covenant must *become* the principle of the relationship thereafter and be its abiding standard. It must be timeless, undiluted by time. It must by its very nature stand against the changings of time.

For these two reasons—that it is total and timeless—marriage is marvelous and holy; that's why we marry with a glad, nearly unspeakable excitement. We surround the event with ceremony. Breathlessly we appeal unto God for blessing. We grow giddy and laugh. We invite more friends than we thought we had; they celebrate with us. We *act* differently now than we usually do, and no one blames us because this thing is so different from common human experience. Even people of an unremarkable faith will feel the need of a "church" wedding, and gruff men cry for happiness.

Yet, that isn't the whole of our feelings up against the wedding, is it? Grown men also tremble, don't they? And women lock themselves in bathrooms.

We approach the wedding with fear, and it isn't just stage fright that weakens our knees. No, some come to the speaking and the hearing of this covenant plain afraid. Why is that? Is it right or common?

Most common. And perhaps it can't be helped. Look again at the two characteristics that make this contract unique—total commitment, timeless commitment—and realize that they occur within a world which is sinful and time-bound. The environment of the vow makes the vow seem hazardous after all.

My total commitment unto another includes not only my worth and goodness, but also my weaknesses and my sinful tendencies. Will I, who fail so often, be able to keep covenant with my spouse in all things? Do I bring her more trouble than treasure? Moreover, what infirmities does my spouse bring to the marriage and to me, since I get the whole mix, the good and the bad together? Never, never did we marry just the piece of a human being—even though it's only bits and pieces we see before the marriage. We marry the other one whole. But always we buy the package before we can open it.

And if the commitment is to be timeless, if I'm bound no matter what the future brings, then my ignorance of that future may terrify me; for here at the wedding I stand peering into darkness, seeing nothing, yet depending for my life upon what is to be. What?—the world will change, but I must not?

Therefore, let two other characteristics attend the marriage contract besides the two already named. Without these next two (which we must choose for ourselves since they are not as intrinsic to the contract as are its totality and its timelessness) we are reckless children indeed to marry. Without them we gamble our lives and our peace with poor odds in a wedding.

3. *Faith.* This is no Christian whimsy, the proper, holy, and expected thing to say. This is a critical necessity, that we have faith in the God who loves the both of us, who encourages such a relationship as marriage, and who is above time. It is only in God that we do touch the future after all, even if we cannot know it, for God embraces in his own knowing the present and the future together: he who is here with us now, as we begin the

relationship, is also, now, at every anniversary of that relationship until we die. He is at the birthing of our children, blessing the event. He is at the tragedies to come (but he's there, by virtue of his timelessness, *now*), supporting and consoling us—therefore, we can go forward trustingly, even to tragedies. God joins the times for us. God comforts and enables us despite our ignorance—and to trust absolutely in him who knows the future is as good as though we knew the future ourselves.

Or else, when our love begins to weaken (as it surely will) we may be appalled by our own weaknesses and paralyzed to take any new steps in the relationship. Fear will cancel boldness when we discover that we had built the relationship upon our ignorant selves alone, and even a young couple can grow instantly narrow, conservative, and "safe" in their dealings with one another. Without faith, the marriage fixes, freezes, atrophies.

Once when I was a tiny child my father put me on a train bound from Chicago to Grand Rapids. I didn't like the idea, and twice I ran off the train before it left. I was homesick already. I was terrified to be thrust alone into the dark tunnel of the future. If I had my way, I was not leaving home and my haven. But this is what my father had to say about it: "I'm going ahead of you. Do you think I would leave you alone? I'll meet you at the station in Grand Rapids. Wait, wait, and see if I don't." And I was comforted, and I was set free to travel. I knew no more about the trip there; neither did I know *how* Dad would beat me there (he had to leave later and was flying). But in place of knowledge I had the *promise* of the one who loved me. He who hugged me now would hug me then. And so long as I loved him and believed in him, I could be liberated to go alone.

So with the couple at the precipice of marriage.

Quo vadis? "Where are you going?"

"I don't know. But if you'll go with me, that is all I need to know."

Quo vadis?

Tecum, Domine. "With you, dear Lord."

4. *Forgiveness.* This is the single most significant tool we have for meeting and for healing the troubles which marriage shall surely breed between us. What those troubles will be, we do not know. But that they will be, we may be assured. And nothing—neither our love, our effective communication with each other, our talents, our money, nor all the good will in the world—no, nothing can make right again the wrongs as can forgiveness.

This tool, so practical and so unequivocally necessary to the healthy future of the marriage, must have its own chapter, and shall.

On the afternoon of August 24, 1968, Thanne and I were married. My father placed his hands upon our heads and blessed us. We rose, locked arms with one another, and walked down the aisle of the country Lutheran church where Thanne had worshipped all her childhood. As soon as we stepped outside, the wind of the fields met us, surrounded us, and snatched Thanne's wedding veil so that it flew up wild above our heads, like a cloud—and Thanne laughed. I have a picture of her laughing underneath this windblown benediction.

I remember now how my heart rose on that veil and on Thanne's laughter. It was a speechless exultation in me, so light that I could fly, so deep that I could cry. All things in that instant were right and good and true—the breathings of my God, who blew the fields, and of my wife, who laughed. My wife. She was—I grasped it in the very whirling of that wind—my wife!

And then, when I brought my eyes down again and looked across the country, I saw that the air was golden. This fascinated me. As the evening came, the day grew not darker but more golden. Why was that? Was it a peculiar kind of mist? Did the atmosphere of Iroquois County carry in itself a myriad, tiny wealth?

And I felt the evening air. And it *felt* like gold.

•PART ONE•
Early Marriage Work

•TWO•

WHO DID I MARRY AFTER ALL?

Idealization/Realization

I intend this book to be both practical and personal—as though I were your pastor and we sat discussing holy, intimate necessities over a cup of coffee. I'll seek to find you and define your marital experience by offering myself, my knowledge, my faith, and my own experience.

Because it is practical, the bulk of the book will be given to the six continuing tasks required of each spouse to build the marriage and to keep it in good repair. Part 3 explains these tasks. But because it is meant to be practical for *you* (or for anyone committed to the hard, holy work of marriage maintenance) I must explain first the most significant tool for the work, the healing gift of God—forgiveness. Part 2 of the book will define what it is, why it is so necessary, and how you may use it.

Yet before we start on either of those discussions, the tool or the tasks, let's begin at the beginning. Let's admit over our coffee that getting married, as good as it may be for those who choose it, is nonetheless a crisis in the lives of newlyweds because it requires radical changes in their habits and behavior, in their assessment of their worlds and themselves, in their priorities, and in their responsibilities. Marriage is an unacknowledged cataclysm to lifestyles. Let's talk a moment about that crisis, what it is and how it may be met.

Thanne and I married on a Saturday. On Sunday she and I and Hadrian drove to St. Louis, moved into a tiny two-room apartment, smiled on each other, and went to bed, newlyweds. On Monday she rose and went to work, teaching retarded children. On Monday I rose, purchased paint, and began to paint the walls of our apartment. Should it surprise you to learn that by Friday she had shed tears and I had begun to experience a spectral doubt over the wisdom of our decision to marry? *Who is this woman? Who is this wife of mine? And what has happened to me?*

The marriage itself begins with the vow, the spoken contract, indeed. But the relationship between two people marrying begins, in fact, much sooner and has already evolved through the period of courtship. Marriage is not the beginning of that relationship; rather, it is a sudden and radical revision of that relationship. It's very important that we recognize and allow for this natural but demanding stage in the progress of things, because our ignorance could turn it into a crisis of unnecessary proportions. But the wise will not be overcome by it.

Marriage immediately forces changes upon the partners, which, no matter how well prepared they thought they were, surprise them and require a new and specialized labor from both of them. This is the fact: the woman does not know who her husband is until he *is* her husband, nor the man his wife until she exists as wife. Before the marriage these people were fiancés, not spouses; fiancés and spouses are different creatures, and the second creature doesn't appear until the first has passed away. Did the courtship last many, many years? It doesn't matter. Were they friends long before they initiated courtship? It doesn't matter. They still can't know the spouse until he or she is a spouse; and there isn't a spouse until there is a marriage.

Even if the partners have lived together before the marriage contract and think they know each other very well, it still doesn't matter. They will change when they marry. Permanence changes behavior, and marriage makes the experimental relationship permanent. No—no amount of foresight avails, since we simply cannot see what is not.

So the recently married couple has a job to do, a good job, a hopeful and rewarding job, but labor nonetheless. And it will take a patient, gentle energy to accomplish this labor well.

I am going to describe both the natural causes of the crisis and the work which can best handle that crisis. But right at the beginning of the discussion I pray that you understand the crisis is common to all couples! No couple needs to fear, in the first year of their marriage, that they've "made a mistake," that they are "in trouble," or that their particular experience is unique. Simply, they have work to do, and God has prepared them to do it. This is the work of *accommodation,* self-adjustment.

For easier understanding, I will divide this immediate work into three parts: (1) *Idealization/realization.* Our idealized image of the fiancé will (must) be replaced by a true realization of the spouse who is; good work, here, will lead us to an acceptance of our spouse, while poor work may lead to alienation. (2) *Mutualization.* The willing and easy part-time mutuality which we maintained during courtship will (must) become a real, realistic, and lasting mutualization of our whole lives, spirits, attitudes, and priorities to each other, so that we do not merely act, but truly are, one. Good work here will be an honest and deep character adjustment, person to person; poor work may lead to disengagement. (3) *Gender differences.* The common, natural differences between the men and women of our culture, often invisible during courtship, become clearly apparent in marriage. Good work will (must) celebrate and make use of these differences. But poor work results from one's disappointment over the differences. If either partner tries to change what cannot be changed in the other, that is poor work; and poor work leads to discontentment in all areas of the marriage.

IDEALIZATION

Love lies a little. Love, the desire to like and to be liked, feels so good when it is satisfied, that it never wants to stop. Therefore, love edits the facts in order to continue to feel good. Love allows me an innocent misperception of my fiancée, while it encourages in her a favorable misperception of myself. If it isn't blind, it does squint a bit. Love idealizes both of us.

This is natural. It isn't wrong or bad. Listen: marriage is such an intimidating commitment that we need a strong inducement to make it; we all need to be persuaded; and the idealization of the prospective partner is exactly that persuasion. My heart, my mind, and all my attention are filled with the beauty of my love alone. Please don't disillusion me with her blemishes. I need this time of pure adoring so much that I wouldn't hear you anyway.

No marriage is the perfect union of perfect people. But if we saw only imperfections before we married (however true they are), marriage itself would seem too great a risk for anyone to take. On the other hand, for those who have the tool of forgiveness, imperfections are rightly dealt with *inside* the marriage bond, after marrying. (This is one reason many who live together before marriage do not marry: they discover their partners' faults without the motive or the means to redeem those faults; so they merely escape; they separate.) The time and the tool for repairing imperfections will come with the marriage. During courtship, then, we compulsively pretend perfection. Idealization is more than natural. It is necessary.

Parents: be careful. When the differences between your daughter and her fiancé are not great or dangerous, you do her damage by trying to "make her realize the trouble with that boy"—and you'll likely fail anyway, because she is, and you are not, in love with him. You would do far better to fit her for forgiving, for the time will come when she will see him as you do. And the training in forgiveness ought to begin very early in her life, especially as *you* model a forgiving attitude before her in your own marital relationship. For the moment, parents, trust it: her idealization of "that boy" is natural and necessary.

I will tell you a truth not absolutely true, but which sustained me in the years 1967 and 1968. I would even sing this truth, so dear was it to me: Ruthanne Bohlmann was a lissome beauty ere we married! Thin, was she? So thin that her legs stuck out of her shorts like toothpicks? Well, but then she was the lighter to carry, the more delicate in my arms; and it made me feel nearly heroic to protect her. I saw her not thin but slender. Besides, it charmed me to find so penetrating a wit in so small a bundle.

And since my own life was so loose, disorganized, I marveled to see how confident Thanne was about the future and how ordered was her present. She was my opposite for practicality; she wasted neither minutes nor pennies nor energy; and this seemed no obstacle to our future union, but aids to the disheveled Walt. Likewise, if she showed no great emotion (whereas I was in a continual turmoil about something), I found peace in the calmness of her eyes, and I stabled myself in the absolute predictability of her schedule and her days. My superior was Thanne before we married, one most worthy *to* marry, my balance, and better than any other woman: Thanne!

For my own part, I put my best foot forward. Was I deceiving her? Of course not. I was showing her what I truly believed myself to be in the generous light of her love—and what I knew I could become, if only for the prize of her hand in marriage. I shaved. I used the cologne she once had noticed. I wore clean clothes—not, in fact, my usual habits, nor my reputation among college friends, but the *me* I would have Thanne to know. Ideal Walt, the Walt whom Thanne might love. When we drove in Chicago traffic I manifested a remarkable capacity to be long-suffering. I was gentle, meek, and temperate, and I loved children. I wrote her poetry when we were apart; and when we were together I made expansive reference in my monologues to goals, dreams, and accomplishments. When she visited my Oxford apartment, I had sprayed the whole carpet with deodorizer, swept the dust bunnies from underneath the radiators, and washed the dishes.

Oh, and when we were together, I laughed much more than usual—a hearty, happy laughter. But that was no deception either (despite my characteristic gloom) because she made me want to laugh, and with her I was happy.

In ways like these do courting couples abet one another in the idealization of their characters. Love can't help lying just a little. But as true as the love is, even so true seems this vision of the beloved. It is not to be blamed.

Nevertheless, the wedding sends them home together, and the days thereafter explode these little lies with fact. The marriage contract declares absolutely, as though they never heard it before: *This is for good; this is forever.*

And soon one begins to wonder whether he wanted so *much* order and so *little* emotion in his life.

REALIZATION

There are three rooms of the marital house wherein the idealized image comes off like a dress or a cummerbund: in the kitchen, in the bathroom, and in the bedroom. The real spouse steps forth; and though she is the same, lo, she is not the same exactly. This, so soon post-ecstacy, is the period of "realization." And it is precisely the sense of permanence which causes it to happen.

Who did I marry after all?

In the kitchen the truer, more spontaneous social habits of the spouse show up, the way he or she relates to other people at the basic, communal level. Look: she has spent a loving afternoon cooking an artistic dinner; carrots and peas give bright, contrasting colors to the plate; mashed potatoes foam lumpless beside them; the meat is tender, the gravy dark, the salad tart with her own dressing—and the careless husband wolfs the whole thing down without a word. Not a peep of praise from him! Worse, he holds his fork in his fist, and he chews with his mouth open, smacking food (oh, what manners shall he teach the children?—never mind that they are two months married and children aren't even ghosts at the table yet). Then, when finally he looks up and asks for more—because he truly liked the meal—he is bewildered to find her crying. Meals and methods of eating signify the beast, or the bird, within.

Look: she talks, while they eat, as brightly as ever she did before they married; but there is something ominously different in the speech. Her conversation is laced with the little stories and opinions he once chuckled at, but they're not so funny now—and the chatter doesn't pause to let a poor man breathe. Or eat. It's full of questions that force him to answer. It probes, like a dentist's pick, into his day (doesn't she trust him any more?); yet more and more she makes herself the topic of the conversation—her work, her friends, the clients she has dealt with, her little vindications in the day. And he notices irritating habits of speech he hadn't noticed before. For example, he can always spot a piece of gossip on the way, because she introduces it by saying, "Bless her soul," or "Now I'm not one to talk, but—" And she twirls a lock of hair around her forefinger. Why does she do that at the table? Then, when finally she asks him a serious and loving question, she is bewildered to find that his eyes have glazed over, or that he is gazing at her as though he'd never seen the woman before.

Who did I marry after all?

In the bathroom the truer physical and personal habits of the spouse appear, the way he or she *is* in the body. Why, she has smells he never guessed that graceful women have. And her plain white face is plain indeed. He hadn't known how lacking were her lashes, mere wisps on the rim of the lid.

But he persists in dribbling a little pee on the rim of the toilet, which leaves disgusting yellow memories of his having been in here. Okay, that's true; but she puts unnecessary frills in places meant for practicality. For example, she's put a fuzzy cover on the toilet lid so that it will not stay up when he's got to go. Does she know how diabolical fuzzy covers are on toilet lids? They wait until the man has started to relieve himself, then suddenly drop shut on the whole operation, mocking his manhood and reminding him that *she's* been here.

On the other hand, he leaves little hairs in the sink, bristles of whiskers, and smudged underpants on the floor. Has he always lived so brutishly? Ah, but has she always lived so vainly? He leaves the mess because she takes an age to primp in the mornings, and he has to scrape everything clean in five minutes.

Who would have imagined he had so much hair all over his body? Or that he never cleaned his nails?

Her toenails gnarl! She picks earwax with bobby pins!

Who did I marry after all?

In the bedroom the truer, unpremeditated behavior of intimacy appears, the way this spouse relates to others on the most personal level, body to body and spirit to spirit. Is he truly patient in sexuality? So he seemed on long spring evenings. Or does he push forward at his own speed to his own satisfaction? And does he consider *his* satisfaction the measure of his prowess? As he acts here, uncovered, so does he act—more subtly and covertly—in the rest of the marriage.

Does she shrink from the encounter rather more fastidiously than she had from mere kissing when kissing was "safe"? Does she cry at unexpected times, showing a delicacy that baffles him because he does not understand all the preliminaries she requires of him before they can get to the point? Jumping through hoops can distract a man, you know. Or does she reveal a sexual boldness so self-assured that the man is shocked out of the mood, having been bounced from the role he had imagined for himself?

There will almost certainly be a period of strain and of searching in the bedroom of the newly married couple (whether sex is new for the partners or not), because successful sexuality expects *both* a complete intimacy with the other *and* a complete fulfillment for the self—and it takes awhile to find out how these two (often opposed) goals can be accomplished. Besides, sexual behavior is unique to each couple. Each couple must learn its own best method; and couples learn that by trial and error. The errors, on the way to discovery, cause the loss of the idealized fiancé. How she or he handles these errors reveals the flesh-and-bones, spontaneous truth of the spouse, the one with whom we are to live forever: realization!

Who did I marry after all?

Now let me tell you a truth that is and was and ever shall be absolutely true: in our little apartment, St. Louis, Missouri, Thanne Wangerin went to bed at precisely the same stroke every night—nine o'clock. No matter the difference of the days, some harder and some easier, some requiring more, and some less, sleep. No matter the marvelous conversations she cut short to get her sleep. No matter me and my late-night habits. Nine! And she always showered first. And she always laid her clothes out neatly!

Suddenly Thanne's prearranged, punctilious life seemed to me a compulsive, cold routine. She was predictable, doggedly predictable, dispassionately, mechanically predictable—and ordered to obsession. My poetic spontaneity was not so much cooled, in the presence of stainless-steel eyes, as positively iced. Neither was she thin nor delicate after the wedding. Thanne was skinny! A dangerous lack of meat on the woman's bones.

I, on the other hand, was to her a stunning mess, so unpredictable as to be unreliable, jeopardizing her peace and her confidence in the future, forcing her to prodigies of planning. And what had happened to her laughing fiancé? Who was this morose, guilt-ridden, night-striding, haunted Raskolnikov hiding in her home? Did I love my typewriter more than I loved her? And how, in the name of cleanli-godli-ness, could I contrive to strew dirty socks through every room of the apartment?

What had I married? A machine?

What had *she* married? An adolescent?

Idealization will surely run upon realization. Visions shatter on the rock of fact. The question is not how we might avoid this crisis, because we can't. It will occur. The question, rather, is what work is required to meet the crisis and to grow by it? For if we think that this revelation of the real spouse is the final truth of our mate and our marriage—and that we've made a dreadful mistake, therefore—then we will move to alienation, one from the other. But if we take this as a natural step in the process of growing one together, we may, with clear sight, move toward acceptance and accommodation.

ACCOMMODATION

When the realization comes, instead of withdrawing in anxiety or blame, praise the Lord and call it opportunity, for now you know the stuff with which this marriage will be made. Understand (this is critical) that you *both* are experiencing the selfsame disillusionment. You are in fact not separate from each other at this moment (though you may feel both separated and deceived); but, having the truth clearly between you now, you are the closer together.

Moreover, you are enabled to be partners involved in the same work. This, too, is important. You are now, more than ever, each "a help perfectly fit" for the other, fellow laborers building the same house, of the same materials—but with different skills. Realization is the discovery of the differences between you, differences at first distressing. But if you see yourselves as partners and not as hostile strangers, you can both acknowledge and celebrate these differences. You can, according to your differing capacities, divide the work of the household, assigning certain duties to certain skills.

Before we were married, self-confident Walt decreed that he would manage the financial affairs of the Wangerins. (Hadn't his father before him, and his grandfather before his father? Tradition approved Walt's decision. Ability did not.) Within two months the Wangerins were defaulting on their debts, though the dreaming, improvident Walt did not notice. Neither did he notice (and to this day does not remember) that within four months Thanne had quietly assumed responsibility for their economy. The organization woman organized, and they are, eighteen years later, solvent still.

Understand, too, that there is no wrong in the experience of realization; there's no sin here for which someone should be blamed, for which someone should feel guilty. No one willfully deceived anyone. Repeat it: the awakening unto truth *after* the wedding is the normal sequence of events. When you speak to your spouse about his or her newly uncovered characteristics, then, resist the tones of hurt or accusation and let your conversation be practical and realistic—grateful, even, for the truth. The tone is all-important for the effectiveness of the talk. And the tone must invite partnership, not division.

And the tone of practical gratitude can be encouraged by this: if the two of you had remained in a prenuptial dream world, your marriage could not work in this in-factual, demanding world. You did not, after all, marry a fiction. You married a person, beloved of God, imperfect indeed, but substantial, real, and vital. Dreams can't nurse you through the coming diseases, can't redeem your coming faults. Dream-wives and dream-husbands would abhor your own imperfections and vanish before your fleshy humanity. But this real spouse of yours can accept and accommodate herself, himself, to the real you. It is most blessed to say, "This Thanne, the skinny one, the conscientious, predictable, clocked Ruthanne—this is the one whom I have married"—because that other Thanne did not even exist. It is good to come down to earth. Speak to one another out of that goodness, and your talk shall be a consolation.

That tone inclines me to listen even to my faults: I am not belittled if we are merely working on a partnership. That tone inspires me to change, to obey the new rules imposed by the presence of another human in my house—because this change does not require an admission of guilt, nor is suffered as punishment, but is a gift of love to one who loves me, and is, after all, simply pragmatic for the success of our marriage. And that tone allows us both to identify and to accept what is irreducible in the other's personality; for some things can never be changed, but it is good to know that soon.

Best of all, that tone encourages me to thank God, even as I am learning certain embarrassing truths about myself (which my spouse discovered in the period of her realization). I may thank God that the marriage has given me someone who can reflect the true Walt to myself—as though I gazed into a mirror—kindly, lovingly, with the purpose of my own improvement. The world would only condemn my annoying characteristics, while this mirror-partner loves me past them.

Finally, you will notice that I am placing the greatest burden for change upon one's *self*. True change, true and effective accommodation, comes from within. Change which is commanded from without merely forces a person into unnatural postures and causes a lasting tension in his being, a tension which may one day explode when he snaps back to his natural form. Accommodation doesn't mean that I require my spouse to be shaped to my expectations, but that I shape me (from my center outward) to her, to him—not to his expectations, but to his very being.

Or else, if neither one of us can change at a certain issue, accommodation means finding creative ways to "accommodate" both personalities despite the differences. Yes, I can learn to chew with my mouth closed. And sometimes (Sundays, in fact, as though it were a sort of date) I can go to bed at nine. But it was years and years before I could acquire simple, human neatness. Therefore, Thanne went shopping. The woman bought five clothes hampers. There appeared in the Wangerin household a fleet of clothes hampers—one for the bathroom, one for the bedroom, one in the kitchen, the living room, and the hall, so that wherever Walt undressed he'd have somewhere to drop his socks.

THREE

HOW SHALL WE LIVE TOGETHER?

Mutualization and Gender Differences

Now we speak of the life patterns of the marrying partners—their schedules, priorities, opinions, tastes. Mutualization is the seeking after the one pattern which will harmonize the two patterns that the husband and wife have brought together. Partners will always play on separate instruments, because they are separate individuals. They will always have a different line of notes to play. It's foolish to believe their lives should be exact copies of one another. Nevertheless, unless they learn to play a duet in the same key, to the same rhythm—unless their lives finally achieve mutuality—a slow process of disengagement will wedge them apart, first secretly, psychologically, and then openly and miserably.

MUTUALIZATION: HOW SHALL WE LIVE TOGETHER?

Like realization, the work of mutualization occurs, for the most part, after the wedding. During courtship two temporary

conditions permit a false sense of mutuality, persuading the fiancés that they are one already. But this is an illusion which the
reality of marriage blows away. Following shock, the good work
may begin.

The first condition is that of most people, whether they are
affianced or not: they do not truly know themselves. They live
by habit and by instinct, mostly unconscious of the nature of
their own existences. They do know some of the characteristics
of their life patterns—those that are most urgent and outstanding. They can tell you what foods they like, what schedules they
usually keep, whether they are "night people" or "morning people," whether their work takes precedence over their recreation
or vice versa. But they may never have considered how that food
is cooked, what emotional schedules keep them, what kind of
atmosphere they thrive in. Some love cluttered, knick-knacky
rooms, while others need bare simplicity—but neither may ever
have considered these needs, as fish likely do not meditate upon
water. Some people compulsively plan the future, while others
take full pleasure in the present. Some must eat lightly but regularly throughout the day, while others eat according to ap-
petite, irregularly. Some crave silence and find it necessary for
intimacy, while others have to talk. Some hold to old customs
and practices, cherishing pictures, memories, and family re-
unions, while others ditch the past joyfully to risk some new,
uncertain thing.

For many, many people, these tendencies are unacknowledged. They *think* they know, but they don't know truly,
who they are—not until their lives experience radical change. A
pinching shoe will finally teach you your toes. The beached fish
learns how good and necessary was the water.

Likewise, during courtship the partners *think* that they are ad-
justing to one another's differences. Each makes certain personal
concessions to the other's schedule, needs, opinion, tastes. Each
of them happily gives up something, and together they suppose
that they are testing their compatability. They even think they've
made a mutual unity of their lives. But in fact, they've been dealing only with what they know about themselves—which is very
little after all. They've achieved harmony only at the surface of
their lives. Below that surface lurks, in each partner, an entire
complex of human needs, unconscious habits, unexamined patterns and desires; and this leviathan sleeps in the blithe presumption that it will always be satisifed, that it shall not be disturbed
even after the marriage has begun. Wait. Wait until the honey-

moon is over when these two monsters will bump against each other. Then they'll wake up.

The second condition which allows a false mutuality before marriage is the willingness of each partner (for the reward that shall come) to *suspend* certain life patterns for a while—but only (each one thinks) for a while. Certain mistaken notions about marriage persuade them to "change" their true lifestyles during courtship. Listen:

"I'll stay up late with him—now," thinks the woman whose schedule sends her early to bed, "and after we're married I'll get my sleep." She assumes courtship to be a fling, a necessary, happy, but temporary concession to her fiancé, which will end when they marry and return to normalcy—*her* normalcy. This is not true mutuality—and, to the surprise of both, will vanish.

Or: "I'll go to the movies with her—now," thinks the man who'd rather watch a demolition derby, "and in time she'll learn to like cars." He expects to change her tastes, to change *her* into the one he truly wants to live with. He doesn't realize that her tastes run as deep as his, and that one might never become the standard for the other. This mutuality will run against hard times.

Or: "I can sacrifice my plans for a career," thinks the woman who has labored for her education, "because I love him so much. I'll shape my life to his." And the intensity of her love may truly persuade her that she *can* surrender this personal desire, while her words persuade him that she has already surrendered it—so he is content, and she is in love. But when the powerful feelings of affection cool in the common business of living together, that desire for a career can reappear as strong as ever, and that mutuality will have been delusion.

This is the false mutuality of courtship: we are, in fact, "playing" at oneness and harmony. It isn't a pretense, exactly. Rather, we "test" liking the things our fiancé likes; and though we might suspect that our own behavior is temporary, we want to believe that the partner's behavior is not. "How marvelous, that the woman is so much like me!" We would be (we will be) offended to discover that she, too, was "playing" at it, whether she knew that or not.

About things we mind very much, we say, "I don't mind—do what you want to do," because immediate feelings and the *desire* for mutuality overshadow deeper needs and the actual lack of mutuality. "Honey, I love your cooking," really means, *Honey, I love you and I'll let nothing come between us.* Yet she smiles at the compliment, feels gratified, and plans to cook this way forever, just to please him. And what does this mean: "No, I don't mind if you go out with your friends tonight; I have things to do in my apartment"? It means, *I want you to think of me as a sensitive, understanding woman, perfect for marrying.* Yet he feels he's been granted permission to run with his buddies as much as he wants even after the wedding—because she "doesn't mind."

This isn't deception. It is a glad "playing" at mutuality. So the courting couple proclaims with full assurance, "We will be happy together; we can tell. We like the same things. We do the same things. We have the same goals. We are one!"

And then they marry. Soon the sweet water turns salt, and the little fishes discover water after all. They marry. Temporary lifestyles, like springs pulled out of shape, snap back to the truer and more enduring lifestyles. "Playing" ceases in the serious business of survival. Now each partner has *become* the other's atmosphere, the spirit and air in which the other dwells, and both are made painfully aware of their different, previously unconscious, life patterns. They marry, and what each "minds" creeps into the conversation. In fact, they were not one:

"Honey, don't you think you should get rid of these knick-knacks?"
"Why? You gave me two yourself last year."

And: "What's the matter? You liked this dress when we were dating."
"Sure, but I don't want men looking at you the way I did then."

And: "Talk to me, talk to me! We used to talk."
"But I could always go home for peace and quiet. Now *this* is my home."

And: "You never shouted at me before."
"You never gave me cause before."

And: "Why do you have to go out with your friends again tonight?"

"I've always gone out with my friends. What's the difference now?"

And: "A wife of mine shouldn't have a job. It makes me feel less than a man."
"Why didn't you tell me you felt that way? If I don't have a job it makes me feel less than a person."

"My mother never did this."
"So what? I'm not your mother."

"Listen, you've got to tell me about your plans. You can't just go out and do whatever you want to do. How can I arrange my life unless you tell me?"
"Hey! Am I supposed to rush home and ask your permission for everything? Trust me a little."

"You spend too much on entertainment."
"Miser! Miser! At least I enjoy my life."

Now, finally, the real facts and the deeper habits are clear: there is much that had never become mutual between them after all. The schedules they compulsively follow, their priorities, their instinctive value systems, the unconscious design of their days, their ways, and their space—the styles of their lives—do not yet harmonize. They entered marriage playing different tunes in different keys. And unless they rise above the noisy discord, they may feel cheated, or criticized by the differences, or imprisoned by their partner's unacceptable patterns. They may try to settle the differences by open argument, or by bossing their spouses, or by nagging. They may harden, proudly, bitterly, into the differences. They may move toward disengagement.

My Lord, how are we going to live together now that the truth is out?

It is important to repeat here what was said in the previous chapter: this crisis, this clashing of two individual lifestyles is not unique in any marriage. To one degree or another, this is the experience of nearly every marriage today (especially since we live in a pluralistic society). There is no fault. There needs to be no blame. No one should feel offended, nor should anyone feel guilty, as though he or she failed to be honest, failed to prepare for the marriage. These attitudes can only hinder the good and effective work that now must take place, because they will confuse the issues. We have not come upon a moral problem, but upon the practical challenge of arranging two lives to fit together—and we could not have come upon it *until* the marriage had begun. Therefore, this is exactly the right time for it. Things are right on schedule. No, nothing's wrong.

But work certainly is required, now. The couple can't ignore the differences and hope they go away.

What work can bring the young couple to mutuality? First to know, and then to nourish, the genuine "oneness" of their marriage.

Know the Oneness

Let's make a careful distinction here. When newlyweds blush and say, "We are one," they may, in fact, mean any of four separate definitions, but only the fourth permits a complete mutualization.

"One" may mean: "We are exactly alike." Some couples strain to duplicate each other, and then suffer the persistent differences or else repress them. They force an unrealistic similarity upon their tastes, their opinions, their priorities, their customary habits. They may do so with the best of intentions; but this "oneness" is no more real than was Adam and Eve's when they covered their differences with clothes. It is a seeming similarity only—a looking alike—which makes the marriage a pretense and will finally tire the partners with pretending. For God created each one unique. To make two beings carbon copies of each other is to deny that uniqueness, the handiwork of God. Neither person could flourish, then, and grow into the special creature God had planned him or her to be, and the marriage itself would stall. It could not enter new realms.

"One" may mean no more than this: one of the partners has taken control of the marriage, and that one will dominates the other. The second will has become silent or submissive or extinct. But this isn't one*ness;* this is one alone. Indeed, there is no disharmony in such a marriage: no arguing, no clashes, no division of opinions, just an evident and absolute order. But neither is there harmony of any kind. The drum has overwhelmed the flute. Then, though one person may flourish and grow, two do not, for the second is always shaped by the character and personhood of the first. And therefore the marriage *as a marriage* does not develop either. The marriage has become the servant of one of the partners.

Neither of these definitions of "oneness" is mutuality. The first is only simulation, the second subordination, and someone is lost for the sake of good order. Mutuality takes two whole humans. The third definition is no better, because it merely plays with words.

"One" may mean: "We have a fifty-fifty marriage, half and half." But mutuality is accomplished by two *whole* persons; and if each partner truly intends to be but the fraction of a relationship (thinking *My whole makes up a half of us*) he or she will soon discover that these halves do not fit perfectly together. The mathematics can work only if each subtracts something of himself or herself, shears it off, and lays it aside forever. There will come, then, a moment of shock when one spouse realizes, "You don't want the *whole* of me? Not the whole of me, but only a part of me, makes up the whole of us?"

So which parts are to be cut off? Who decides? This turns marriage into a procrustean bed, where those too big are cut to fit. And often the partner of the stronger willfulness consciously or unconsciously swings the knife, for someone finally must decide *how* the two should fit together; so we are, in practice, back with the second definition after all. This third definition sounds better than it is: "Fifty-fifty means that we take turns at deciding things." I will believe that so long as no one feels that the "turns" are cheating him out of his own presumed rights and privileges; thus, good feelings can continue. But sin destroys such sharing. And I repeat: mutuality must acknowledge the wholeness of both partners.

The fourth definition, then. This asks that you think in a new way. Up till now we have assumed that there are only two beings in a marriage, the husband and the wife. In fact, there are three complete beings in a marriage—you, your spouse, and *the relationship* between you, which both of you serve, which benefits each of you, but which is not exactly like either one of you. This relationship is itself very much like a living being—like a baby born from you both. It has its own character. It enters existence infantile, when you speak vows to one another. It comes cuddly and lovely, but very weak and in need of care and nourishment. As time goes on, as this baby-relationship grows up, it becomes stronger and stronger until it serves and protects you in return. This "being," this living thing, this relationship which needs you both (the whole of each of you), but which is *not you* (it is not the two of you added together, because it is distinct from either one of you)—that is your "oneness." Serving *it,* you both enact a harmony. You are co-laborers committed to the care of a single (third!) life between you. You are each a whole, unique, free creature of God. Yet you are one.

Now, then: when you look upon your marriage, you are not just looking upon one another (possibly feeling at odds with one another), but upon this third being which requires the complete attention, all of the wisdom and skills, and the holy prayers and faith of you both.

Nourish the Oneness

This is the real work of mutuality. This brings your various lifestyles into harmony (without canceling either one, without a forced similitude): that you have realized a common purpose together; that you are both committed to the nurturing, not of oneself and not of one's partner, but of this third being, the Relationship; and that together you seek the wisest ways to do so—and you do them.

Serving this Relationship, neither partner has to feel that change was imposed upon you; rather, each of you offers your various talents and the best of yourselves to the Relationship. This becomes a willing offering, never fearing that your spouse is "getting more than he deserves." Why? Because both of you benefit in the Relationship's good health. Now neither of you must submit humiliatingly to the other; rather, each *chooses* to serve the third being, the Relationship.

Listen: when a baby cries in the middle of the night, do the parents bicker and neglect their baby's needs? Not if they love it. Or do they blame one another because the baby *is* a baby, helpless, in need of human care? Of course not. Instead, they willingly adjust their lives in order to nurse the infant; they adjust without accusations because the baby's needs are no one's fault, and their dear one is more important to them than their own desires. Each trusts the love that the partner also has for this child. They adjust their lives, feeling in no way oppressed by such necessity.

Likewise, when the marriage Relationship (like a baby!) here at its beginning cries out for attention, even at unexpected and inconvenient times, the husband and the wife can sit down together as co-laborers, partners (not as antagonists), and willingly each adjust their lives in order to nurse this Relationship to maturity and to strength. If they work together for the sake of this third being, they can adjust without complaint: no one is whining; no one is grasping; no one is losing something unreasonably, or being oppressed. Both apply their separate skills, and each respects the judgment and the offering of the other.

There is a world of difference between: "You must include me in planning our future, because you hurt me when you neglect me; you destroy me, my sense of worth," and: "The Relationship needs our planning, but I can help you in that, because I know some of its needs: I've got a thought or two about its future." There is a world of difference between: "You wasted my money! How am I going to buy food? When do I get a dress?" and: "I've been looking at the budget. How can we increase the percentage for groceries?" The issues are no longer personal. As *both* see it that way (not as accusations, but as problems to be solved), both may apply their creative minds to the common questions. You will not pitch ready-made solutions at one another (which sound very much like commands) but will pose questions for the consideration of both.

In this way a husband will use his wisdom and ability when he best can solve a problem—but never command just because he is a man. Likewise, a wife will use her experience and talents when they best enable her. Each of them can willingly allow the other some charge of this mutual, beloved being, the Relationship.

In this way spouses do not need to become *like* each other, mimicking one another's opinions, tastes, and habits. Their differences shall have become too important to lose, their various skills too respected to ignore. On the other hand, their schedules will, naturally, meld together; their priorities will become mutual not by the imposition of one on the other, but because the single priority of the baby-marriage has been accepted by both. As they work toward a more harmonious integration of their lifestyles, they will fight less (since they focus less upon one another) and they will confer more (since they focus more on the being which requires both of them).

And when one defaults in his or her new duties to the marriage, the spouse need not take that personally either. Again, there is a world of difference between: "He failed me," and: "He failed the marriage." If he fails *me,* I might be so hurt that I can't speak to him. Or I will shout, shutting down all wisdom, both his and mine. Anger gets in the way. The true issue—and the Relationship—shall be forgotten in the midst of feelings. But if he fails the *marriage,* I can still speak to my co-laborer, without the distortion of wounded feelings, about the baby who wants our whole and cool attention—and he can listen to me after all, since I do still respect his abilities and am asking him to use them for the benefit of the thing we both love: the Relationship.

Finally, as a baby rewards its parents with healthy laughter and burblings and many tokens of love, so shall the Relationship, thus nourished, reward its marital guardians—with stability, trustworthiness, warmth, and security. So a little mutuality encourages more and more mutuality. As the marriage blesses you with a harmonious sound, you'll play your instrument better and better, for the sake of the sweet sound alone, and you will marvel that your spouse could play so well.

The third piece of the work of accommodation comes from gender differences, the natural dissimilarity between man and woman that becomes clearly apparent only after the marriage begins.

WHAT HAPPENED TO THE MAN (THE WOMAN) I MARRIED?

In our present culture (though this is changing) men are bred to have an "instrumental" character, while women develop an "expressive" character. (Not all men are "instrumental" nor all women "expressive." This is a general classification and not a rule. But the sexes fall commonly enough into these categories that we may handle the difference here according to gender.) These tendencies are radically different from one another, but during the period of courtship the difference is hidden. After marriage that difference pops up as a rude surprise. First it must be understood and then it can be managed by the early marriage work.

The "instrumental" character is a pragmatic person. He focuses upon a future goal and needs to believe in the practical value of that goal. He justifies a present activity by what it shall accomplish in the future. He can be very patient doing precious, little things—so long as they shall ultimately prove productive. He likes the words *progress* and *useful*. His values are utilitarian. "What good is this?" means "What good can this *produce?*"

The "expressive" character, on the other hand, is a more artistic person. She focuses on the feelings and the activities of the present—for their own sakes. She needs no future goal; it is enough to take pleasure in the moment. She is content and patient doing precious, little things because the doing has its own value. To be "in touch with one's feelings" and to say so is living in itself; she asks no more, nor even understands the necessity of progress, production, or utility; these demands feel deadly cold to her, and distracting. "What good is this?" means to her merely "What *is* this thing, anyway? Help me know and feel it." Her values are relational. She doesn't know the word *useful,* but loves the word *you.*

He lives in the calculating mind. She dwells satisfied within the heart.

He would grow vegetables—and grow them efficiently—for food. She grows roses for their beauty, whether anyone sees them or not, and can weep at the color red.

He studies in order to gain employment. She reads to live the story.

He rests in order to be prepared for tasks the following day. She loves her bed; sleep is good, simply because sleep is good.

He (and now we come to our point) courts to get married; but once he's married, the purpose of courtship is accomplished and he moves on to other, more productive, things. She, on the other hand, courts and kisses for kissing's sake; and once she's married expects simply that the kissing will continue between them forever.

Before the marriage, these two characters look exactly the same: both are glad to spend time holding hands. Both find value in quiet moments together. Both seem content, seem pleased, seem fulfilled *merely to be together.* And he speaks such "sweet nothings" in her ear. Yes, he likes roses. And she weeps to have found one man in a thousand who is patient, gentle, kind, and loving, who doesn't want to use her.

They look alike; but they are not alike. This instrumental man has made a worthy instrument of courtship. He can do all he does because it is, after all, useful: it shall produce his goal of marriage. The marriage of the future justifies these cuddling activities in the present. They are not sweet "nothings" after all, but whisperings calculated to persuade her to the altar. Please don't think evil of this poor fellow. Again, this is not a conscious deception. In fact, he likely presumes that she is like himself and, like him, intends to continue these foolishnesses only so long as they have practical consequence; after that he expects them both to progress past nonsense to the real business of living.

Then comes marriage, and the goal of "being together, doing nothing" is fulfilled for the instrumental personality—and doing nothing, thereafter, is a senseless thing to do.

Then the wife is chagrined to find that he has forgotten flowers and dispensed with touching for touching alone. (Why must he always touch her, now, with sex in mind? Why must there always be an ulterior motive for every gentle gesture, ruining the goodness of that gesture?) Now she feels used, indeed, and very mistrustful of the man who has two faces. Sex begins to feel like a job, a duty, since he seems to care only for the climax (his purpose) and not all the valuable foreplay (her purpose). Was he lying to her all through the courtship? Or what has changed the gentle man she'd learned to love?

Well, no, he wasn't lying. And nothing's changed *him;* it's just that the circumstances have changed. The goal that made him patient has been met.

For his own part, he is also chagrined by his wife. Why has she so suddenly become emotional? Why does she cry so easily, now, and withdraw from his touch as though he were brutish or dirty? What's wrong, that she keeps wanting to go back to the past and do all the old things over and over again? Didn't she ever mature beyond her adolescence? Is she stuck in some earlier stage? Did I marry a child? Let's get *on* with the marriage. And no—I do not understand the importance of flowers; I'd rather buy a lube job for her car; it costs less and means more. Lord, I never knew she was so hypersensitive. Doesn't she like me—or appreciate all I do for her?

But the woman hasn't changed either. Simply, she had expected marriage not to revise their relationship, but to preserve what she had valued in it before.

What, then, is required but the work of understanding? I repeat again (and again) that our natural differences are good and ought finally to be celebrated. As one body must have both a calculating mind and a feeling heart, so one marriage is blessed with mind *and* heart; these are not antagonistic elements, but complements one of the other. It would be a cold couple who could not glory in a purple sunset. Do not belittle the cry in her throat, thou pragmatic man; participate in it! It would be a stagnating couple who could not risk new ventures nor plan against the future. Do not dismiss him as hard-hearted, thou sensitive woman; benefit from it! Let each one teach the other; but let each attitude temper the other's. The thing which you do not know by nature is not, therefore, valueless. Be willing to learn it. And the thing which you do naturally know, but which your spouse does not, is not the only good in the world, proving him a nincompoop for ignorance. Take patient time to reveal it to him. Be glad that your marriage has two eyes instead of one, and let both of you see through both of them. With two eyes wide open, the marriage can see depth. It gains perspective.

Most important: don't judge your spouse as evil. He did not deceive you. She is not now loathing you. It took marrying to reveal these varying characteristics, the "instrumental" and the "expressive"; marrying did this thing, not some devious action of your partner. But marriage is the perfect arena in which to join your differences, for marriage gives you time and the lasting willingness both to realize that the other's tendencies are, after all, good, and then to take that goodness for yourself.

Oh—and here is how I know that men may be "expressive" while women may be "instrumental": Thanne took a long time to understand the value of poetry. And I was the one who wondered why she grew so businesslike two days after our wedding, going to work, forgetting me. Mine is the womanlike soul; hers the manlike. Come, let me tell you what a purple sunset did for me and Thanne and Hadrian . . .

·PART TWO·

Forgiveness

·FOUR·

WHAT KIND OF RELATIONSHIP IS MARRIAGE MEANT TO BE?

The Divine Ideal

---

*I*t's a truism that marriages must have communication, that husbands and wives must learn to talk honestly with one another and to listen well. A truism: almost no one is ignorant of the need. A truism: though people think, when they utter the word *communication,* they've delivered themselves of something profound; they have in fact said something nearly meaningless. Of course communication is necessary. Likewise, it's necessary to know how to handle a steering wheel before driving a car. But drunks know how to handle steering wheels; and drunks drive cars—into other people. And certain teenagers are both skilled with the wheel and rash with the car.

The most crucial issue in a marriage is not *that* a couple communicate, but *what* they communicate.

Sadly, humanity is sinful and self-centered. One may communicate very well his personal desires and satisfy himself that he's done the right thing, when in fact he's just made unreasonable demands upon his wife. Or she may communicate with exceptional facility her anger—dropping him to the floor with a verbal bullet. "We had a good talk. We got it all out into the open." Yes, and you stunned each other in the process. "I told her what this marriage needed. I told her coolly, carefully, and clearly. Things will change now." But change—if "what this marriage needs" is no more than what you *think* it needs, or what *you* need—may be that all the griefs intensify. And this may bewilder you, that good communication should have such distressing consequence.

Let there be communication, indeed.

But let the thing communicated be *forgiveness.*

There is no tool more practical to marriage maintenance nor more important than that both husband and wife are capable of the reparation of forgiveness. But, despite our self-confidence, it is not a tool any of us knows by nature or uses by instinct. Oh, we know the term *forgiveness* well enough; but we confuse its meaning, and we must acquire the skill of using it.

Therefore, I'll devote the second part of this book to an explanation of that tool by answering three questions: Why is forgiveness so necessary? What is forgiveness? How do we practice the miracle of forgiveness in our marriages?

Apprentice yourself to me awhile. Be prepared to study patiently the part that follows, and the reward of your labor will appear in your relationships. No carpenter, no shipwright, no cooper could have shaped the wood properly until he had learned to use an adz. But how could he learn to use the thing, if he didn't even know what the word *adz* meant? In the beginning, most of us understand the term *forgiveness* no better than we do the strange word *adz*. In the beginning, at the wedding, we're wide-eyed children after all.

Why is forgiveness necessary among us? Because it can return us to the ideal that God had intended for marriage, the ideal our sin destroyed. Let's start our study of forgiveness, then, with that divine ideal.

WHAT KIND OF RELATIONSHIP IS MARRIAGE MEANT TO BE?

Loneliness hurts. I mean that literally, physically. I can put my hands on my stomach and feel the place of the pain of loneliness. But I also mean the worst kinds of loneliness: bereavement, the

child's unspeakable homesickness, or the lasting, hopeless loneliness of despair. These things deaden something in the human,
and they hurt.

Sometimes I imagine that loneliness is the vulture that attacked Prometheus when he was chained to a rock on Mount
Caucasus. The vulture pierced him at the abdomen and all day
long chewed on his liver with a bloody beak. All night long the
poor man's liver grew again, so the next day was no better than
the last, and day after day the pain was the same. Loneliness feels
like a thick, internal bleeding. And worse: the lonely are vulnerable to every little hurt of the world as though each hurt were a
blow.

In the year before I knew Thanne well, my first year in Oxford, Ohio, I lived in a small town of strangers, in a tiny effi-
ciency apartment, in a constant confusion about my personal
worth, and in solitude. Every other student was confident, unthreatened, easy in the company of others, and healthy. I was
not. I was overwhelmed by a sense of exile and by the suspicion
that this would never end, that I had just entered the real world
and discovered what life would be like forever. I did not feel
equal to the demands of graduate school. Every new assignment
accused me as incompetent. Throughout the fall and the winter
of that year I withdrew into my room. I was lonely. And it hurt.

If anything troubled the simple schedule of my day, I felt as
though I would burst into tears. The snow itself seemed to suffo-
cate me, and little criticisms in red pencil on my papers were
intolerable. All this is embarrassing to remember, but it is all
true: loneliness is as debilitating as a cancer. It's like a parasite, a
worm forever feeding in your vitals. When I bumped my head on
the corner of the cupboard door—no more than a little knock—I
suffered the whole range of emotions from fury to pitiful tears.

I didn't clean the apartment. I didn't wash my sheets or get a
haircut. I could hardly persuade myself to shower in the mornings. I said, "So what? So what?" For whose sake should I be
clean? No one, in the silence of the nights, said, "For my sake,
Walt, because I love you."

Finally, there were mornings when I didn't go out to teach my
freshman classes. I let the students sit and wait and wonder. So
what? Why should I teach them? All responsibility was swallowed by the unanswerable question, *Why?* If it had no answer, I
had no reason to go. And it had no answer because the question
really was, *Why am I living?* No one, in the silence of those
mornings, touched my hand or glanced across my room or even
existed to *be* that answer for me: "Because I need you." *Why am*

I here at all? No one is there to assure the lonely: "Because you are important to me. Because you are worthy. Because I love you."

Like a parasitic worm, loneliness feeds on the spirit—and kills it. It is an existential misery. When the question *"Why?"* has no answer, neither does the question *"Who?" Who am I?* If all that I do is meaningless, so am I.

Personal meaning and human value arise only in relationship. Solitude casts doubt on them. Identity, too, is discovered only in relationship. Lacking companions at the level of the soul, I finally cannot find my soul. It always takes another person to show myself to me. Alone, I die.

The last entry in my diary that year is cryptic and melancholy. "With joy's departure," I wrote, "is not sensitivity's, though perhaps it should be. With joy's departure is the arrival of an emptiness. Wanhope."

Wanhope is an ancient word for despair.

Then praise the dear Lord God who understood the dread of this human condition, so common to so many of us, and who in his mercy killed the killing worm by granting us a means for the knowing of our own lives: companionship.

It Is Not Good for Anyone to Be Alone

So said the Lord, and then he gave his creatures a gift so necessary and so universal that we seldom even think about it. He gave Eve and Adam to each other: he gave to every individual *community*.

Listen: particular and loving relationships are more than merely "good"; they are an essential quality of life. They affirm the individual's being. They assure him that he is. They both support him physically and define him spiritually. They give him a special place in the world, and they acknowledge the good purpose of his presence in that place. It is more than comfort we receive from other people: it is identity, so I know who I am. It is being itself, and the conviction of personal worth.

Have you noticed the words which Old Testament people use when someone important calls them by name? They don't say, "What?" or "Yes?" They answer with the curious sentence, "Here I am." So much is in that sentence: readiness to respond, a willing servitude, an offering of oneself to the other. But I rejoice in an even deeper meaning.

For there are times when Thanne and I lie abed at night, nearing sleep. Almost we float apart from one another; sleep is so private an activity, and darkness seems to close us into ourselves. But then Thanne whispers, waking me: "Wally? Wally?" And suddenly the fact that she has called my name—that she knows my name and can say it, that she whispers it in the trust that I will hear her—makes me to know *me*. Her voice, her word, her presence startles me with the knowledge of selfhood. I distinctly realize, in the tingling darkness, that *I am*. Moreover, I am not lost; I am not elsewhere or lonely or slipping into unreality, or else dead. No, I'm *right here*, in bed beside her, in this special place, enveloped in her sleepy love. Oh, that is a marvelous feeling—of being: an unspeakable gift of God.

Thanne merely whispers, "Wally? Wally?" And like Abraham when the Lord had called to him, like Samuel running to Eli in a Shiloh darkness, my soul responds with the thrilling knowledge, and the whole sentence: *Here I am*. I touch the woman's shoulder with my own. It is enough. She had nothing to say but my name. I had nothing else to do, but to be.

The worm is dead. (Ideally, the worm is dead. Remember: this chapter describes God's intentions.) God cancels loneliness in community.

All community has this beneficial effect for the individual. Friends affirm her, parents identify her, colleagues praise and depend upon her, neighbors support and acknowledge her. She needs people in particular and loving relationship. Marriage, surely, is not the only relationship of community; nor do we mean to argue that everyone must marry—only that every individual has, as a gift from God, the opportunity to discover herself and to come to self-conscious life within the network of human community.

Nevertheless, it was a man and a woman whom God joined in the beginning. And that joining, called a "cleaving," took precedence even over the relationship of parents and children. Marriage specifically was a gift of God. And marriage we may take as the most primal paradigm for any other relationship of community. It is marriage which we can characterize according to the creation account.

Therefore, we may ask now: tell us, Genesis, what is this archetypal relationship like? Or rather, what did God want it to be? What is marriage in its ideal condition?

A Helper Fit for Him

It doesn't say that God would make "a lover" fit for him. Marriage is not romanticized in the creation account. Its ideal

purpose is not one of sweet feelings, tender moods, poetical affections, or physical satisfactions—not "love" as the world defines love in all its nasal songs and its popular, shallow stories.

Not a lover, but "a helper." Marriage is meant to be flatly
practical. One human alone is help-*less*, unable. But "two are
better than one," says Ecclesiastes, "because they have a good
reward for their toil. For if they fall, one will lift the other.
Again, if two lie together, they are warm; but how can one be
warm alone?" Marriage makes the job of survival possible. This
is a purpose distorted if either partner thinks that feelings are the
most important purpose, or lasting romance the good reward.

And the fact that a spouse is termed a "helper" declares that
marriage was never an end in itself, but a preparation. We've
accomplished no great thing, yet, in getting married. We have
not *completed* a relationship (though many a fool assumes that
the hard work's done with the wedding and turns attention to
other interests). Rather, we've established the terms by which we
now will go to work. And it's in this "helping" one another that,
ideally, we will grow more and more to be one. We're not one by
magic. We're not truly one because the preacher, or we ourselves, said we were. But we grow one as our goals become the
same, and as we labor together toward those goals, helping one
another.

But Among the Animals Was Not Found a Helper Fit

Neither are we one because one spouse dominates the other,
overwhelming her goals with his own. Neither the husband nor
the wife is beast, or bird, or cattle to the other.

Beasts of burden conform to their owner's desires, bearing the
drover's loads, plowing the farmer's fields. Or beasts (the wild
animals, the untamed animals in the Genesis view of the world)
may be forced to submit to human will. This sort of creature,
and this sort of relationship, is not "fit" for a spouse.

Birds fulfil the aesthetic side of the human's superior nature,
beautiful in their plumage, thrilling in their song, the focus of
human dreams to fly, to soar, to be free of this drudge existence.
But neither is a spouse "fit" only to be a beautiful object, a lovely
but idolized thing, a "hunk" to show off, or a gracious goddess
who satisfies my sense of my own importance.

And *cattle* are considered personal property—the domesti-
cated animals of Genesis. In fact, the word *cattle* is a cognate of
the words *chattel* and *capital*, as in "capital gains." Animals may

be the possession of another human being, but a spouse was never meant to be.

The slow may make up speed by riding horses; so the horse is a help. The weak may make up strength by driving oxen; so the ox is a help. The blind use dogs. The thirsty milk cows; the hungry keep hens and slaughter steers; the sentimental fix affection upon cats. Humankind has always made up its lack of skills in the skills of animals. But that purpose (completing one's *self* by gaining the talents, characteristics, skills of another human) is not fitting for a marriage and is dangerous wherever it is found, because it reduces the spouse's role to that of an animal—something to be used. Only one being was intended to dominate in a marriage, but that one was neither of the partners. It was the Creator himself—God.

What sort of "help," then, is the spouse "fit" to be?

At Last, Bone of My Bones and Flesh of My Flesh

There is a shout of joy in these words. Right here, precisely here, is the end of loneliness. For Adam has found another being so much like him that she is, in fact, *of* him. And finding her, who has he found? Why, himself!

Ideally, the spouse is to be the "help" of similitude, of *likeness*. (This is only half the "helpfulness"; but understand and rejoice in this half first.) Husband and wife act as living mirrors to one another. When I look at Thanne, I discover myself, because Thanne is at the same time reacting to me. If she is reacting truthfully—and if I look upon her in true humility—I will find my talents in the praise of her eyes. I will see my needs in the sympathy of her chin; my personal characteristics will appear in the expressions of her face, in her posture and her words. I am I in Thanne! And she is she in me. And where better to view the truth of my self than in one who neither flatters nor scorns me, but knows me well and lovingly?

This mirroring is a most practical "help" to all my work, for I will be wise to my strengths and watchful of my weaknesses thereafter. Neither falsely proud nor falsely inferior, I can make realistic, efficient decisions.

When Thanne's eyes, looking upon me, are wounded, then I may know that something in me is injurious. When Thanne's eyes, looking upon me, are consoled, then I may know that I am consolation. And when Thanne's eyes merely look upon me, then I may know that I am: the gift of the knowledge of being! "Wally? Wally?" And I answer: "Here I am." This is a "help" most "fit" to me—to me specifically—one no chattel nor slave nor employee could ever be.

It is significant that Adam, seeing Eve, makes a pun in Hebrew on the words *man* and *woman*. *Ishshah* (woman) develops the word *Ish* (man) to its fullness, whereas *Ishshah* takes its root from *Ish*. Each word completes itself in the other. The pun implies that each spouse may find himself and herself in the other.

But the help of likeness is counterbalanced by another help.

They Were Naked and Not Ashamed

Nothing was hidden between this man and this woman. He was a man, she was a woman, and the sexual differences blamelessly, nakedly, showed. Behold: the differences were good!

What kind of "help," ideally, is the spouse to be? Also the help of *unlikeness*. It is because the man and woman were different that they could be both a sexual and a spiritual match together. If they had been exactly the same in every respect, they would not have "fit" into a single whole, but would have remained two duplicates, and separate.

Marriage both celebrates and uses the differences of its partners; this makes the partners necessary to one another. Is one smarter, better educated than the other? Good! That's not a matter of superiority nor an index of importance; rather, brains are that one's gift unto the marriage. When we married, Thanne's intelligence became my intelligence; she fit her wisdom to my foolishness, and we became one. Is one more sensitive than the other, quicker to weep, quicker to sense the mood of the moment? Good! My perceptions into the human drama and my artistry were my gift to our small community; they became Thanne's; they fit perfectly into her practicality, and she is not ashamed or threatened by the difference.

No two partners in a marriage are—or were meant to be—precisely alike. Each will have talents and tendencies the other does not have. Ideally, these differences are not a hindrance to complete unanimity, but should be searched out, identified, made naked unto one another, and celebrated. So do two begin to weave into one, working together by a wise division of labor.

Sexually, the differences yield a happy sensual satisfaction first—and after that, offspring. Physically and spiritually, these differences first "satisfy" any lack in the individual partner, a pleasant experience in itself (*satisfy* in Latin means "to make full"): this is the end of loneliness. Then, second, they produce the fruit of a shared labor.

So: the relationship of marriage is meant to be practical, each spouse a "help" to the other. And that help "fits" them perfectly together because they are *like* each other, and at the same time *unlike*.

In the Image of God . . . Male and Female He Created Them

What then? Did marriage have nothing, in its ideal purpose, to do with love? No, it had very much to do with love, but not in the merely mundane sense of good feelings and warm affection.

The image of God was reflected in created humanity, in male and female together (not merely in a man, or in a woman). In this we are like God, that we may love completely and unconditionally, emptying ourselves *of* our selves for the sake of our beloved. (Read Philippians 2:5–8 to see in Jesus the clearest expression of divine love, the love which God intends among humans and in marriage, a love radically different from the pale, self-serving concept of worldly love. *This* love requires self-sacrifice.) In this we may bear the image of the God who created us, that we have the capacity to love. It is when we love that we reflect God's image.

But in this we are unlike God—who could exist in serene solitude and still be love—that we must love someone else (not ourselves!) to love truly. That's why no single individual can completely manifest the image of God. Our love must have an object; there must be two in relationship to fulfil God's image.

Thus, marriage is the perfect arena in which the divine image—and love—can grow. As each partner loves the other more than he loves himself; as each sacrifices personal desires for the other's sake, or personal satisfactions for the good of her spouse; as each reveals the mind of Christ, doing "nothing from selfishness or conceit, but in humility counting the other better than" himself or herself, then the mind of their Christ appears in their marriage. It becomes visible. The purpose of marriage, then, is to allow us to nourish this holy love. More marvelously, the purpose of marriage is to manifest our God before the world. Lo: Thanne and I *are,* when we love each other with true humility, the image of God!

And when we love each other—when we are each a help unto the other, in likeness and in unlikeness—then we are in fact also loving God, whose holy ordinance we are obeying. For this is how he loves us, by giving us all good things, all the things we need for healthy, daily existence. (What else is Eden?) And this is how we love him, by obeying him in everything.

Marriage, finally, has very much to do with love.

FIVE

HOW DOES SIN DESTROY THE MARITAL IDEAL?

The Reality

---

*B*ut after we had been married many years, I woke one night to a dreadful truth.

I mean literally that I woke from a sound sleep, confused, ignorant of what woke me. My eyes popped open, though I didn't move a finger, and I stared through darkness trying to remember if I had heard a gunshot outside, a door slam, a child in the bathroom. I remembered nothing, none of these things. There was the silence only, and I felt an enormous emptiness as though the breath were being sucked from my body.

We lived in Evansville, then; I was often troubled by the obligations of my ministry; and I thought for a moment that plain worry had wakened me. But the church was not on my mind. It was a greater hollowness than my members had ever caused me; and this is the truth: I was afraid. Stiff on my back, stiff on my pillow, I murmured, "Thanne? I'm sorry, Thanne. Would you wake—"

But then I understood. Or at least I understood a part of the truth.

Thane wasn't in bed beside me. The bed was empty, her covers turned down.

"Thanne?"

It was two o'clock in the morning. "Where are you? What's the matter?" Thanne loves sleep. She's a champion sleeper. And if she's not feeling well, if that's all it is, then why do I feel so frightened?

I got out of bed and crept through the hall, through all the rooms, and began to suffer the odd notion that she was nowhere in the house. This wasn't a silly premonition, though I told myself it was; this was nearer the truth than I'd wanted to believe.

"There you are!" I said with relief. I found her in the living room, a dark form sitting in the corner of the sofa, her knees against her chest, her arms hugging her legs, her face turned sideways to stare at pale light outside the window. "What's the matter? Can't you sleep?"

She didn't answer me. She didn't move.

"Can I get you something? Milk?"

She didn't so much as shrug. I crept around her, to see her face. Her eyes were open; her mouth was pulled down at the corners.

Now my silly premonition began to have its reason, and the emptiness in my chest swelled. I didn't have proofs. Thanne hadn't said a word. But the emptiness seemed to be between us. I felt very clumsy, suddenly, and very afraid. Thanne was so small. Thanne was so sad. The pale light shined in tear-tracks on her cheeks.

Well, I couldn't just stand there, full of uncertainty. I reached my hand to her knee. When I touched her, I thought she trembled and I pulled back. Then my own body seemed gross, and I felt foolish, my hand hanging in the air. So I told myself that the trembling was just my imagination, and I reached again.

Without moving a whit, in a clipped, brittle voice, Thanne said, "Don't touch me."

Immediately I sat down opposite her and—I couldn't help it—groaned.

A long, long silence lasted between us. Thanne was crying without a sound, her eyes wide open. I was searching for something to say. I could not leave her and go back to bed, not like this. But I felt as though I were burning in the furnace of her silence.

I said, "Thanne—" I cleared my throat. "Thanne, what did I do?"
She didn't answer.

I said, "*Please,* Thanne, tell me."

She said, "Nothing."

It was a response. I'd heard her voice. That was worth something, so I pursued it. "Not nothing, Thanne." I said. "It can't be nothing, if you're like this. Won't you tell me what I did wrong?"
She didn't answer.

"You've *got* to talk to me," I pleaded. "What am I supposed to do? Guess?" But I was ready to defend myself against any accusation she might deliver. I leaned toward her, intense. "If we don't talk, we get nowhere. Ruthanne, this is stupid!"

She snapped, "Leave me alone!" Now she was trembling visibly. Even in the dim light I saw her chest heave.

But she had spoken. I came toward her from my seat, yearning for her to speak some more. "Is that what I do? Do I leave you alone?" She shrank from me. "Please, Thanne! Please, Thanne, tell me—"

But she stood up. She hissed, "You! You! You're *all* talk. What good would talking do?"

I said, "But I don't even know what—" I said this to myself. Thanne had run on bare feet away from me. She threw herself into the bathroom, slammed and locked the door. All these things I heard in the darkness. And then I heard her burst into angry tears. When I stood outside the door, I saw that she hadn't even turned on the light.

I went back to bed. And this is what I thought, even in my stupid ignorance: Thanne was lonely. She was truly, violently lonely—though we were married, and though I did in fact love her. I recognized the signs from my own experience: the worm was not dead after all.

O dear Father in heaven, who gave us marriage to abolish loneliness, why should such a thing be, that my wife, the source of my own self-knowledge, suffers loneliness?

But this is the consequence of our sinning.

I'll say it plainly: sin destroys the divine ideal of the marriage—not just the little sins of a few people, but the sinfulness of humankind. Finally we will define the forgiveness that can heal the hurt of sinning. But first we have to understand sin itself. Therefore, back to the book of Genesis we go.

You Will Be Like God

Eve is the matriarch for all humanity. Her choices prefigure ours. In her we may see ourselves in order to understand what sin is and what it does, specifically, to marital relationships.

What is not particularly significant is that this picture of the primal sin contains a woman. What is, however, significant is that the woman was alone. Aloneness (not loneliness, but a willful separation from supportive relationships) makes one vulnerable to temptation and to the suspicion that one might pursue and satisfy one's own desires, neglectful of one's spouse. Separation—physical, emotional, spiritual, financial; the persistent hiding of habits, of important matters, commitments, possessions; the separation of one's *self* from one's spouse—is not in itself wrong. But it is dangerous.

This is what the serpent said to the woman alone: "You will not die. . . . You will be like God."

Here is the sharpest, most concise statement of sinful desire, and the core of all sinning: to be like God.

But why should the satanic promise be so enticing? Wasn't Eve already like God, made, with Adam, in his image and after his likeness? Well, yes, she was—but not in the way that self-centered people would wish to be.

First, no human alone is like God. The true image of God is reflected in the loving community, people with people, male and female together. The image of God is printed upon the marriage whole, when it is as it should be, but not upon either individual partner *of* that marriage, whether male or female. "You will be like God" is the desire for sole self-importance, to be a law unto oneself regardless of the presence of others—to be complete in and of one's self, as only God can be. Independent. Free! Needs exist only as that one has needs; the needs of others are mere irritations, for all others are seen as lesser than this god-self.

Second, to be truly in the image of God is not, at the same time, to possess the authority of God. Rather, it is to participate in God's supernal authority by means of humble obedience to him, by humbling oneself to one's spouse—even as Jesus was both obedient and humble before all humanity. But "You will be like God" is the desire personally to possess divine authority over others, over everything. Such authority turns one's own desires (even one's whims) into commands for others; thus, one's wish is seen as the *law* of the relationship. As God makes and enforces orders without explanation, merely because he is God, so does this godlike person force his or her will upon the marriage; other people are seen as good and righteous only so long as they do those wishes.

When Eve took of the fruit of the tree and ate, the attitude here described became her faith, her perception of truth and of reality. (Every faith, whether true or false, whether good or bad, believes its principles without clear evidence; it merely and steadfastly believes what cannot be rationally proven. The sinner does not need proof that he is a god. He simply believes it.) Eve's action of taking and eating turned a tendency into a fact. Sin is this godlike attitude; sin is the action that comes of it. This is the monster that enters the marriage, destroying the ideal the true God has established.

Knowing Good and Evil

The serpent told Eve that she, like God, would know good and evil. But didn't Eve already know these things? Yes. She knew it was good to obey God and evil to disobey, because disobedience would bring death. But the serpent (sin!) offered her the knowledge of good and evil *as God saw them*—that is, sin wants to decide what is good and what is evil through its own opened eyes; it wants to decide these things *for itself!*

You see, now that one is a god, one declares that what is good for oneself is "The Good," good for everyone, for the world. And one takes for granted that what hurts oneself (whether it be to dig too much in the garden, or else to go without sexual satisfaction for a while) is "The Evil," evil for everyone, for the world. The godlike person ascends to the seat of universal judgment and has the right (simply because he is a god) to criticize the world according to his own personal standards.

But the ideal marriage relationship depends upon a humble obedience to the true God's declaration of what was good and evil. It is just at this point that sin completely ruptures that holy design. For the godlike person feels quite qualified to accept what he likes of that design and to reject what discomforts him. Yet the godlike person assumes himself to be righteous (oh, sin is insidious) because he feels that he is still being obedient. And he is obedient. But he has chosen to obey the false god of Self.

She Also Gave Some to Her Husband and He Ate

Adam ate as well. No one is free of this sinful attitude. No one is able *not* to act upon it. All husbands and all wives are tainted; and it is likeliest the spouse who says "I, at least, am holy" that is more blinded by sin than the other.

But there's a deeper meaning in Eve's action than the universality of sin. She is saying, "Do as I do." Further, she is saying, "Be as I am." The godlike person wishes to make the world—and this marriage—in his or her own image. The true God must be cast out for good (for my good) and for good (forever).

Now that one is like God in some things, one wants to be like God in all things—and wants all things to be like himself. Little images of the true God are distressing to have around. A truly good wife is a constant criticism against the godlike husband; the better she is, the more he is convinced of her evil, because her very being opposes him. Therefore one tries every means available to "make" his spouse his own—his own possession, his own devout worshipper, his own image. "Be more like me!" (And if she will not conform, then she is "contrary," and he is righteous in self-pity.)

Thus sin enters not just into one partner but into the *marriage*, into the relationship.

And then this is what is:

In the Day That You Eat of It You Shall Die

Well, no: they didn't, and we don't, immediately expire upon the sin. But we do begin the grievous process of dying. Awake and aware (if not fully comprehending the reasons), we suffer the perishing, the passing away, of the good order of God, the good life of his ideals, "The Good" itself. It is this suffering which characterizes human relationships. We chose for ourselves a deific, supernal *one*-liness. We chose to be like God, who can dwell in divine solitude. But we are only creatures, not the true Creator; therefore, we did in fact choose for ourselves intolerable *loneliness*.

Loneliness, you will remember, is a dying. God was right.

And this is what is:

They Knew That They Were Naked; . . . and Made Themselves Aprons

Do you remember the "help" that God intended husbands and wives to be for one another?—the help of *likeness* (each an honest mirror to the other), and the help of *unlikeness* (a pooling of their separate talents, a celebration of the differences)? By sin these are destroyed.

Both Eve's and Adam's eyes were opened. Both the godlike husband and the godlike wife choose to decide good and evil from their own, separate perspectives. So, his good may seem her evil, because it diminishes her. And her good may seem his evil, because it jeopardizes his personal fulfillment. How will they solve a difference if they are two gods in the same household, obeying two separate codes of law, each as righteous as the other? And how will they truly reason with each other, when gods do not need to explain, merely to command?

Such partners are not helps *to* each other. Rather, each demands help *from* the other; and each feels that she or he has a right to the help. He has a right to her body: aren't they married? She has a right to change plans without telling him: aren't they married, after all? He has a right to be heard in his household. She has the right to privacy in her own house. Self-importance gives them these rights. The marriage was made to serve—*me*.

What, therefore, happens to the help of likeness?

When the likeness between them is self-importance (and not a common obedience to the same God) it causes an intense distrust. The husband is convinced that his wife does everything with the motive of building herself up, easing her life. How does he know this? Because he knows himself and she is like him—isn't everyone? Therefore, he does not trust what he sees in her. If she flatters him, he suspects it. If she criticizes him, rejecting the things he has called "Good," he calls her selfish. In true pain the husband cries out, "My wife doesn't understand me!" And how does he feel then? Why, lonely. They are spiritually separated, as though each had put on clothes to hide from the other. The marriage, meant to abolish loneliness, makes him even lonelier than before. "She thinks only of herself."

More subtle still, the husband may be right, but not in the way he thinks. It could be that the wife who breaks her back to please her husband has deep within her the selfish motive that she cannot live in a tense household, that she is trying to relieve the tension for her own sake. Therefore, she tells him what he wants to hear and shows him what he wants to see: she mirrors to him not his true self, but his own false picture of himself. And of herself she reveals nothing, hiding both anguish and her private motives in the clothing of smiles, a (sometimes manipulative) servitude, and Christian goodness. How does she feel? Well, when she cares to admit it, lonely. Together—but separate—they suffer the selfsame dying.

And what of the help of unlikeness?

The differences between two gods become threats and weapons to enforce the personal will. One either uses his superiority against the other, or else fears her superiority against himself. So she has an able tongue; now, however, it no longer speaks for him, helping his own slower speech; now it is sharp and cuts him like a razor when he cannot think of a word in his own defense. So he has a strong arm; now, however, it is no longer a support for her weakness; now it is a brutality to support his own demands, his "rights."

Unlikeness makes one feel strange or endangered—"different" to the point of alienation. At the least, unlikeness draws pity or snorts of scorn or blank, uncomprehending looks. Therefore, the partners strive to seem the same. They dress themselves in "like" opinions, in "like" habits, in "like" tastes and goals—but at bottom this sort of sameness is a truce and not the truth. They have become ashamed of their nakedness.

Then, truly, "in the day that you eat of it you shall die." These spouses spend a great deal of energy denying much of the truth of themselves, of their own natures, repressing it so that they may live life with as little pain as possible. So close to another human being, yet so isolated. So lonely.

In Pain You Shall Bring Forth Children, Yet Your Desire Shall Be for Your Husband

This, then, is the irony that characterizes the marriage relationship as a consequence of sin: that one's desire should also cause one's pain. It is a paradox that the good of bringing life into the world feels so bad, that it feels, in fact, like dying.

But it's an irony not restricted to women or to childbearing; birth is just one example of the same condition which affects all human relationships. Sin, the arrogant, personal drive to godlikeness in authority and solitary self-importance, has so snarled the marital bond that, though we will always desire to live with another human, yet living together causes pain. We *will* want it; but it *will* hurt us. We may produce a marvelous good in marrying (just as a woman brings forth a marvelous baby), but we will produce it through tribulation and labor.

"Men!" said the wise old woman, shaking her head. "We cain't live with 'em, and we sure cain't live without 'em."

"Women!" growled the ancient philosopher, spitting against the stove. "You love 'em and you wantta leave 'em—both. It's a puzzle, surely."

And together they spoke the truth.

And He Shall Rule Over You

Yet marriages survive, despite the sin that troubles them and isolates the partners. How is this, if the sin has not been cleansed? In his curse the Lord God announced the pattern that would preserve them, though he was no longer speaking the ideal: he was defining a realistic necessity caused by the loss of the divine image among us. "He shall rule."

The significant word here is not *he,* but *rule.* When two conflicting wills engage to live together, it takes *rules,* a law, and a single dominating will to keep them together in spite of themselves. Whereas there *should* have been sweet agreement, a humble care, a unifying equality in which each emptied himself for the sake of the other, there must now be a code of law imposed upon the marriage—imposed with the rights of judgment and the persuasion of punishment. It compels a unity of sorts, though it can't cancel human misery and it will not fuse two beings truly into one.

Where does such a law come from? Often from outside the marriage. From the legislated decrees of the state; from the mores of one's immediate culture and community (which are stronger as that community is smaller, more watchful, and more conservative); from the marital ethics taught by one's church, as churches interpret scripture and their own traditions; from the explicit agreements of the spouses themselves (and then each one's conscience is the stick for such a law).

Usually the law for any single marriage is formed from a combination of these sources. The benefit of legal structures upon marriage is that they restrain the sinful tendencies of the spouses, protecting them from themselves. They make it right to talk about "rights." But the sadness is that legalities cannot transfigure the spouses; they cannot change their natures, cleanse the sin, and atone their souls. The effect of the law is always negative. The law restricts; it does not empower. It can punish; it cannot encourage. It holds back the hand; it does not feed the heart, so that this heart might willingly nourish another. And the more evident sadness today is that as the law grows weaker, individual willfulness grows stronger. Fewer marriages endure after all, and more divorce occurs.

Again, where does this law come from? Often, too, from within the marriage. That is, the spouse of the stronger will *does* "rule over" the partner to one degree or another, by open command or by a hidden manipulation. So the marriage survives; but its humans are no longer whole. Something of each is repressed or lost or amputated.

Even so has sin disfigured the good ideal God had offered us. We were meant, in our relationship, to be his image in the world;

and the holy evidence of love was intended as the purpose of our marriages, the product of our *help*fulness *fit* for one another—our oneness. Instead, love has been replaced by law. And a failing law has produced a sad statistic: a mass of failing marriages.

And yet—we remember the ideal design. It is an extraordinary human faculty, that we can remember even back to the beginning. Even when we cannot see it, we *know* the ideal and yearn for it. A tension exists, then, between the reality of the world and the holy image in our minds. So the question comes with urgency: is there no alternative? Is there no means given us by which to be transfigured, to be redeemed from our sin/legalistic condition, truly to figure the divine face, divinely loving, in our marriages again?

Well, the Lord Jesus entered the world to redeem its reality, and to forgive.

By forgiveness the same Lord Jesus can enter a marriage, to redeem a relationship.

·SIX·

WHAT IS
FORGIVENESS?

The Divine Absurdity

---

*H*ow long can a silence last? Long. How long could Thanne continue not talking to me—not talking, at least, of matters crucial to our spirits and our relationship? Long. Thanne had a gift for silences. And after the night when I found her awake I suffered a bewildered misery.

Oh, I was such a fool in those days. But I was working blind. What could I do, if she wouldn't talk to me?

No: I was a *fool* in those days. I did not see that even my efforts at healing hurt her. Well, I wasn't looking at these present efforts, only at past actions to find the fault; but, in fact, the fault was consistently there, in me, in all that I was doing. Therefore, I kept making things worse for all my good intentions. I was a walking fault!

At nights she always went to bed before I did. When I came to the bedroom, carefully shading the light from her eyes, doing everything possible to care for her, I always found her turned away, curled tight on her side, at the very edge of the bed. Her cheek was the only flesh I saw, and the corner of her eye—

closed. Was she sleeping? I didn't know. I was scared to ask, scared to wake her if she was, and scared she wouldn't answer if she wasn't. I got under covers cursing creaky bedsprings. And my heart broke to see the cheek I could not touch. Her skin was no longer mine.

"Did you sleep well?" I asked in the morning, as casually as I could.

Thanne was growing pale, gaunt in her thinness, drawn around the mouth (from so long, so pinched a silence). Her hair broke at the ends, dry. She fixed breakfast for the children in her housecoat. Her poor ankles were flour-white.

"Did you sleep well?"

I stood by, eating toast. Ministry always grieved my stomach. On the days of difficult duties (preaching itself tore me up; counseling was forever an uncertain affair dead-ending in human sin; funerals were the worst responsibility of all) I would eat a scrap and leave.

"Did you sleep well?"

Thanne flashed me a glance as sharp as a scalpel. "I didn't sleep," she said and slapped eggs on plates. Her tone said volumes, but left the interpretation to me: *because of you.* Or, *What's it to you?* Or, *You ask me just to rub it in.* Or, *Why don't you just go to work?* I could take my pick. I left for work.

But I was not a bad man, was I? I didn't fool around with women—that's worth something in this world, isn't it? I didn't fritter away our money, or beat her, or even talk back to her. I wasn't a drunkard. What I was, was a pastor! I had given even my professional life to God. I was a good man! Then where was the problem between us?

All day I argued my defense in my own mind. All day I truly suffered a stomach pain which felt very much like homesickness, an intolerable loneliness. It prickled my back to think how much I loved Thanne; but it drew my gut into a knot to remember that we were not talking. And the knot was guilt; but the knot was self-pity, too. For God's sake, what did I do?

In the evening I planned to prove my goodness to her. I vacuumed the living room. With mighty snaps, I shook out all the rugs of our house. When the children had gone to bed (so quietly, so quietly, like mice sneaking beneath their parents' silences) I noticed that Thanne hadn't yet done the dishes. *Good!* I thought. *My opportunity!* And I rolled up my sleeves to help her out.

But when I was halfway through the pans I felt the hairs on my neck stand up—as though the Lantern had haunted our kitchen.

I paused in the greasy water. I turned and saw Thanne standing in the doorway, glaring at me in silent fury, her thin arms folded at her chest.

She hissed, "You're just trying to make me feel guilty." She disappeared from the doorway and went to bed.

No—but I *thought* I was trying to help. The dirty pans beside me made me sad.

And then I pulled a trick so callous and offensive that I can only tell it here as a confession. What I did was right for the sermon that Sunday morning. I always preached sermons with a certain dramatic staging in order to serve the point, and this particular gesture was perfectly reasonable for worship. But not for Thanne. I wasn't thinking of Thanne. Or rather, I kind of hoped that a gesture so right for preaching might benefit me at home, too.

I was preaching, I think, about love. I was focusing, I think, on the necessity of gift—the giving of one's heart. Thanne and the children sat near the front of the sanctuary. While I preached, I likened the heart to the blood-red rose. And in order to signify the symbol visually, I walked to the altar and drew a rosebud from one of the vases there. Preaching, still preaching, I descended the chancel steps and moved among the congregation toward Thanne—whose mouth pinched tighter the closer I came (but I was preaching and did not notice). There, in a triumph of sermonic illustration, in front of the entire assembly, I handed Thanne my rosebud.

She took it. Instantly I knew my error. She took it, glaring at me. She took it, and her chin began to tremble. She took it, and her eyes glistened with tears—but she did not bow her head or give a single indication to the people around her that she was crying. She held her head high. She took my rose and dropped it to the floor.

That afternoon she made no dinner at all. She left the children with me and drove away alone.

She was so small. She was so independent to be driving God knows where in the car. I loved her so much, and I ached so horribly with her pain, and I was so perplexed as to why she hurt or what in the world I could do about it. I suppose that if I'd been alone, I would have panicked and gone after her, not even knowing where to look but hating inactivity more than the fruitless looking. But I wasn't alone. I had the children.

Thanne had left me with three responsibilities: to watch over the children; to cook their Sunday dinner; and to make some decision about the party we had planned for the evening. Rich and Donna Nordmeyer were scheduled to visit us for food and games and devotions. This was our regular practice; once a month we gathered to support each other. And we played a game called Risk.

Well, I cooked and we ate dinner, the children and I. But because the afternoon stretched toward the evening, and because Thanne wasn't coming home, and because games seemed alien to the mood of our household those days, I made the decision to cancel them. I telephoned Rich and explained that something had come up; we couldn't meet that night. I "fixed" it.

At six-thirty, a half hour before the time of our party, Thanne drove into the garage, got out of the car, closed the door, and walked to the house. I watched her in the evening gloom. She came into the kitchen, laid her purse aside, and began to remove her coat. The kitchen was full of shadow. I hadn't turned the lights on yet.

I said, "It's all right, Thanne. I made it easier for us."

She gave me a tight-lipped glance.

"I called Rich and told them not to come tonight," I said.

And that was the end of our silence. Thanne is little. Thanne can be as quick as a stiletto.

"You—" she whispered. "You!" she snapped. Her eyes blazing, her face broken by the final assault, one wound more than she could tolerate from me, *"You always do that!"* she cried. "Those are *my* friends! I needed my friends!"

With her coat half on, half off, she stood furious in the middle of the kitchen and fired at me old, old anger, a fusillade of grievances, the pain that had been eating at her, mutely, from the inside. She was frightfully articulate: God had given her a tongue, or anger had. And she did not love me then. No, she did not love me then. Each of us was very much alone. She used the word *hate*. And for the next fifteen minutes she described in particular detail what her life had been like for the last few years. She told me why she couldn't sleep the night I found her in the living room. She used the word *hate*, and she accused me as the cause of all her sorrow. And she was right.

When she was done, when the words simply ran out because there was no more to say, Thanne went upstairs to the bathroom. I stayed alone in the kitchen. And I knew one thing for sure; and one thing I guessed at. And one thing both of us wouldn't even think about.

I knew for sure that Thanne was right. I had sinned terribly against her, sins which I will name before this chapter is done, so you will understand that it wasn't a single act or a number of acts: it was I myself. I was sin.

And the thing I guessed at, while I stood beside the sink, was that I could live without love. I mumbled the words to myself in order to hear them: "I can live without love." I was, I thought, defining the rest of our lives. I was imagining our marriage as a structure containing no soul, no life nor breath. "I can live without love": a sort of a vow and a preparation. I was imagining the days we would spend together hereafter, our passage through the years with, but not *of,* each other. I was testing my resolve, I think, staring through the kitchen window to an evening darkness: I can survive; "I can live without love." Because I deserved no love! It was a righteous punishment.

And the thing that neither one of us would even contemplate was divorce. We were stuck with each other. Let the world call that imprisonment; but I say it gave us the time, and God the opportunity, to make a better thing between us. If we could have escaped, we would have. Because we couldn't we were forced to choose the harder, better road.

WHAT IS FORGIVENESS?

Forgiveness is a sort of divine absurdity. It is irrational, as the world reasons things, and unwise. But "has not God made foolish the wisdom of the world?" It is a miracle maker, because it causes things to be that, logically, empirically, have no right to be. For-give-ness is a holy, complete, unqualified *giving.*

Let me define that "giving" more clearly. Then let me speak of the source for such a marvelous impossibility.

Giving Up

Forgiveness is a willing relinquishment of certain rights. The one sinned against chooses *not* to demand her rights of redress for the hurt she has suffered. She does not hold her spouse accountable for his sin, nor enforce a punishment upon him, nor exact a payment from him, as in "reparations." She does not make his life miserable in order to balance accounts for her own misery, though she might feel perfectly justified in doing so, tit for tat: "He deserves to be hurt as he hurt me."

In this way (please note this carefully) she steps *outside* the systems of law; she steps *into* the world of mercy. She makes possible a whole new economy for their relationship: not the cold-blooded and killing machinery of rules, rights, and privileges, but the tender and nourishing care of mercy, which always rejoices in the growth, not the guilt or the pain, of the other. This is sacrifice. To give up one's rights is to sacrifice something of one's self—something hard-fought-for in the world.

Giving Notice

But forgiveness must at the same time be the clear communication to the sinner that she has sinned. It may seem saintly for the wounded party to suffer his pain in silence, and it is surely easier to *keep* that silence than risk opening wounds; but it does no good for the marriage, and it encourages no change in the sinner. He, the one who was sinned against, must speak. "Giving notice" means that he will reveal to his spouse, as clearly as he can, what she has done. No, the purpose of this revelation is not to accuse: it is to impart information. Nor does he disclose the sin by acting out his hurt in front of her (that wants to punish her by increasing her guilt; but he has already separated her sin from his own hurt). With love and not with bitterness he explains both her act and its consequences, remembering always that this communication is for *her* sake, the sinner's sake, and showing always in his countenance a yearning love for her.

This, too, is sacrifice. To react in a manner opposite to vengeance (the natural desire of human nature), to risk reopening wounds, and to seek to heal the one who sought to hurt—these are sacrifices of one's self.

Giving Gifts

Forgiveness is, at the same time, a pure, supernal giving: the receiver doesn't deserve it; the giver wants nothing for it. It's not a *thanks*giving, because that's the return of one goodness for another. It's not a purchasing price, not even the price of marital peace, because that is hoping to buy one goodness with another. Forgiveness is not a good work which expects some reward in the end, because that motive focuses upon the giver, while this kind of giving must focus completely upon the spouse, the one receiving the gift, the one who sinned. The forgiver cannot say, "Because I have given something to you, now you must give something to me." That's no gift at all.

Rather, forgiveness is giving love when there is no reason to love and no guarantee that love will be returned. The spouse is simply not lovable right now! Forgiveness is repaying evil with kindness, doing all the things that love requires—even when you don't *feel* the love; for you can *do* love also in the desert days when you do not feel loving.

Only when a pure, unexpected, unreasonable, and undeserved gift-giving appears in the marriage does newness enter in and healing begin. This is grace. Only when the spouse has heard his sin, so that he might anticipate, under the law, some retribution, but receives instead the gestures of love—only then can he begin to change and grow in the same humility which his wife has shown him. Finally, gift-giving is the greatest sacrifice of all, for it is the complete "giving away" of one's self.

SACRIFICE: ARE WE ABLE?

All three types of "giving" together define the full act of forgiveness; all three must be present at once in the same act.

If one hasn't truly "given up" his legal rights and expectations, he will "give notice" and "give gifts" grudgingly. The forgiver will still expect some reward for his goodness and may grow severely disappointed if all his good efforts seem, in the end, to come to nothing.

If one hasn't truly "given notice," the forgiveness may indeed be unavailing and the sinner may never change, because she will suppose that she has a right to her husband's "gift-giving," and his love will seem no wonder to her at all—though, coming undeserved, it should seem an astonishing wonder.

And if one isn't truly "giving gifts," if one isn't loving truly (even when there's no reason for the love), then the whole burden of change is left up to the sinning one, who has just been notified of her sin. But someone sick can't heal herself very well. Therefore, newness does not enter the relationship.

Together these three elements make forgiveness a sacrifice indeed. Are the offspring of Adam and Eve able to sacrifice themselves? This is a question of crucial importance. Are we able to sacrifice our whole selves for the sake of someone who hurt us? And even if we think that we *are* able, is what we are a sufficient gift?

The apostle Paul didn't say that love bears some things, that love believes only in the best things, that love hopes for a reasonable period of time, or that it endures for a while. No, love is a divine absurdity. It is unreasonable. Paul said, "Love bears *all* things, believes *all* things, hopes *all* things, endures *all* things." Love is limit*less*. For-give-ness is to give infinitely, without end.

But look at us! We are but created creatures. There comes a point when we grow tired in a difficult relationship: there is an end to our emotional rope. The wife says, "A person can take only so much"—and she speaks truthfully. The husband says, "There's nothing left in me to give you any more. *I've reached my limit!*" He isn't lying. We are limited, after all.

This is our human predicament: we are able to sin infinitely against one another, but we are able to forgive only finitely. Left to ourselves alone, forgiveness will run out long before the sinning does.

In fact, we cannot sacrifice enough to heal the one who hurts us. We are not able to forgive equal to our spouse's sinning—not when such giving must come solely from ourselves. But if forgiveness is a tool, it is also a power tool whose power comes from a source other than ourselves. We may use it; we may carefully and self-consciously apply it to our spouses; but Jesus Christ empowers it. He is the true source of its transfiguring love. And the love of the Son of God is infinite.

Jesus Christ, the Primal Source and the Power of Forgiveness

In order to forgive your spouse—and so to heal the broken relationship—first forget your spouse. The primary relationship is between you and God; what happens there will affect what happens in your household. First, it is you and God alone.

And behold: with God, *you* were the sinner! Ever before your spouse sinned against you, you sinned against the mighty God. You, like Eve, demanded the personal, self-centered authority that belongs to God alone. In your own life, you pulled God down from his throne, then sat in that seat yourself, becoming at once your own god and God's own enemy. At best you used God as your servant, making your prayers a list of demands, the good things you wanted him to do for you. At worst, you recreated the divine being in your own image, rejecting God's revelation of himself, resisting his commands as you would resist a tyrant, hating him. In either case, yours was so monstrous a sin that you should have died for it. The sentence and the consequence was death, no less than the extinguishing of your life—and no appeal.

When we speak in terms of life and death, we are speaking of infinities. Death is infinite, an endless separation from God and from the life that has no end. You chose, by your sinning, an infinite solitude.

But God responded with an infinite love. This is the measure of his forgiveness: that it was more than equal to your sin—and is therefore measureless.

The dear Lord God did not turn you over to death. He sent his Son into the world (into the enemy territory of your own life) to do what? To *forgive* you. And it is marvelous to note that all three elements of forgiveness (the same ones you must bring your spouse) were purely present in Jesus' sacrificial act on your behalf.

Jesus "gave up" his rights—and so removed you from the world of law to the world of mercy. Jesus "gave up" his rights. Though in the form of God, he "did not count equality with God a thing to be grasped, but emptied himself, taking the form of a servant." As a servant he lived in the flesh. Moreover, he humbled himself to death, even death on the cross. Do you die *a little* for the sake of your spouse? Jesus died completely for your sake—died the death you should have died. This is mercy, that the divine dictum "In the day you eat of it, you shall die" became "though you were the one who ate of it, Jesus died instead." When he gave up his rights, he transferred you from the world of doom to the world of life.

Also, he did this publicly; he did this in the flesh, where everyone could see it. That is, he "gave notice" both to humanity and to you: that you sinned, what your sin was, and what its consequences were—his own suffering, holy grief. The evident righteousness of Jesus' life revealed that *your* sin sent him to the cross, not his own. And just as his glance to Peter, after that disciple had denied him three times, drove Peter out of the courtyard to weep bitterly, so through his Scripture did Jesus glance at you, persuading you of your personal fault.

Finally, he did all this in grace, as a free gift for you, loving you with a love you did not deserve. "Giving gifts." He himself received nothing for the sacrifice. You received everything—though you could have paid nothing for it. You received life—infinitely. In Jesus Christ you do possess the *infinite* love which you need for your marriage. As much as you could sin, so much did he forgive you. He bore and believed and hoped and endured *all* things. This is the primal sacrifice.

Now, thou servant possessed of a measureless bank account—now remember your spouse again, whose sin against you is a pittance (however painful it may feel), whose debt is a denarius, measured in pennies.

When Christ is the single most solid reality upon which you stand; when in faith you find the source of your own life in him; when you yourself do dwell within his loving mercy and his forgiveness, then you are empowered to forgive your spouse, infinitely. Christ is the well from which to draw the water for your thirsty wife or husband. But this must be remembered: only as you know Jesus' limitless forgiveness *for you* (that first!—that personally!) are you able limitlessly to share forgiveness with your spouse (that second—but that personally as well).

But then what? Then you *become* Christ's forgiveness for your wife, your husband—for Jesus loves her fully as much as he does you. It isn't you at all who produces this forgiveness; it is Christ in you, whose divine forgiveness is forever. His was the real death, his the real sacrifice. Therefore, you do not die at all; you merely mimic the archetypal forgiveness which Jesus accomplished on the cross once for all time, once for every marriage and for every sin that any marriage suffers. Are you able? Well, if you yourself are not the one who is dying; and if you are losing nothing now (having lost it all in Christ before), of course you are able to love the one who wounded you. Of course you are able to forgive.

The Divine Ideal Revived

"Love one another," Jesus said, "*as I have loved you.*" This is the love enacted on the cross, the sacrificial and self-emptying love, the love of forgiveness. Sin destroyed the image of God in human marriages. But with the gift of mercy, seized by a strong faith, sin now becomes the opportunity for the image of God to be resurrected again in human marriages.

The wife who turns her face, filled with a forgiving grace, upon her husband shows him, too, the face of Jesus. Each spouse becomes God's mirror to the other—first the reflection of God, and then the reflection of that other.

And if my wife shows God to me (especially when I realize that I do not deserve love) then my wife herself will seem to me a gift of God. She not only brings gifts—she *is* a gift! Suddenly my own love for her leaps up to a higher plane; I will handle her as a sacred, holy thing, an Eve I had no right to expect. This marriage should have died—but it didn't! That she exists at all, that I did not lose her (as rightly I should have) by my sinning, shall wring from my soul an honest gratitude. Do you understand how the very nature of the relationship is transfigured by forgiveness?

When both the husband and the wife are thus humbled by the forgiveness of their Christ, they are also humbled before each other. The individual attitude of godlikeness is gone in the true God, killed by guilt and feebleness, buried under mercy. With it goes the individual's arrogant presumption that he can himself decide what is good and what is evil: what he thought was "good" nearly destroyed them. When *both,* then, are obedient children of the same good God, the differences between the spouses are no longer threats or weapons or a shame; but, like children in innocence, they may blamelessly be naked before one another again, celebrating and sharing these differences. If one can truly trust that the other will forgive him, then he need no longer hide portions of himself under an apron of lies and hypocrisy; he can be fully honest and forthright before her. And if she believes in her own (her Lord's!) ability to forgive "all things," then she will not blind herself to the realities of her husband's character; she will not need to maintain denials or fantasies, but may see and hear and know him completely for what he is. Truth, not lies or suspicions, dwells between them. And what is the practical benefit of such clear-headed honesty? Why, that they can work *together* on the common projects of marriage, that each one, once again, is a "help" perfectly "fit" for the other.

DEUS EX MACHINA—DEUS EX VENIA

What did I learn that Sunday evening in our kitchen when Thanne broke silence and burned me with my guilt? What did I hear from the small woman grown huge in her fury, half in, half out of her coat, while the daylight died outside? I learned her grievances. I heard what her life had been like for several years, though I had not known it. I saw myself through *her* eyes, and the vision accused me.

And I learned what caused her silence in the first place, sending her out of my bed a month ago to sit in the dark of the living room and in sorrow.

"It's all right, Thanne," I said when she first came into the kitchen. "I called Rich and told them not to come tonight."

Her eyes flashed. "You—" she whispered. "You!" she snapped. "*You always do that!* Those are my friends."

"Thanne, I do not always—"

"Always! More than you know. You decide my whole life for me, but you hardly pay mind to the decisions. You do it with your left hand, carelessly. You run me with your left hand. Everyone else gets the right hand of kindness. Everyone else can talk to you. Not me. The left hand."

"Thanne! I'm not a bad person. I do everything as well as I can. What have I done to you? I try to please God. I'm a good pastor—"

"A good pastor!" she spat the words. "You *are* a good pastor, Wally. God knows, I wanted you to be a good pastor. But sometimes I wish you were a bad pastor, a lazy pastor, a careless pastor. Then I'd have the right to complain. Or maybe I'd have *you* here sometimes. A good pastor! Wally, how can I argue with God and take you from him? Wally, Wally, your ministry runs *me,* but you leave me alone exactly when I need you. *Where are you all the time?*"

I didn't answer.

Then this is what she told me in the darkening kitchen that terrible Sunday evening. This is what she made me see: that this good pastor carried to the people of his congregation a face full of pity—

—but at our dinner table my face was drained and grey. At the dinner table I heaped a hundred rules upon our children, growling at them for the least infraction. Our dinners were tense and short.

This is what she made me see: that I could praise, could genuinely applaud, the lisping song of a child at church—

—but I gave the merest glance to Mary's Father's-Day card, in which there was a poem the girl had labored on for two weeks straight.

"That poem said she loved you, Wally."

Thanne said she knew how much I hated to visit the jail. But I went. And it never mattered what time of day or night. Yet I did nothing that I hated, nothing, at home.

For counseling and for sermons, my words, she said, were beautiful: a poet of the pulpit. But for our bedroom conversations my words were bitten, complaining, and unconsidered. We talked of my duties. We talked of my pastoral disappointments. Or we hardly talked at all.

"How often I wanted to tell you of the troubles here at home," she said, "of my mistakes with the children."

But I was doing the Lord's work—the Lord, Thanne wailed, whom she loved dearly. So what could she say to me through all of this? How could she find fault with a divine command? I *was* a good pastor.

If she was discontent, then, who could she blame but herself? Over and over again she had told herself that she was being petty and selfish. And that's how she endured, by accepting the blame. But that's when the chipmunk's smile began to die on her face. And that's when Thanne began to die, a constant crab in her own eyes, truly dissatisfied and truly guilty for it. Bad Thanne. A bad person.

There were times she despised the children just for being children and for being there. And because she knew what a vile mother she must be to feel like that, she turned the despising inward.

But there was no one saying that he loved her then. There was no one pointing out her value after all. There was no one forgiving her or freeing her from confusion, from this horrible captivity. And how could someone as sinful as herself take anything away from God?

"Wally, where were you?"

She wanted me to see—but she didn't want me to see—her suffering. I shouldn't see the wickedness (yet I should, she thought, to forgive it); I should see her *need*. And I should see it on my own. If she had to show me, how little I loved her then, or how little she was worthy of my love. I should see it on my own; she shouldn't have to tell me. How could she explain what she didn't even understand? But in fact, I was seeing nothing at all those years. I didn't notice that Thanne had lost her smile—though I could smell a parishioner's sadness from halfway across the city!

"Why didn't you stop me then?" Thanne cried. "Why didn't you ask, 'What's the matter' then? *Wally, where were you?*"

I was ministering. I was a whole human, active in an honorable job, receiving the love of a grateful congregation, charging out the door in the mornings, collapsing in bed at night. I was healthy in society; she was dying in a little house—and accusing herself for the evil of wanting more time from me, stealing the time from God. I laughed happily at potlucks. She cried in secret. And sometimes she would simply hold one of the children, would hold and hold him, pleading some little love from him until he grew frightened by her intensity, unable in his babyhood to redeem her terrible sins. And sometimes she cursed herself for burdening a child, and then she wondered where God had gone.

In those days the smile died in her face. The high laughter turned dusty in her throat. Privately the woman withered—and I did not see it.

But the event which broke Thanne altogether, the little sin which was more than she could take, had occurred one evening when Rich and Donna came to our house for our monthly game of Risk. This was one month before the game I canceled. One month before she told me all her sorrow.

For me the night was no different from any other; but for Thanne it was a turning point. It shut down our marriage.

We played Risk on opposite teams, Thanne and I, so she sat across from me. The game progressed. I relaxed. I leaned back and spread myself in my chair, feeling this to be a very good party. I made jokes.

But I made them at Thanne's expense, oblivious of their effect on her. And she saw how much my very being belittled her. If she was dying, her husband was not altogether blameless. He was killing her by small degrees and scorn.

"Thanne's my little 'possum," I said. "Do you know that the woman sleeps curled up like a 'possum? And she never, never has trouble sleeping. Oh, I wish I had it so easy."

Rich laughed. Donna laughed. We all knew how exhausting was my work.

"Thanne's the best critic of sermons that I have," I said. "No one sharper nor more voluble than her, yes sir. After every sermon I ask her, 'How was it?' You know what she tells me? Every time she answers, 'Fine.' That's it. That's all I get from her. A regular Samuel Johnson."

Rich laughed. Donna laughed. Everyone knew who was the true talker of this family—and it was just like Walt to name some author no one else had read.

And when Thanne was clearly beating me at the game, I let it be known that I didn't mind. I turned that into a jolly joke as well. I said, "See how serious she gets at games? Thanne plays for keeps. Why, I remember once when we were courting—we played Hearts together, just the two of us. I absolutely infuriated her by passing her the queen of spades—twice. This woman hissed. Remember, Thanne? I think she trembled, she was so angry. Well, ever since then I let her win at games. I don't want a 'possum mad at me."

Rich laughed. Donna laughed. Thanne did not. But I didn't notice the silence. I enjoyed myself immensely that night. No, I didn't at all mind the losing. In fact, I was glad to give Thanne the gift. I went to bed quite satisfied with life and with the night. Thanne went to bed, too. But that was the night she did not sleep.

This, in the kitchen one month later, is what she told me: she heard my breathing beside her, and she realized that she did not love me. For a while she condemned herself for making too much of a little stupid humor. But it didn't matter how small the sin was. She didn't love me anymore, and that caused her tremendous sadness. She got up and left the bedroom. She went into the living room and sat curled on the sofa, alone and in the dark, and she was dead. And when I came in smelling of sleep and asking what the matter was, she didn't want to see me. Worst of all, the worst thing in the world, my touch repulsed her. My touching her made her cry.

And this, with all the pain and all the pleading of her soul, is what she demanded when she finished telling me all these things: she cried, *"Wally, Wally, where were you all that time?"*

But I could only stare out the kitchen window at the gathering gloom and answer nothing. Poet of the pulpit! I had no words whatever to say. Nothing. Oh, Thanne, I am so sorry.

"I have to hurt you," she said. The strident voice had turned to whining by now. She wasn't shouting any more. She was just unspeakably sad. "I had to hurt you to make you notice me. I hate it. I hate it! And when you do notice me, what do I get? Wally, you are so selfish. At least I know it when I hurt you. You don't even know. I get a red flower in front of the whole congregation. Oh, Wally!"

She told the truth. All this was the truth—and now she was done.

I said, "I love you, Thanne." So little evidence. So foolish. I said, "I will always love you, no matter what."

Thanne went up to the bathroom, not to cry, just to get ready for bed. She was all done. But I hadn't moved so much as a finger. I stood in the kitchen, burning in my guilt, keeping my whole body still. How could I *not* have seen so much—especially since I did, truly, love Thanne? This was a mortal mystery discovered too late. How could she have suffered in the same house, in the same *bed* with me, and I stay so utterly ignorant of her torment? There was no reason for this, except that I am abjectly sinful—and she is right. Oh, Thanne, I am so sorry—but what good does that do? No one should grieve alone. My wife, you should never have grieved alone.

I stared out the window, and I said to myself: *I can live without love. I can because I must. I've killed Thanne's love for me. Jesus, how I miss her smile! I can because I should. I deserve nothing less than loneliness, no less than to endure the same thing she did.* Now it was dark outside, and I still did not move. I can live without love.

After that Sunday night we returned to our silences again. She cooked, and I ate her food. I always received it, those days, as a pure kindness that she would still cook for me—and that she never spoke evil of me before the children. But we didn't speak to one another, except in the gravest politeness.

I didn't so much as brush her back when I crawled into bed. And once in bed I lay stone still for fear of shaking the mattress and waking her. Did she sleep then? I don't know, though she looked sallow and sick in the daylight. For my own part, my heart hammered all night long. Sometimes she rose in darkness to pace the house; and then I cried because the bed was empty and because I could not help her in her hurt: I didn't have the right even to try. I restrained myself in silence. I played with the kids. I preached, a purple hypocrite, the poet of the pulpit. And always the tears trembled just behind my eyes, even at church. But I could live without love.

Thanne could not forgive me. This is a plain fact. My sin was greater than her capacity to forgive, had lasted longer than her kindness, had grown more oppressive than her goodness. This was not a single act nor a series of acts, but my being. My sin was the murder of her spirit, the unholy violation of her sole identity—the blithe assumption of her presence, as though she were furniture. I had broken her. How could a broken person be at the same time whole enough to forgive? No: Thanne was created finite, and could not forgive me.

But Jesus could.

One day Thanne stood in the doorway of my study, looking at me. I turned in my chair and saw that she was not angry. Small Thanne, delicate, diminutive Thanne, she was not glaring but gazing at me with gentle, questioning eyes. This was totally unexpected, both her presence and her expression. There was no reason why she should be standing there, no detail I've forgotten to tell you. Yet, for a full minute we looked at one another; and then she walked to my side where I sat. She touched my shoulder. She said, "Wally, will you hug me?"

I leaped from my chair. I wrapped her all around in two arms and squeezed my wife, my wife, so deeply in my body—and we both burst into tears.

Would I hug her? Oh, but the better question was, would she *let* me hug her? And she did.

Dear Lord Jesus, where did this come from, this sudden, unnatural, undeserved willingness to let me touch her, hug her, love her? Not from me! I was her ruination. Not from her, because I had killed that part of her. From you!

How often had we hugged before? I couldn't count the times. How good had those hugs been? I couldn't measure the goodness. But *this* hug—don't you know, it was my salvation, different from any other and more remarkable because this is the hug I should never have had. *That* is forgiveness! The law was gone. Rights were all abandoned. Mercy took their place. We were married again. And it was you, Christ Jesus, in my arms—within my graceful Thanne. One single, common hug, and we were alive again.

Thanne gave me a gift: She gave me the small plastic figure of a woman with her eyes rolled up, her mouth skewed to one side, the tongue lolling out, a cartoon face. I have this gift in my study today.

The inscription at the bottom reads: *I love you so much it hurts.*

·SEVEN·

HOW DO WE PRACTICE FORGIVENESS?

Steps to Accomplish the Necessary Miracle

Most of our errors about *how* to forgive arise from fear or from faithlessness. We are personally afraid to confront the sinner openly with his sin. If the sin hurt once, don't we risk a second hurt by exposing that sin? Or we doubt ourselves (or the God within us), doubt we can handle it right, doubt the righteousness of our emotions, doubt that forgiveness can do any good after all.

So we avoid true acts of forgiveness by the simple expediency of changing its definition. We call things "forgiveness" which aren't; we do those lesser things and feel that we have done enough. But we haven't.

—*Forgiving is not just forgetting.* That which truly happened and truly hurt is never truly forgotten. We may pretend we've forgotten it—but then it will pop up at dangerous, inappropriate times, when the sin will control us instead of our con-

---93---

trolling the sin. Or we may sublimate it, swallow it down into our subconscious. But then we shall have diminished the marriage itself.

If Thanne had "forgotten" my sin against her, she would have denied a very real piece of her husband (however grotesque that piece) and would have buried very real events. Only *part* of our past could she recall after that; she would spend energy ignoring and editing the rest; she would grow tentative and careful to remember only the right things. Over time she would end in a psychic prison, unfree. Also, only *part* of me could she recognize as worthy to be her husband. Since my sin was not an aberration, but my true self, she would have to cut away pieces of my being (ignoring, forgetting them) to accomplish this sort of "forgiveness"; and soon she would be married to a partial person. In the end we'd have a marriage unholy and unwhole.

But forgiveness is meant to make us whole again.

—Time does not heal all wounds. Neither is forgiveness a silent, patient waiting for the sinner's change (no matter how faithfully the wounded one may pray for that change). Even as sins do not appear by magic (they are the real stuff of human nature), so they will not vanish by magic. God himself had to *do* something about the sin of the world. The notion that time heals wounds may make us seem saints of patience; but in fact we are ducking a dreadful responsibility. Sinners seldom change spontaneously.

Forgiveness requires the action of the forgiver.

—Forgiveness is not merely our own change of heart. "I don't hold it against her any more," says this sort of forgiver. "I don't feel bitterness or blame. It's better between us, because God has cleansed my soul." This is good, commendable, righteous, and godly—for that spouse. But the marriage is not lived out in the soul of a single partner. It exists, in fact, in the events of the relationship between *both* partners. There the sin occurred; there forgiveness must be effected—openly—or the relationship will continue to bear the injury which one partner has ceased to feel. It is the marriage whole that needs healing, not just the wounds of one.

Therefore, forgiveness is an act involving as many people as acted out the sin.

—Forgiveness is not kiss-and-make-up. More clearly: a good experience at lovemaking does not expiate the sin that

occurred in some other area of the relationship. Good sex isn't proof that *all* is good between us, though it may be, for a while, a good narcotic to numb the areas that are not good. It's an emotional red herring, distracting you from the sin that needs, at some time, specific attention and a good deal of energy. Make love. But make time to make lovely again that which has turned ugly between you. Forgiveness can't be received until the sinner knows her sin clearly *as* a sin, knows what it is and what it has caused.

Forgiveness is an act, involving both sinner and forgiver, and focusing self-consciously upon the sin.

—Forgiveness is not merely the words, "I forgive you." If forgiveness is spoken but lightly, the sin will seem to the sinner something light, hardly worth the notice. Her repentance will equal the tone of her forgiver, not the real depth of her sin. The significance of this act must be equal to the damage which the sin caused; I'm afraid we cannot avoid the complete, revealing encounter. It must have its own time, and its own place, and the full attention of both parties. And it will, always, at least at the beginning, cause pain: to the sinner, since awaking guilt is painful, but guilt persuades repentance; to the forgiver, who loves the sinner after all and hurts to see her hurt; to the forgiver (and here the last word is set into my definition of "forgiveness") because *forgiveness, involving both sinner and forgiver, and focusing self-consciously upon the sin, is a sacrificial act.*

FORGIVENESS

The complete act is divided into six steps. I'll explain each step in its sequence with this promise: the more you understand the act of forgiveness, and the more you practice it in the fullness of these six steps, the more habitual it will become. Finally it will arise from your own nature, from your soul and from your faith.

One other word before we begin. Please know that it isn't your spouse's sin which crucifies you, though you might have thought so; rather, it's your loving willingness to forgive. *That* was the cross of Christ, the cross you take up when you deny yourself and follow after him. Therefore, forgiving will not immediately soothe your pain; instead, it introduces a different pain, a much more hopeful pain because it is redeeming. You do "deny yourself" and die a little in order to forgive. Pride dies. Fairness dies. Rights die, as do self-pity and the sweetness of a pout or the satisfaction of a little righteous wrath. You take leave of the center of the marriage and of your own existence. You die a little, that the marriage might rise alive.

1. Be Realistic

This is a preparatory step, performed within yourself alone, preceding anything you might say to your spouse.

Listen to this: "She's an airhead. She just doesn't think. She always leaves something unfinished, so the battery's dead when I want the car, or I can't find my screwdriver, or I get the creditors on my back. She drives me crazy!"

Always, you say? *Always?* And she is a woman truly incapable of thought? Do you mean that? Was she as malicious as you are angry? And when you erupt in front of her, what do you plan to accuse her of? Existence? But what was the specific fault on this particular day?

Listen to this: "He doesn't love me; he never touches me; he doesn't want me around. He never notices the children except to bark at them. He puts his shoes on the sofa. He hit me once. He's just like all men."

Never? Do you mean *never?* And do you know all other men in order to class this one with them? And which sin is the sin before you right now? There's a radical difference between a muddy boot and a brutal fist.

Unless you spend time and care to make an absolutely realistic assessment of the sin itself, unless you act from the truth alone, forgiveness will be swallowed up in exaggerations, emotions, imprecision, fusty attitudes, and war.

Be realistic. Ask three questions.

—What was the sin exactly? Identify the immediate sin without the heat of emotion, focusing on what was done rather than how it made you feel. Identify that sin without leaping to conclusions regarding the character of your spouse.

—Against whom was the sin committed? It's not a silly question, even if you first felt this sin as pain inside yourself; for the sinner may, in fact, have struck at himself more than at you— and your pain may have come because you love him. You will act differently, if he's the one suffering destruction. And if the sin was against you, then against which part of you? Your authority? Your trust in him and your love? Your body? Your plans—or simply against your desire to enjoy a quiet day? Learning this will teach you just how grave or how incidental was the sin, and will temper your response.

—What exactly are the consequences of the sin? What exactly was destroyed or damaged? The sofa? Your pride? A car battery? The future of your children? Sometimes the true proportion of the sin has been lost in your *perceived* proportion of the sin. When the heart is hurt, the eyes are blurred by tears, and the world itself is distorted.

If this first step is accomplished carefully, you will cleanse yourself of the errors which muddy and confuse an accurate forgiveness. You will save yourself from adding sin to sin, attacking your spouse under the guise of a "Christian" forgiveness.

It's a common error to dump a thousand grievances into the pot of a single sin—and then all the remembered offenses of a marriage are summoned as testimony to how miserable your life is. But on that particular day, it was *one* sin. That one wants its own attention, its precise identification, and its cleansing. If that one sin represents a persistent fault in your spouse, an attitude and not a single act, then focus only on that attitude. Name it in your soul, recognizing that it's not the human whole whom you would change (or he will think you think him wholly bad).

By the three questions, protect yourself from the error of exaggerating the effect of the fault. In spite of your feelings, "She *always*" and "He *never*" are usually lies. Once you believe them, just because you spoke them, you divide yourself further from your spouse by dividing yourself from the truth. Good dialogue is crippled. The sinner will respond to your exaggerations not with repentance but with a self-righteous defensiveness—with argument and a rejection of your charges.

By realistic analysis, protect yourself from the error of blaming the person closest to you for *all* the sins you've suffered in a day. When does he put his boots on the sofa? Well, after your sister hung up in your ear. After your accounts didn't balance at work. After another driver cut you off, then honked at you. By then you've become one jumping nerve in a hairshirt, so a boot on the sofa can feel like physical abuse. Wait! Exactly what was your spouse's fault that day?

Finally, protect yourself from judging something to be a sin which isn't—which is, in fact, your own disappointment in his failure to meet your (perhaps unreasonable) expectations. Your husband grew heavy. Your wife grew fat. But you had married a body trimmed to athletic proportions. You took pride in the beauty and dreamed it would last. Obesity, then, hurts *you*, very much like a sin against *you*. But is it, really? And even if the condition causes your spouse to smell, offending your nose, causes your spouse to sleep more, offending your sense of duty, causes your spouse to buy more clothes, offending your budget, what *is* the sin? Against whom? With what specific consequences?

As a physician must first make an accurate diagnosis before prescribing treatment, so must you become realistic about the sin before acting upon it, or the latter state may be worse than the first.

But I don't mean to imply that realism will always reduce the sin to something minor. Often enough your pain shall be just and the sin severe. But then your assessment at step one must include one other significant realization: that the sin against you was also a personal sin against God.

This knowledge will temper all your action with mercy. Your face will show an urgent care for him, not anger against him—because he is in danger. To malign the image of God in you is to injure God himself; your spouse has broken God's commands, has chosen his own will above the will of God. The gravest consequence of his sin, then, is not what you suffer, but what he, whom you love, might suffer. How can there be vengeance in your actions, or how could you distort the truly holy motives of forgiveness, if your spouse is David of Israel and you no more than the prophet who charged the king with his adultery? How could you punish your spouse, if she is Gomer and you are Hosea, sent by God to take her from her prostitutions and bring her home again?

2. Remember Your Own Forgiveness

This step (still your private preparation) is the equalizer, leveling in you any sense of superiority over the sinner, to whom you are more similar than to the righteous God. The apostle Paul remembered both his outrageous sinning and his weaknesses in order to bring nothing to his beloved or his enemies but the crucified Christ. Take time to remember your own particular sinning; remember the specific and healing grace of God for you. Remember, and you'll find it difficult to approach your spouse in pride—not even in the arrogance of a greater spirituality. (How sanctified do some seem who forgive—and how hypocritical.)

Recall: that though you may have done it in another form, you too have sinned the same sin as your spouse. Is he self-centered, putting himself before others? So have you been (so *are* you, if you balk at forgiveness for any reason—because "he owes you an apology," because "she should get a little of her own medicine," because "he's had his turn, it's my turn now"). Is he cruel? Oh, break your shell in true confession: so were you once.

The sins we see easiest in others we learned first in ourselves; we know their behavior and their signs from the inside. Though they deny the personal fault, gossips spot gossips a mile away, as wolves know wolves by a familial scent. Is he neglectful? Impatient? Judgmental? Self-indulgent? Jealous? Scornful? Abusive? So, sometime and somewhere, were you—

Recall: that if you did not commit the sin against your spouse, yet you did, once, against your parents, your adolescent classmates, your friends, your colleagues at work, the teller in the bank, another race, another class of people, the poor. Or you did in your heart what you didn't have the temerity to do openly with your hands.

But recall these sins *not* to torment yourself, rather to rejoice in the forgiveness God has given you—you personally—since God was always at the other end of your sin, and did not return judgment for iniquity, but mercy. In this step discover two things: first, that you and your spouse are not enemies, but wanderers in the same wilderness, two people very much alike, sent to support each other's weaknesses. Second, that *you are able;* you are not too small; you have forgiveness more than equal to your spouse's sin, since it comes from God, to you, and through you for the one who sinned against you.

3. Sacrifice Your Rights in Prayer

Christ came to you when he forgave you (remembered in step two). But Christ becomes visible in you, so others might see him there, when you *do* as Jesus *did*.

The world says (and your worldly flesh agrees) that it is your legitimate right, your dignity, and your duty to bring suit against the one who injured you, to press her until she has redressed the wrong, to accuse her, to punish her until her hurt at least is equal to yours. This is just. This re-establishes the order her sin destroyed. This places the burden of reconciliation totally and righteously upon the one who started the mess—

—and this is not forgiveness. As scandalous as it seems to the world (as painful as it is to you), forgiveness places the burden of reconciliation upon the one who suffered the mess.

Even before you face your spouse, it is absolutely necessary that you pause and self-consciously surrender the world and all its rights. You drop legalities. You die. Can you in fact do this on your own? Not often and never well. Only Jesus purely whispered from the cross, "Father, forgive them, for they know not what they do." Therefore, it is Jesus who must love you in this step. It is Jesus who frees you from yourself, emptying you of your own will even as once he emptied himself. It is Jesus who divorces you, not from your spouse but from the law, to place you fully under his light of grace. Here your faith, shaped by serious prayer, comes to life, for this is done in trust alone; this is Christ's act and will therefore reveal Christ *in* your actions. You will demand of your spouse nothing *for yourself*. Anger has vanished from you; vengeance is gone; love alone is left. This is no less than the contemporary miracle, a conundrum to the world, a sign of divinity.

But it is critical that this sacrifice occur first, because even an unconscious bitterness will make your words to your spouse a boiling oil and not the oil of mercy. A cornered creature is remarkably perceptive. She will sense the hidden attack and (still living under the law) grow defensive. She'll fight the hurt you bring her. The division between you two will increase, and you will say, "See? I tried to forgive, but she is incorrigible." But you will not have tried truly.

No, forgiveness is not a simple speaking of the correct words. It is given only when your whole being, your tone, expression, gestures, and intent seek the other's healing. Then her defenses will not be roused, but puzzled rather, bewildered, and finally dropped as unnecessary. Love, when it is unexpected and undeserved but present nonetheless, is always confusing and subversive of hostilities.

When Thanne stood in my study, looking at me, the whole woman was purely present. There was no cunning in her coming, no trick, no strategy; there was the gentle spirit of my wife, unprotected, unashamed. And when she said, "Wally, will you hug me?" any defensiveness in me collapsed. Because who had spoken to me? My judge? No, my Jesus.

4. Tell Your Spouse the Sin

You and she alone.

Set the stage. Be very intentional about this important conversation and not haphazard or snatching at the opportunity whenever "the time feels right." Make it a time when no other people or distractions will interrupt. You know best the quiet periods of your day and your relationship; and you know the places in your home where the atmosphere is serious. Surely, you won't be watching television when you talk, nor folding clothes, and there won't be some appointment fifteen minutes away. This talk must come to its own conclusion. Is it in the kitchen where you've had serious talks? Talk in the kitchen. Or do you share your secret thoughts in bed, *without* one of you departing too soon into sleep? Talk in bed.

Talk. And your talk shall have two clear parts to it. (1) What her sin is. (2) That you forgive her. Let the second follow immediately upon the first. In fact, begin by saying you have *two* things to tell her.

What shall you say of her sin? Exactly what you learned of it in the first step of forgiveness, in the analysis. You will be specific, explaining both the sin and its consequences to yourself and to the marriage. You say this not so much to persuade her of it, but that she might hear and understand: this is the sin; she did it, is responsible for it; and it hurt.

This is the step that gentle people shrink from and angry people exaggerate. But it absolutely cannot be avoided. How shall you speak of the sin? Completely. Avoiding no details. From its beginning to its end, which was your hurt. The sinner must have her sin set before her *as* a sin, as *her* sin, as an undeniable fact, so that she can choose to confess the fault her own. She will not change otherwise.

How shall you speak of the sin? Certainly not reproducing the hurt in your voice! That feeling has been laid aside; the hurt is here only in the explanation. How shall you speak? Not whining, not attacking—but not mechanically either, as though you had withdrawn your love and your soul from her. Let your words be said, as Paul exhorts, "in a spirit of meekness," which is a fruit of the Spirit and which includes kindness, courtesy, graciousness, humility. Your whole being can radiate love for your spouse, even while you talk. You might touch her, forestalling her urge to argue; that way she will *see* and *feel* your second point even before she hears it. That way, too, you persistently communicate to her the joyful hope that sins do not end blessed relationships, however they may hurt it in the passing: she need not, then, sense threat when you speak of the consequences of that sin, as though some retribution were yet to come.

And how shall you speak of the sin? Why, with a perfect faithfulness in your spouse's change, her repentance, her coming righteousness, and her value to you—*even before these things have happened!* For it is your trust in them that shall call them forth and give them place. This is how Jesus forgave you, seeing you as righteous even while you were yet his enemy. This is how Jesus forgave Peter on the seashore after the resurrection, commissioning him to "feed sheep" and "tend lambs" even before he, Peter, was fully grieved for the sin of denying his Lord. The

Christian acts in paradox, believing the thing before it is—so that it may be. Your faith in your spouse opens up a holy little room within your relationship, wherein she may then enter. And what if she doesn't repent? Well, you believe in it anyway, against the future.

Then the second part of your talk will be to say that you forgive her. This has already been communicated; nevertheless, it wants its own words, too. You now do more than explain; now you persuade. With all your heart you desire her to trust (1) that the hurt is gone. Where did it—could it—go? To the Lord Jesus. It is yours no longer and does not trouble the marriage. (Remember, the issue in this conversation is not your hurt, but your spouse's sin; that remains the more dangerous of the two.) And you desire her to trust (2) that you do not hold the sin against her. Judgment and reproach are gone, and with them went punishment, retribution, tit-for-tat, or any gesture that might make her, the sinner, hurt.

That's it. That's enough to say at this step.

It's true that forgiveness is rightly received only by the sorrowful, confessing, repentant sinner. It is also true that this conversation will not spur all spouses to such penitence. But it is not, then, your duty to punish her till she repents. That's God's business, who will accomplish it in surprising and unforeseen ways. Your duty is to speak the sin and the forgiveness.

I know that the world supposes that remorse comes by accusations, and contrition by chastisement. But where the soul is concerned, the world is wrong. Such methods only harden the sinner in her concern for herself, either causing her to fake a confession so that she hurts no more (but her soul remains unchanged), or else causing her to justify herself and grow angry, retaliating. In God's economy, a true and loving forgiveness, when the injured party had every right to punish, confounds the sinner's logic of laws, bewilders her expectations, and dismantles her defenses.

5. Follow Words with Action

More than merely saying the world was forgiven, Jesus performed forgiveness. He not only proclaimed our righteousness; he set things to rights. This, now, is the actual reparation of the marriage.

And as Jesus forgave always in the role of a servant, so do we forgivers continue even now as the servants of our spouses. "If I then," said Jesus, "your Lord and Teacher, have washed your feet, you also ought to wash one another's feet. For I have given you an example, that you also should do so as I have done to you." These roles do not suddenly reverse at this point, granting us the privilege now to *be* served by the repentant sinner. Nothing is owed us, because the law has been displaced by mercy.

And your *serving* love will be the most persuasive, potent proof to transfigure the sinner. This is absolutely necessary to the process of healing—to integrate the blessing into your daily life, or else the moment of forgiveness will vanish like a dream in waking.

The speaking of forgiveness will have one of several effects:

Best of all, your spouse may repent and truly realize her forgiveness on the spot. Then your service to her will be to give thanks to God for the good thing he has done, for this will encourage your spouse to believe that it is God, not you, who is the source of the stability of this marriage.

More likely, something of the sin will continue to taint your spouse after your talk. She may admit the sin but doubt the depth and reality of your forgiveness (and so she will suffer guilt). The guilty live in dreadful uncertainty. Because of their own unworthiness, the good world may collapse around them—and they are helpless, they feel, to sustain it. They caused it, and they deserve the collapse. In despair they may do nothing at all to help your relationship. Or in abject shame, they may rush to and fro doing *everything,* trying to "make up" for their sin. Now—right now!—your quiet, continuing, stable service to your spouse, your cheerful, utterly sincere, and humble service to her, is irrefutable evidence that your love is unqualified. It does *not* depend upon her at all, yet is for her wholly; it is love indeed. The Prodigal's father gave him what the guilty son knew he did not deserve: rings and shoes and a party. The father did not dispute his son's guilt, since guilt was natural and right. But by love he stripped him of his guilt (though not of his humility) as though it were a dirty shirt. Serve her. Serve the guilty one. Had you cooked for her before she knew her sin, when she took your cooking for granted? Continue even now to cook, and you will serve her body and her soul together. Your most common service, if it continues sincere, will strip the guilt and reveal precisely where certainty was in the marriage all along.

"You don't hate me?" So say her eyes when you set the plate before her.

"No, I never hated you." So says your food.

And she, by eating it, says, "I believe you."

The cut is healed.

But your speaking of the sin (between you and her alone) may have the opposite effect. Instead of guilt, your spouse may feel attacked, as though you were doing to her exactly what (you say) she did to you. Then the result may be her anger, her defensiveness. She will be living squarely in the world, according to *its* standards and criteria, which are the law. That is, she will watch you thereafter through narrow eyes, to catch you in your own sinning, to gather proofs that you had no right to condemn her, and so to discredit your judgment against her. She will seek to support her goodness by your wickedness.

Now more than ever your good service to her will feel like (and will be) a sacrifice, serving the undeserving. But now more than ever it is necessary that you do it with an unmixed willingness, and with love. Let your common, true, and daily service be a stumbling block—a scandal!—to her worldly and sinful interpretation of existence, just as the cross of Christ is a scandal to trip up the wisdom of the Greeks. You may need to continue serving a long time. You may need to endure her testing it, since she will not believe that it is pure, but that it must have some deeper, self-serving motive. ("He can't be for real!") So it may go unrewarded, it seems, forever. But *so long as she knows her sin* (whether she admits it or not), that sin and this servitude will place her in an impossible contradiction that can only be resolved by her repudiating the world's legalistic standards and accepting as real the merciful standards of God.

The world cannot rationalize a truly sacrificial and persistent love. Indeed, the world cannot abide it. But the world is forced to deal with it only as you perform it—endlessly. It will cry out against what it can neither change nor abide; so the anger and the frustration of your spouse may increase. But yet you love her! Yet you feed her! Yet you remember her with gentle words and gifts. Yet (even and especially under these conditions) your kindness, seeming so meek, continues indestructibly strong, divine, of Christ, *is* Christ—until she (or he, if it is your husband) breaks on the headland of a holy goodness. And then she may suffer (as Paul did on the way to Damascus) a period of lonely exile, because her world has failed around her! But that is good. That is the deeper guilt. And now your service (continuing still!) invites her gently from the fraudulent world of law into the merciful kingdom of God's grace.

All along. Whom has he seen in you all along, unrecognizing? Why, now he knows that it was never you at all, but the face of the Jesus who loved him.

"Wally—" impossibly, absurdly, miraculously, "—will you hug me?"

Two final thoughts before we give the sixth step its own chapter.

Not always will steps four and five redeem the sinner from sin. Sometimes the sin will be mortally destructive both of the marriage and your lives; sometimes the speaking/serving combination proves ineffective while the sin continues to destroy. Chemical dependencies, physical abuse, a heart as hard as onyx in its self-centeredness, sins whose roots are psychological and as deep as the sinner's childhood—these, finally, may need a more severe mercy. We will speak to them and to that mercy in chapter 15, "Healing the Abuser."

And finally: all I've said so far in these steps of forgiveness has implied that you were the one aggrieved, the one sinned against. Don't let that deceive you or lull you into a sense of your own righteousness. As your spouse sins, so will you; and then the entire process of forgiveness will be transposed. Be prepared yourself to be confronted, when she will come to tell you of *your* sin; if you have learned these steps well, you will ease her labor and honor her sacrifice. You will understand the hurt you would cause her if you grew defensive and unrepentant. More importantly, you will already know that the source of her forgiveness is the Lord of both of you—so you will not need to doubt it nor fear to be vulnerable, humiliated, in confession. You are in a mighty, marvelous, and merciful presence. Before God it is both right and safe to be meek—for this is the one who lifts up sheep and bears them on his shoulders.

"Wally, will you hug me?"

I hug you? Sweet Jesus, the better question is, would you hug *me?*

She did. And he did. And this is the truth: they lifted me from the ground of Golgotha to the height of the cross and to the shoulders of the shepherd. It took my breath away, because I had said, "I can live without love." I had expected that the rightful end of the sheep was to be slaughtered, to lie down and die, not to be laid on the neck of the Lord.

·EIGHT·

HOW DO WE PRESERVE THE GOODNESS GAINED IN FORGIVING?

The Covenant

---

*T*hanne and I did not suddenly become giggling newlyweds on the day that followed her remarkable forgiveness. I slept in a sweet relief, yes. I pushed myself close against Thanne in the bed that night, rejoicing that we could touch again, merely touch, that I could feel her warmth and her skin against mine, and feel that I had the right to do so after all. Thanne is so still in bed. She lies so quietly and loves her sleep. But she is so *there* beside me— and her eyebrows are even, and her closed eyes are contentment. All the world has one still center in Thanne's sleeping eyes, and all my life has a leash to keep me there. I look at her when she sleeps. I circle her, and am still.

But in the morning I went to work—happy in my heart, no different in my schedule or my actions. *All is well,* I thought in jubilation. It never crossed my mind, though, that *nothing is changed.* I counseled. I kept appointments. I contemplated buying Thanne a rose. But did not. After all, there were bad associations. I rushed home to snap up a dinner, grinned silly on Thanne, and rushed back to church for meetings.

That night she was (wasn't she always?) in bed by nine. Since I returned after ten, I kindly did not disturb her, but went to my study to read. At one I went to bed.

Between her eyebrows Thanne has two lines, verticle wrinkles. You won't see them in our wedding photographs; they appeared some time after the days when the air was golden. In fact, they're more than wrinkles: they are creases of changing depths. They gauge the silent soul of my wife, sometimes a quizzical print on her brow, sometimes deeper than a knife-blade.

If Thanne was sleeping when I went to bed that night, she was sleeping with knife-blades in her forehead. She was frowning. She can sleep and frown. It may be sound, but it does not satisfy. And it is no center I can circle in contentment—except I hold the handle of that knife.

But this was the difference that night: there was more between us than my fault and her hurt. I knew that. I had experience of that. Therefore, I had the boldness to waken her.

"Thanne?" And again, "Thanne?"

Her eyes opened pale blue, the irises tiny.

"Thanne, are you dreaming?"

"No. I don't think so."

"Thanne, are you happy?"

She did not say no. She did not answer. She did not stop frowning. She was not happy. All my joy grew nervous and uncertain. I lay back on my pillow. Ah, things don't change in a day, do they? But she did not close her eyes again.

"What's the matter?" I said.

Silence.

"Did something go wrong today?"

She said softly, "No."

"What then?"

And this was another difference of that night: she talked.

She said, "It's the same thing, Wally. It's the same old thing. You bounce back so quickly. You bounce so high that you leave me behind. So you're glad. I'm glad you're glad. But your very gladness means that everything's just the same as it was."

She said this slowly, in disconnected pieces over a period of time; and I lay breathing beside her, hearing her, not answering. She talked, but for a while she might have been talking to herself, because the situation seemed to me impossible. My happiness was her distress. So what was the alternative? That we should both be miserable?

She said, "The only way I can get you to see me is to ruin your gladness." So we were thinking the same thing. "But I love you, Wally. How could I keep being mad at you? How could I hurt you to make you notice me? I can't. So it's bigger than us," she said, emotionless, hopeless. "And everything stays the same. Be happy," she said, and she closed her eyes, but she was frowning. She meant, *Be happy without me.*

She meant, *Be Wally.* She meant it much in love and much in despair. She herself could foresee nothing but a personal sadness, especially since our dramatic confrontation merely seemed to approve all that had been. She meant, *You'll never change.*

I lay a long time quietly. A silly thing went through my mind: *how much sleep Thanne's missed these days. She's going to get sick if she doesn't sleep more.*

And maybe she did fall asleep again. I didn't know, because she just closed her eyes and remained motionless.

Can I touch you, Thanne?

Don't ask.

Can I hug you again, Thanne?

I'm sleeping. I'm gone. How can you hug me if you can't find me?

So forbidding the swords of sorrow between her brows.

But so dear was the woman and so deep my need not to leave her, but to comfort her, that I began to talk in spite of myself. In my talking I searched for anything to offer her. Before I was done I had made her a promise. I had given her a cup; but I had not yet kept the promise, nor was I sure whether she'd even heard the promise—and, if she did hear it, whether she could believe it. Therefore, it was an empty cup, worth nothing on its own, waiting for worth to come and fill it.

I said, "We need to be together." I meant that with all my heart. And I continued, "We need to make the time to be together. What I should do," I said—but would this insult Thanne?—"What I should do is make appointments on my calendar for you. Oh, forgive me for sounding so businesslike. But I should write it in my schedule book."

I said, "Every night we'll spend the hour before supper together. I'll be home and we'll talk together. I'll write that in my book. What do you think? That doesn't demean you, does it? Maybe it does. But I'll do it." I said all this to the ceiling. And I said, "We'll spend a weekend together, you and me alone. Two nights, three days, away from home. Count on it. This year, next year, all the years. I'll be with you. I promise you I will."

That's what I said. That was my promise, my covenant: a cup made not of clay, but of time; a cup not to be filled with water, but with our presence, one for another.

I said it, and I felt somewhat better—as though I'd actually done something already, though in fact I had done nothing. I went to sleep.

Years later I learned that Thanne had heard. Poor, disappointed Thanne had heard the promise. She heard, too, how quickly I sank to a deeper, steadier breathing.

"Well, it did you some good to say so anyway," she whispered. "That counts for something."

In the days that followed, I came home before dinner. A full hour before dinner. And I sat on a stool in the kitchen while Thanne cooked. And this is how I felt: artificial. The little talk we made was mostly forced, and Thanne was mostly silent. Well, our lives had been different in the last years, more divergent than we realized; we had little in common after all. Worse, Thanne was simply not sure whether she could trust my care for her or my change. It would be a risky thing to reveal herself to the one who had hurt her and could hurt her yet again. She did love me. She had rediscovered it and told me so. But I don't think we were friends much.

The cup, the daily hour, continued empty for a while.

But even if it was empty, it was *there*. It became a fact, a form in our lives and in our relationship. First it had to be that form—and then it might, when the time was right, be filled.

I kept coming home. Even when we didn't talk, I came. It was simple labor, the keeping of a covenant for its own sake, because it had been promised; there is no excitement in this part of the story.

But the mere persistence of the cup caused Thanne to begin to trust it. If I was there yesterday, then I could be there tomorrow—therefore, she might risk a word or two today. And she did. Thanne began to talk. She began to believe that I would listen. And I did. The more she talked, the more I *wanted* to listen, and the more my own talk wasn't merely self-centered.

It is a wonder when your beloved trusts you enough to give herself to you again, trusts you with her weight, her treasure, and her life. In time the cup, which had proven itself, began to fill with the serious liquid of our lives. What a valuable vessel is a cup, a covenant!

Now, though we may be separate in the morning, the ideas that occur to us apart we save for the hour when we will be together, because we trust in that hour; and it is as though we'd been together the whole day through. If Thanne suffers another sin of mine, it needn't swell in secret until it explodes. The cup is there for it, a place for it, and I drink from the cup, both the medicine that wakens and purges me, and the love with which she nourishes me.

THE COVENANT

Be realistic: change doesn't happen in a day with a single act of forgiveness. Be realistic, not depressed by that thought the day after you forgave. And then be wise. You have right now the opportunity to give a concrete *shape* to your relationship, to establish between you certain promises and certain habits which will characterize your interaction hereafter, which will give a foundation to your mutual trust, and which can forestall this sin's recurrence.

The event of forgiveness is not yet complete until you agree upon a covenant—almost a renewed contract—defining your future behavior together. Surely, you have at this point a deeper knowledge of one another; you know the destructive tendencies which previously were hidden; you know something of their causes and you have felt their consequences—and this is, now, a knowledge common to *both* of you. (A mutual recognition of one another's deeper personalities is a blessing of enacted forgiveness!) You are wiser. Moreover, each of you has, right now, a greater willingness to change, to make very practical commitments to the marriage. The forgiven spouse yearns to give thanks; the forgiving spouse rejoices in return and renewal. You both are "in love" as you have not been for many a lonely day. Finally, you are able to talk about persistent faults without shame or blame, realistically.

But you are not yet in heaven—and good sense and good feeling, if they are not translated into specific patterns of behavior, may pass away with time until they are a distant nostalgia.

Remember the "help" of "unlikeness"? Well, it is clearer now which of your spiritual strengths fit your spouse's spiritual weaknesses. Help each other in the difference. Establish a covenant between you. For example, what signal will you give her the next time she veers close to her sin? If the sinning begins compulsively, she may not be able to recognize its coming. How, then, can you be the eyes she doesn't have? And how will *she* receive your signal? What will she do to prove that she understands? Define the roles of both right now, so that when it is necessary to perform them, each of you understands that the action is done with love.

Or how will the two of you plan to diffuse his anger before it grows uncontrollable (if that is his temperament and his sin)? Will you take a walk? Will you ask him to write down, with logic, clarity, and examples, an analysis of his mood; and will he promise to do so, in order to subdue his passion with mental activity? I don't know the actual patterns your covenant should take; you will fit these creatively to your own particular personalities, his need, your resources. But I do know that the covenant should prepare for you to bear his weakness.

Or if you know now that certain conditions of your lifestyle have caused sin in one of you, how will you rearrange the times and places, the atmosphere and the expectations, of your habitual activities? Do certain friends of yours have a pernicious effect on your wife? Or is it the lack of society that troubles one of you? Then which of you is more flexible to make a change (the stronger to the other's weakness)? Which of you will find new friends for the sake of your spouse? Or what social activities can broaden a narrow existence?

Has one of you perhaps neglected to praise your spouse, to affirm him in his labor, to acknowledge in obvious and precious ways her significance, to celebrate the person that the other is? Then name now the means by which such affirmation will come in the future, and the times, and the ceremonies. *Make a covenant together,* consciously and carefully, not doubting its value and its intent just because your actions aren't "spontaneous," but planned.

In these plans, in the trusting and the keeping them hereafter, your particular marriage finds its outward form and its shape—like a cup. By the grace of God, you've turned a trouble into a good. The cup/covenant may seem empty at first, and your action artificial. But time and patience will fill it with good spirit. What began in sinful separation has through six steps of forgiveness become the growth, the maturation, the development of that little baby, your relationship, into a healthy being between you. So now the baby is strong. So now the baby will carry you.

That year of our resurrection Thanne and I spent three days alone at a cabin in Kentucky. It had a tin roof, and the rains came down. In my memory, love sounds like the ceaseless drumming of autumn rains on a metal roof, both light and loud, so loud sometimes we couldn't hear each other; we could only *be*. And it smells clean. And love has an October bite—the same sharp chill that bit us on county roads in rural Illinois so long ago.

We couldn't talk; but by then we didn't have to talk. Thanne read P. D. James while I read *The Pilgrim's Progress*. We sat before a fire, in separate chairs, in a holy, drumming dry—and in love.

And here is how I know that the covenant finally contained the both of us wholly, that we had grown together truly: on such a weekend, without fear of deflation or loss, Thanne spoke aloud a dream that would alter our lives completely. She entrusted this tender portion of herself to me. She said, "Wally, what if I went back to school?"

But she already had her B.S. in exceptional education.

She said, "I want to earn a degree in computer science. I think I'd like to work full time."

Do you see how much the woman had come to trust me? Why, she believed in beginnings again!

I said, "And who will do the cooking after that?"

Thanne smiled prophetically, knowing full well who was about to do dishes, and cook, and scrub floors. One tooth peeped out between her lips, exactly like a chipmunk's smile. She said, "What do you think of my idea?"

·PART THREE·
Marriage Work: The Continuing Tasks

•NINE•

"FAITHFUL UNTO DEATH": WORKING WHILE THERE'S LIFE

I didn't think hard about the marriage vow before I made it. Neither was I unfamiliar with it. The words were common and seemed right enough; and I was sharp enough to know that, though I spoke them *before* the pastor, the witnesses, the people and God, I spoke *to* none of these. I made the promise *to* Thanne alone. I knew, too, that these words were not merely ceremonial, a sort of ritual formula to signal a solemn moment. They were supposed to mean something. I knew that I was communicating a particular thought to Thanne (and she to me) as a surety against the future. From this point on, until we die, I was going (I said) to do, or be (or not do, or not be) something—and she could count on that.

"Something." It's that *something* which I hardly considered— a shocking oversight, really, since this was one of the rare life-time vows I would ever make to another human. This was in-tended, by my voluntary commitment, to qualify all my actions thereafter, shaping me, defining "Walt" in all things, not just "Walt" when he was with Thanne, because I wrapped my whole life into that vow. And if I didn't truly intend that vow so comprehensively, why then, all my vows and all my words are compromised. Who can trust anything I say, if neither Thanne nor our hand-picked witnesses could trust that?

"Something." What was that *something* which I promised? In what would I be faithful to the slender Thanne?

Well, I think I thought I was talking about sex. I was announcing that I would fool with nobody else, forever. On a higher plane, I think I thought I was talking about romantic and spiritual commitments: "Keep me only unto thee." I would not become entangled in dangerous affections with other women; I would "love" no one else as I loved her—and she could count on that. And I know that I thought the vow to be mostly a negative one, a promise of what I would *not* do. If it was a positive vow (a promise of something I would do) this was only the vaguest, most ineffable sort of doing: "I give you me. It's you and me forever."

And that was meant to satisfy the woman? That shapelessness was to shape our lives together forever? I did better than that for every employer who ever hired me, promising with bold clarity precisely *what* I intended to do for them, defining the deeds they could count upon.

But everybody smiled when I gazed into Thanne's eyes murmuring, "I promise you my faithfulness." Everybody nodded. One or two dabbed at a tear. Nobody noticed the lacuna, the blank spot, behind my precious words. Everyone understood that Walt was promising to be Thanne's husband. But if anyone seriously wondered what that meant, they never mentioned it to me.

Perhaps Thanne, the instant I'd recited, "And I promise you my faithfulness," should have seized my hands and cried, "Stop!" Perhaps she should have demanded that we sit down in the front pew before I went a syllable further, then fixed me with a terrible stare and said, "You promised me your 'faithfulness.' Wally, what *is* that, exactly? Seeing that my life depends on it, maybe you could explain yourself, poet of the pulpit! It would relieve me a little."

She didn't, of course. We were both children in expensive raiment, children caught in a cosmic episode, both of us acting chiefly on faith.

But the question isn't out of place.

And, finally, it can be answered—though the answer is seldom perceived until the marriage has lost its golden sheen and taken on its common colors in the daylight:

I promised her a positive thing after all. Yes, I would *do* certain things. And so did she to me. I promised to accept certain responsibilities, to perform carefully, continually—*faithfully,* so that she could count on it!—certain tasks on behalf of the marriage, and so on her behalf as well. I promised to do work. Specialized work. Relational, marital, practical work.

And the tasks I promised to do (whether knowingly or not— that makes no difference) are not so mystic that they cannot be defined.

Belatedly, blue-eyed Thanne, I can and I will explain myself to you—though you didn't ask.

The third part of this book presents the six tasks to which a husband and a wife committed themselves by their comprehensive vows in their wedding. I'm not much concerned about the various wordings of these vows, but about the intent, about the nature of healthy marriages, and about the mutual work which keeps them healthy. "Faithfulness unto death" means working while there's life.

In practice, these tasks are not easily divisible. They entwine and qualify each other. Spouses are engaged in several at once, even in the moment of a single act. But we will divide them here in order to name and analyze them—and in order to reveal the *complete* responsibility of either spouse. No, sir; no, ma'am. Having done one thing, you've not discharged the whole of your obligation. It is when you both work at all things that the marriage is made sturdy against storms external and internal. So we count up tasks to the number six, and we pray that each partner sees the sum as his and her own *Haustafeln,* or table of duties.

But before we take them one at a time, it's important that we make clear each partner's best attitude toward all of them together.

These are not six "laws" of marriage. They are not meant to burden you as with new commandments, which, if you don't keep them perfectly, accuse you and cause you guilt. In fact, the identification of these tasks is meant to *relieve* you!

In any job, ignorance is the most heavy shackle—like leg irons halting you. If you know you are to do something, but know not what that thing is, the job itself seems continually oppressive. But when finally you learn what that something is, and that you are able to do it, that job becomes your own—your place in the universe, your opportunity for development and self-expression, your challenge for accomplishment, your value. Then it feeds you, body and soul. So are these tasks meant merely to identify what has been true all along. And you can do them. You are capable.

But these are your tasks. They are not six rights which either partner might claim of the other. These, most emphatically, are not six demands a wife may make of her husband, or a husband of his wife. Rather, they are the six areas of work to which your marriage vow has obligated you, *your* service to the relationship, *your* glad opportunity for a whole participation, *your* livelihood therein.

Most marvelous of all, these are a means by which you may, within your marriage, serve the Lord. It is the Lord you serve when you serve his child, your spouse. It is the loving Lord you serve when you cause his image to be manifest *in action* in your household—the Lord who "came not to be served, but to serve, and to give his life as a ransom for many."

Then let no one, reading these tasks, think: "Yes, he should be doing this for me." For if anyone imposes them on the other, the marriage will suddenly be locked in the law; and then stern standards of judgment will have been established, commandments after all, which any spouse will finally fail to keep. The marriage will deteriorate to criticism, complaint, self-righteousness, and dissatisfaction. These are not rules for your partner's behavior.

Rather, let everyone reading these tasks exult: "So this is how I can bless my spouse! This is what I can most effectively do for her!" For if everyone makes a free gift of these services, the marriage will be characterized by willingness and a holy grace, and every act performed may seem pure kindness, unexpected, undeserved. Where there are no judgments, there is no question of failure; and the spirit of gratitude casts out the spirit of criticism. What an abundance will that marriage seem to have, where each receives more than either asked for!

With this attitude, it is more than a motto, more than a little plate affixed to your front door, more than a devout and meaningless phrase—it is the very nature of your most incidental act within the marriage that:

"AS FOR ME AND MY HOUSE,
WE WILL SERVE THE LORD."

TEN

THE FIRST TASK:

Truthfulness and Dependability

"*T*ruthfulness and dependability" might at first glance seem adjectival nouns, abstract conditions only, and qualities of being. In fact, they are jobs. They are, together, a task requiring our careful work—and they will have a very definite effect on the relationship. When this task is conscientiously accomplished, it produces in your spouse the dear and necessary fruit of *trust*.

Each marriage begins with a period of trust; but it is a limited period. For a while she will trust you just because she loves you; for a while he will trust without evidence, because he wants to. But finally that trust must find a more solid ground—and in most marriages it must be *re*produced since it is so commonly broken by the natural shock of living together and truly discovering one another. Now the task takes on its significance.

TRUTHFULNESS

Truthfulness regards your speech to your spouse:
—that it hides nothing in lying;

—that it neglects nothing important;

—that it distorts nothing, either consciously or unconsciously;

—that it communicates as accurate a picture as possible of anything it chooses to offer, whether of the world, or of yourself, or of your spouse.

Such watchfulness of talk takes work, not only to resist the impulse to keep things to yourself, but also to train yourself in choosing what to say and how to say it most effectively *for the sake of your spouse*. Though God gave us tongues, we are a race lazy at speech; though he gave us eyes, we are lazy in observation; and though he gave us hearts, we are inclined to be self-centered.

What, specifically, is the work required here?

Certainly, truthfulness means that you do not willfully lie. That hardly needs explanation or an argument, does it? Surely everyone realizes that lying is the dry-rot of any relationship, destroying it at its center until it is no more than a hollow form. A crisis, when trust is most needed, brings the whole house down, liar and spouse and all.

Besides that, truthfulness means that you've taken careful time to examine yourself (the speaker) in order to identify truly your experiences, your feelings, the observations significant to you. And then you've found and you practice the best methods of communicating these things to your spouse—in words that he or she can understand. That's work.

The truthful husband (or wife) does not neglect to express the essential events of the day he spent apart from his spouse—however tired he generally thinks he is, however alien his world and his language may seem to her, requiring interpretation. To keep silent about his experiences, and therefore about his own being, is to shirk a necessary work. The truthful wife (or husband) does not make decisions which affect the family without including her husband in the early stages of that decision.

Unless the partners *volunteer* such talk, unless they clearly reveal the changes occurring in their lives, their spouses may be exiled from both the change and finally the life—till one day a wife complains of her unforthcoming husband, "I just don't know him any more!"

And when a husband asks his melancholy wife, "Honey, what's the matter?" the truthful wife will answer. Despite the silence she yearns for, despite the real difficulty of putting deep feelings into words, she works; she answers. Self-examination is always work. Self-revelation seems sometimes perilous. It is easier to forget the day, not live it thrice—once in reality, again in thought, again in conversation. It is easier simply to suffer a gloom than to try to understand it, easier to lie a little: "Nothing's the matter. Forget it." But an easy silence causes dis-ease in the end, not trust.

Truthfulness means that, when you talk, you make a most careful bridge of your words. This requires *two* cares, really: care for the topic, to get it right; and care for your spouse, that she/he hear it right. That's work. For example, a blizzard of unconsidered words may be a glad release of personal emotion, but it can also blind your spouse to the true cause of that emotion. Either he ends up feeling as strongly as you do, but not knowing why (frustrating!), or else he confuses himself with the cause and wonders what he did to make you feel so bad. Work is the self-restraint that does not merely "dump" on a spouse but labors for clarity of explanations. It doesn't only seek a comrade in feeling; it honors the spouse with understanding.

And truthfulness, when the topic is specifically your spouse, does not attack. Always it is meant as a benediction, a good word seeking his or her well-being. She is the object of this truth: it is true *for* her, on her behalf; it is true *to* her, to what is best for the best in her. This is something much more elevated than the "truth" that is mere fact; it is aware of the very spirit and purpose of your relationship. Too often, "Hey, babe! I'm just telling you the truth, just being honest" is justification for personal criticism. Under cover of the virtue of honesty, it's meant to wound, to snap her into shape, to improve your own life (pretending, perhaps, to improve hers). In other words, such truth is neither truth*ful* nor true to the purpose of your marriage.

What then? Does truthfulness restrict you in praising your spouse only, to agreeing, approving, commending? Of course not. That would become its own sort of lie. You'll not conceal a truth which might truly improve your spouse. If you don't speak it, who will? Who better could he or she trust than you? But you will know (or you must labor to discover!) your motives *truly*. If your purpose is criticism only, who sooner will he *mis*trust than you? And then the marriage whole will suffer. Rather, speak that truth in sincere love. The motive of your speaking will be as evident to him as the words themselves. Surely, you will not drive this truth, some blemish in his character, like a nail into his skull with mean repetition, or twist your face to show how much it troubles you.

So, what is the work here? To assess your motive—if to pick and criticize, shut up. Likewise, the work is to assess the purpose of the marriage *and* the best in your spouse, so that when you do talk it will promote both. That is the labor of the spirit of truthfulness.

What sort of trust, then, does truthfulness produce?

That your spouse believes in her heart, "He tells me all." And further, "What he tells me, he tells me truly." Such trust produces security. And security produces peace.

DEPENDABILITY

Dependability is truthfulness in action—in your actions. It regards your promises, whether spoken or unspoken, and your spouse's reasonable expectations, that you will in fact do what you pledge to do, that you will fulfill anticipations. It secures, now, the future in *deed*.

The future is always cloaked in the darkness of our ignorance; we move into it by calculated guesswork and by faith; but the less we can guess by present evidence, and the less we can believe in those who move with us, the more fearful we are to move at all. In a sort of terror we may be paralyzed, unmoving—till we sit in a stony conservatism and wait for the future to come and get us. That is, we cease to risk, cease to make the significant decisions, cease in great measure to live.

And the world at large defrauds us, promising promises it never intends to keep. Advertising uses, but does not love, us. Friends disappoint. Governments propagandize for their own purposes. Economies rise and fall in mystery. Superiors walk on the heads and hearts of their inferiors as on rocks in a stream. This is a sad, familiar litany, but its very familiarity witnesses to the instability of the present, the treachery of the future. There must be something upon which we can depend in order to plan, to act, and to live.

You, loving husband; you, faithful wife: you may be the light which illuminates the future and frees your spouse confidently to enter it. But only insofar as you are dependable. Otherwise you *are* that world to him or her.

Dependability requires a careful work:

—to make your promises wisely, realistically, according to your true abilities, according to your spouse's real needs;

—to remember the specific promises and your general marital duties in a hectic world;

—to make these promises a fixed priority in a world that will entice you persistently to other interests (she sings like a Siren, does the world);

—and to accomplish all the little pledges ungrudgingly, gracefully. Each is a nail. Behold: you are building a lodge against the future, a structure in which to house the marriage hereafter.

Let me enflesh this, first, by a negative example:

There are people who, to escape the burden of today, make wondrous promises against tomorrow. These people live in their words alone; they are infants in responsibility. More than their bond (*less* than their bond) they think their words themselves are deeds! In fact, that are pleased to believe that by promising something they have already accomplished something.

"When we have children," says such a husband earnestly, sincerity softening his eyes upon his wife, "I promise I'll cut back at work and spend more time at home." He is earnest. But the emotion that trembles in his voice is due, at least in part, to an awe at his own wonderfulness. *Aren't I a good husband,* he thinks wordlessly, *being such a good father? See how I understand my wife's needs?*—this, ever before she is pregnant or he a father in fact.

Then a long time passes before the child is born. When the child arrives, more time passes while the wife waits for him to cut back his work, as he had promised. And in that time this husband has (1) been promoted in his job, (2) forgotten the intensity of his feelings in making the promise so long ago, (3) used up the credit it earned him in her eyes, having already enjoyed her gratitude and praise (what more adoration could he earn by actually cutting back at work?), and (4) noticed that she isn't as alluring as she was before the baby came. He's also less inclined just now to sacrifice on her account, and the home isn't as pleasant either, what with a tiny human making noises and smells and demands. In fact, this home is less inviting, now that it needs him more than he needs it.

So what? So precisely when his pledge ought to come due, when most she needs to depend on him (having planned this baby *on the strength of* his promise!), he defaults.

"Honey, I had no idea what would happen at the office. How could I read the future?"

But that is exactly the purpose of a promise: to assure stability *in spite of* the uncertain future. To make that future certain and readable after all. Of course he had no idea what tomorrow would bring. Neither did she—until he made his promise. But because he caused a trust which he also betrayed, she will be doubly suspicious of the future, twice as isolated, and full of doubt. The opposite of trust is doubt.

And doubt breeds doubt. If your spouse can't depend on you to keep your promises (truth in your actions), he will soon doubt the truthfulness of all your talk, whatever its topic. Doubt breeds a general separation; and one who is undependable forces another to be fiercely *in*dependent.

Do you see, then, that dependability is, first of all, a personal and spiritual labor? It is a struggle, in fact, against self-centeredness, against thinking you have the right to follow your own immediate moods, to satisfy your own feelings. (Children may sometimes shirk duties for a present pleasure—"If it feels good, do it"—but you gave up childhood when you married and vowed faithfulness!) Now your previous pledges must shape your activities, your schedules, your priorities, and your labor. Dependability requires that you will sometimes sacrifice the unforeseen opportunity, that you will decline certain personal advantages, that you will not be blown about by every whim or new event. Rather, you yourself will control the day's events according to the marriage's expectations upon your promises—not because your spouse commands you, but because those promises do. Is this submission in marriage? Obedience? Yes. Is it the submission of wives to husbands, or of husbands to wives, so that one might dominate the other? No—but of either partner to the pledges which he or she made both to and for the sake of the spouse. *It is the purer submission: submission to relationship.*

And this is the blessing it provides: that when one is dependable even in the small things (making a bed every morning, for example), the spouse is inspired to trust in all things. So a whole world may be foundationed on the head of a little deed—and cosmic peace upon a little promise kept. What an astonishing return upon a penny's investment!

Thanne loves Pachelbel's "Canon." She tells me that it softens the hard day, softens the knots inside herself, softens her to gentle peace. She dips her head, shy at her own metaphor, and tells me that this tempered music makes her feel, when it surrounds her, as though she's a lump of bread dropped into milk. The bread swells till you can't feel the edges. So does her soul fill up with the "Canon."

One night in the spring of 1983—one morning, in fact, in the small hours of the morning—I was listening to a recording of eighteenth century music, trying to relax, trying to find sleep, when Thanne came down to my study because of the music, Bach, Mouret, Handel. I had a little reading lamp above my chair, so my book was bright but the room was dark, and she was dim in the doorway, watching me. She asked the question before I could.

"You can't sleep?" she said.

Like a ghost she floated upright in the deep black doorway. I always feel a tiny shock of joy to see her when I hadn't expected it. I grinned and didn't think to ask her the same: *You can't sleep either? It's two in the morning.*

"No," I said. "I can't sleep." It's a common problem with me—but not with Thanne. I should have asked her the question.

Instead, I told her at length why I wasn't sleeping. But that's all right, too: I made her laugh. I made her sputter that high-throated helpless laughter that sounds like water gone up her nose. Fifteen years married, and that laughter was still my benediction.

"Well, I read that if you imagine a tranquil scene," I said, "you can tranquilize yourself to sleep. Put yourself into the scene and it will relax you. I tried that tonight. It worked—sort of."

She floated three steps in from the doorway. My light cast orange shadows on her face.

"Well, so I imagined I was in a winged glider, wheeling through the sky, sailing on silent thermals," I said. "I made the whole sky blue and perfectly quiet, except for the breezes—and I began to relax. Then I looked down to enjoy the scenery. I imagined a great green forest below me. I was looking at a carpet of giant fir—and I was relaxing. But I thought I'd fly closer to the forest, and I wanted *all* of me free in the air; so I imagined that I was in a hang-glider."

Thanne's shadowed face was smiling. That's such a good sign.

"I flew right over the trees," I said. "They slipped beneath my stomach. Then I thought, *But what if the wind dies? What would I do?* And I answered myself, *Well, I could land in a tree, couldn't I?* And I did. A sort of test. The wind died; I lifted the nose of my hang-glider, dropped, and grabbed the top branches of a tall tree. It bent under my weight, but I held on. And then I started to climb down, branch by branch. Oh, Thanne—when I came below the canopy of the forest I found that the branches ran out. Between me and the ground was forty feet of bare trunk! There was *no* way down! I panicked. My heart started to pound, I broke out in a sweat, and I wasn't relaxed any more. I was tense in bed. I had imagined myself into such a predicament that it woke me right up and I couldn't sleep at all—"

And Thanne was laughing. Dear Thanne was choking on her laughter. I had told this as a serious story, seeking sympathy; but she turned it into such a ridiculous joke that I burst out laughing, too.

"Wally, you are so stupid!"

And I nodded, roaring at two in the morning. My imagination was a dangerous companion.

Thanne sat down in her laughter and gazed at me.

"So," I shouted, "I had to get up. I had to come in here and read to console myself after the crisis—"

Just then Pachelbel's "Canon" began to play on the stereo. All at once Thanne's laughter stilled and the smile vanished from her face. She continued to gaze at me, her eyes made huge by deep shadows; but in a moment I saw the glint of tears in them, points of light from my reading lamp, and I grew quiet too.

I thought the "Canon" had moved her, so I held my peace until the music was done. But I was wrong. Thanne's tears are like golden carp in dark water. Where do they come from? How deep do they go?

The record clicked off, and the room grew quiet, but Thanne didn't cease her weeping or her looking at me.

Finally she whispered, "Wally, I'm afraid."

Ah, that's right! Neither had *she* been sleeping at two in the morning.

"Why?" I asked.

She looked down. "Next month I graduate. In the fall I'm going to hunt for a job. That's why."

"Thanne, you have no reason to be afraid," I said. "Look at all you've accomplished so far. Who goes back to school with as much confidence and success as you have?"

"That's not it," she said.

But I thought she should have taken some satisfaction in that. Computer science was a totally new direction for her education. And she had flourished in these last years. Good study, good grades, the high approval of her professors, an orderly pattern to her days: these things had smoothed the creases in her brow and brightened her eyes. She had looked beautiful, dressed for the world in fall and winter clothing. She had a *reason* to dress for the world, persuaded both of her significance and of her capability.

"You'll do very well, Thanne," I said. "God's given you remarkable talents and a self-possession—"

"No," she said with her head down.

"Yes," I said. "He *has*. Look at your grades—"

"No!" she said again, and she raised her eyes. "It's not me. I'm not afraid because of me. It's you."

"Me?" Not herself. Not Pachelbel's "Canon," but *me*.

"How," she whispered, "can I trust you?"

"Well . . . I . . ."

"If I'm going to get a job, I have to depend on you. I can't keep the house and a full-time job together. And I'm afraid to commit myself to any job just to fail at it. I won't even go job-hunting, Wally, unless I can depend on you right now. What I'm scared of, I might have done all this for nothing."

"Thanne," I said, "don't you think I'll help you?"

She gazed at me. She said, "I think you want to help." She meditated quietly awhile, and I didn't interrupt the thought. She'd made a concession, at least, to my good intent. "Wally," she said, "you get hung up in imaginary trees." She said that with honest, parental affection.

"Oh, you can't judge me by that."

"I think so, Wally. You're distracted even when you drive the car. Your mighty mind isn't always in this world. But I feel like *I'm* in your tree, looking down. There were times, you know, when you weren't there to catch me."

"I know," I said. "I know. I remember."

"And this is the point, Wally," she said. "It won't be enough for you just to 'help' me—sometimes to relieve me of my work. I'd still be responsible for it, planning it, making sure it got done. It's not just the doing that tires me; it's the obligation. Do you understand?" she said. "I can't still supervise. You have to take the jobs and the responsibility. Do you see?"

But this was the wonder of that conversation early in the morning: Thanne trusted me enough to talk with me, to disclose without fear (even without accusation) her most serious concerns. I took strength from such faith in me (for faith it was!) and in our limber relationship.

Do you hear how the tears had passed from her voice by now? Do you hear how the fear found calm even in its expression? That meant she knew I was listening to her—which was itself a trust in me. How could I break that trust?

I said, "What do you want me to do?"

Now, I believe that her next words came from the top of her head. She might, with longer thought, have chosen other expectations. But right then the issue wasn't so much *what* I would do as *that* I would do it and so prove dependable. What she said became my pledge.

"You could make the bed in the morning," she said, drawing her robe around her. "You could cook."

"Well, I will."

Little things, but monumental promises! Fundamental, in fact. From that day forward a good portion of our marriage rested squarely on this: that daily, every day, I made the bed. The promise could not be the fine-spun stuff of my intent and my imagination alone. Daily, every day: it was the persistence of the job that made it worthy of her trust; the very doing of it was more valuable than all the poetry or protestations or stories I could make for her, since truth is in the doing.

Do I need to mention that in our house I am now responsible for cooking, for scrubbing the kitchen, for parenting children? Well, these have their value between us, surely. But it was the making of the bed that taught me *what* value, and encouraged Thanne to trust. Upon her education, yes; upon the good brains God had given her, and her thrift, and her skill at organization, yes; but also upon my daily making of the bed, Thanne has built a career.

And we have built a marriage.

A little active dependability proves much of truthfulness; and truthfulness produces trust.

And trust bequeaths the following blessings upon the marriage:

THE CLEAR MIRROR

Who are you? What are you—what kind of person? How do you know these things?

Identity, as we've said, is discovered in relationship. Simply, as other people look at me, acknowledge me, make space for me in their days and their lives, I am persuaded that I am. I have existence. I become conscious of my *self*. But among others and against them, I become conscious of my self's limits as well, my boundaries and my *shape:* I learn my definition. *How* other people look at me communicates *what* I am—not only what worth I have, but also what characteristics I truly possess.

If I walk down a crowded street and no one looks at me; if I work in an office where no one greets me; if, when I return home, my family takes me for granted, then something of me vanishes. If I do not exist for them, I die a little in myself. I look in a mirror and see nothing. I lack significant evidence of my own being.

On the other hand, every smile turned toward me shines on me; I live in its light; it illuminates my being. When friends touch me, I literally feel my *being* in that touch. A hug, a simple warm embrace consoles me with existence. It says, "You are, and you are here, and you are dear."

Eagerly, then, and persistently I seek myself in others' eyes. Both shrewdly and unconsciously I read my character in the curl of their lips, the bend of their bodies (to me?—away from me?), in the tone of their conversation with me. I do not truly know that I am funny until someone laughs. I may not know that I am brutal until someone cries.

In the fifth grade, Alice Kleinhans whispered, as I walked through the classroom, "He walks like a girl!" Was she telling the truth? It didn't matter. I heard her. I saw myself in the reflection of her giggled sentence. In my mind, I was one who "walked like a girl." Alice Kleinhans, eleven years old, had given shape to another human being.

Edward Dinkmeyer casually confirmed that shape. We were playing softball. I had hit the ball to left field—an able swat, I thought—and was running to first base. But Edward cried out, "We don't mind if you carry the piano, just don't stop to play it!" It was funny. I laughed. But it was also defining—and I saw myself a most unable runner thereafter. This was who I was: physically inept.

On the other hand, my high school creative writing teacher, whose name was James Barber, returned a story of mine with the comment: "Wangerin can write the eyes out of a turkey at fifty paces." I heard that, too. Surely he will not remember it today; but that single assessment made me, *made* me, shaped me, formed me in my own mind as a writer—and I committed prodigious energies to the craft on the strength of his fleeting reflection.

Even so does the careless world mirror the individual to himself and tell him who he is. But that, precisely, is the problem. The world is careless, unconcerned for the truth, despite the incisive effects of its judgments. Therefore, we desperately need one human being whose truthfulness has been proven in dependability, whose truthfulness we can trust, who neither mocks us nor flatters us but reflects us accurately. Therefore Adam *needs* Eve in order to know Adam, and I need Thanne, and a spouse needs her spouse.

Say it clearly, then. The blessing of—and the necessity of—truthfulness in marriage is no less than that one assures the other of his or her identity. It is an existential gift. In Thanne I find myself; if Thanne is truthful, I can withstand all the false reflections of the world. I can recognize them *as* false. In point of fact, I do not walk like a girl; but I know when my rear end threatens to spread to embarrassing dimensions, because Thanne points out how my pockets buckle to accommodate the bulge. And I can never grow vain in literary accomplishments so long as Thanne reflects the reality of that talent in me: "Wally," she said, "you get hung up in imaginary trees."

And I protested, "Oh, you can't judge me by that."

But she was not dissuaded from the truth: "I think so, Wally. You're distracted even when you drive the car"—your writing habits have their dangers. This, too, is who you are.

If the spouse is not truthful, who will be? If the spouse is undependable, then we are cast back upon the world, or else upon our own inaccurate assessments of ourselves, upon vanity or a crippling inferiority. If the spouse is a distorted mirror, we will live a lie. Who am I, really?

Truthfulness and dependability grant the spouse a self—at least a working knowledge of that self.

A SAFE HAVEN

The ability to trust creates a sense of security even within a chaotic world.

A house is built of wood and brick; within my house I am protected from summer thunderstorms and the winter's chill. But a home is built of trust and the assured stability of human relationships; within my home I am secure against the shocks of a haphazard, hateful, fraudulent world. Let one human, please, be truthful to me, that I might safely trust but one. No, I do not plead an endless praise of me, but truth told in love. Inevitably, I will doubt the praise. But it is in trusting that I am consoled and find a place of peace.

I have seen what uncertainty and mistrust do to people. When they cannot count on the systems of their community, when they see that the general motive of the world is selfishness, and when they suspect that nothing *has* to be what it says it is, that anyone might be deceiving them, (1) they fear the world, as though they were strangers in a strange land, and feel helpless. Or (2) they fight back; they themselves become selfish and uncaring on the premise that all existence is "dog eat dog." In either case, the security of a trustworthy *home* could have protected them, strengthened them, and kept them virtuous in spite of the instability outside. People need to experience trust in order themselves to be confident and truthful. The dependable marriage is a fortress—not to keep them from the world, but to steady them, to strengthen them for entering into that world.

Do you see, then, how utterly necessary it is to be truthful to your spouse in all things? Even little lies destroy trust, turning this spiritual shelter, this home, into a house merely, turning your spouse out, as it were, into the cold.

The husband says he will be home at five. Instead, he comes home at seven. To his way of thinking, this is a small fault, hardly worth talking about. If he had been this late for a business appointment, he would have called his boss to explain; but he takes his wife's understanding for granted. And he will see her soon enough. In fact, he sees her all the time.

Yet when he comes into the kitchen, he is astonished to find her crying. And when he tries to comfort her about the overdone dinner, he is further bewildered by her tone. She is angry!

She says, "You do this all the time."

He denies the accusation. He truly doesn't remember how often he's broken the incidental promises, simply because he hasn't paid that much attention to them.

But she begins to count off specific examples, and now he is shocked. How can she remember? Why should she take such specific offense over so minor a matter? "Isn't she," he says, "overreacting?"

No! She isn't overreacting, and the matter isn't minor. Neither is she merely angry, nor is it the ruined dinner that troubles her. She is frightened! It is not an exaggeration to say that her world is crumbling. Security itself is endangered by his carelessness, and she fears that their home is not essentially different from the rest of the careless universe. Her tears and her instincts are perfectly right: if he is faithless in the little things, how can she trust his faithfulness in greater things? Or how can she trust him to know the difference?

"I promise I will be faithful to you unto death." That vow was comprehensive, unqualified, and included faithfulness in everything. Every "little" promise kept is a new nail in the entire structure of the home, to make it proof against an outrageously deceitful world, to build trust, and by trust to build one sure place of peace.

As much as your spouse needs refuge, even so much will you labor to be dependable.

PREPARATION FOR COMING CRISES

Henry and Alice had a workable marriage. Nothing at all seemed wrong between them, nothing neglected or unsatisfied—

until their only son wandered out of the back yard and, a half-mile away, slipped over the bank into the Ohio River. The currents drew him in; the river floated him downstream; three fishermen found his body gently bumping against the shore.

Not immediately—one year later—another living being followed the boy to death. Henry and Alice's marriage ended in a mute divorce. There is a direct connection between the two catastrophes.

When the crisis struck them, so did a terrible irony. In their sorrow, both Henry and Alice needed a constant reassurance and love; both needed support and the gentle consolation of someone healthy, stable, and faithful; and both needed it from the one most significant in their lives—the spouse. But precisely because of the sorrow and their great need, neither one was healthy enough or stable enough to give it to the other. The crisis had undone them both.

Therefore, in the year after their son died, each felt less and less loved, more and more alone. Each asked the other in a hundred ways for proofs of support; but because *both* were asking, neither could answer. Both began to doubt; both suspected that the other's neglect was purposeful and sinful.

Alice said, "He blames me. He doesn't say so, but I know he does."

Henry said, "She doesn't understand how much I hurt. She thinks I should spill my guts like her. The way she looks at me, I can tell she thinks I just don't care. No, she doesn't know me."

Alice said, "He's not even trying any more. He's withdrawing."

Henry said, "She doesn't let me touch her. She hates me."

They both said, "There's no love here. None. What's the use?"

Well, if he loved me, wouldn't he show it?—

—Wouldn't she show it, if she loved me, now more than ever?

The irony described here is not at all uncommon. Whenever a crisis strikes a marriage, both partners hunger after the love neither partner can fully express just then. And very few marriages escape some sort of trauma. Why, even the move from one city to another can precipitate loneliness, confusion, instability—and a crisis.

But that the crisis should end in divorce, as it did for Henry and Alice, is not inevitable. They may have had a workable marriage before the death of their son; yet it lacked the one thing that could have survived the silences of unanswered questions: trust. They did not completely trust each other's hidden self. Trust sustains love and the relationship even when there are no immediate evidences of love and a relationship. Trust is a "believing in" one's spouse. This faith is, itself, reassurance and support and consolation precisely when the spouse can offer none of these things. It is "the substance of things hoped for, the evidence of things unseen." Once more: trust absolutely resists suspicions, and it waits until the spouse is healthier and can respond; it believes in that response long before it comes.

Trust is marital protection against the crisis.

Two personalities will work through their griefs in different ways. One may go cold and quiet, while the other spouts emotion. Trust blames neither way, but waits. A wife may reject sex for a while; a husband may fail at it. Trust doesn't take that personally; it waits. A spouse might miss dinner schedules or let the house grow messy or else become compulsive about cleanliness. Trust overlooks the irritations—and waits.

In this way, through waiting (such a difficult thing for inveterate "fixers" to do!), the marriage survives; for the one who heals first acts first to heal the other, but neither pretends to know the other's mind when that mind remains unspoken.

Please learn this crucial fact about trust: it cannot suddenly be created during the crisis! Husbands and wives, you can't cause trust when you can't show love. Faith in one another must be established *before* the crisis ever strikes, when things are normal and workable, so that it is already a natural, durable element of the marriage. *The proofs for trusting must precede the need for trusting.* You cannot spend what you do not already have.

And the strongest trust is built by the smallest actions, the keeping of the little promises. It is the *constant* truthfulness, the continued dependability, the remembrance of minor things, which most inspire confidence and faith.

O Thanne, that you might believe in my love during the desert days to come, I do this little thing, I make the bed this morning too. Then you will know me and wait for me, even when my soul is hidden from you.

·ELEVEN·

THE SECOND TASK:

Sharing the Work of Survival

---

*T*he word is "sharing."

The task is to *share*.

That a married couple must work in order to sustain themselves and to survive needs no argument or a chapter in this book. You work in order to live, whether you're married or not. You earn a salary, fix the plumbing, dust the living room, wash the windows, shop, fry eggs, raise children—you work.

But the specific marital task, the careful labor of a husband and wife, is to make all that work a *shared* proposition—to make of their myriad duties, jobs, and toilings one single work (not two, not many) in which you both participate.

Be careful: to share a salary is not to share the work.

To receive the benefits of someone else's labor is not to share the work.

(I know a fellow who, if his wife is not home, is constitutionally incapable of rising from his chair and fixing a sandwich for himself. He can't. He doesn't even entertain the notion. He waits until his wife returns, then asks her for the sandwich and therefore satisfies himself that they share. "Because I need her so much," he explains.)

To share in procreation, even to share love for the same children, is not to share the work.

Certainly, to share space in the same house is not to share the work which maintains the marriage inside that house.

On the other hand, sharing does not require that spouses be duplicates of one another, equally able to do the same jobs, periodically switching positions.

Nor need they do everything together.

Remember: three beings live within the construct of the marriage: a wife, a husband, and the relationship between them. When all the wife does and all the husband does are done to serve the third being, the relationship, when each detail of their toiling is a service to *that*, then they are sharing. Surely this will ask for a wise division of the labor; nevertheless, each remembers the spouse not only in but also *by* everything he or she does. That is, not only does the husband sometimes think of his wife while he works apart from her; but all his action—all of it—is offered to their relationship, almost as a holy, sacrificial offering, the fruits of his hands being placed upon the altar of their unity. Since the relationship embraces them both, so does his labor. They share it.

Of course one is not always conscious of it—but it is possible to tap quarter-inch holes in a metal piece on a radial drill press *in celebration of* one's marriage, in service to that marriage, and so in remembrance of one's spouse. This is sharing.

I have a distinct memory of walking out the kitchen door with a letter in my hand, and of Thanne's calling me back to ask a solemn question.

The letter said that a publisher wanted to print my novel, *The Book of the Dun Cow.* I was thirty-three years old, had been writing as long as I could remember, and was therefore not yet completely convinced that the letter was real. It was too sudden, too businesslike to persuade me of radical changes in our life. I'd written the novel at odd hours in a corner of the basement as a task my nature demanded of me. I had been so private about the project that it was halfway done before I showed it to Thanne. I was afraid that it would fail and I would be embarrassed. There were too many unpublished manuscripts already in my past, all of them shaming me. If *The Dun Cow* was to be one more shame, I wanted to suffer it in private. I didn't want to disappoint Thanne as well.

But then the publisher sent this letter, indicating interest and offering a contract. I read it and doubted it at the same time. I did not comprehend the meaning, didn't even try to imagine my manuscript as a book, felt no rush of joy within me, and certainly couldn't consider consequences. I began to wander out the back door that July afternoon, the letter in my hand. I think I planned to mow the lawn—

But Thanne said, "Wally?" and I was surprised by the searching, serious expression in her eyes.

"Yeah?"

She paused a moment. She said, "This isn't going to come between us, is it?"

Right easily I said, "Of course not. How silly." I frowned: "Why should it?"

"Well," she said. She shrugged. She did not look consoled. "You're an author now."

"We'll wait and see about that," I said. The term was too exalted. I didn't accept it. "But so what? What's the difference?"

She didn't answer. I touched her shoulder and went outside, disbelieving.

But Thanne's fear (fear it was) was not unfounded, and she was perfectly right to search. If "my" writing had not been "our" writing all these years, but private and personal, would my success in fact be *our* success hereafter? Thanne understood the significance of that letter from her first reading; she saw the consequences of a book published, whether it did well in the marketplace or not. It would authenticate my writing; it would turn an avocation into a vocation; and what might have been defined as a hobby before would now become, by its public recognition, a work. An acknowledged commitment. A serious occupation.

I thought Thanne was worried about celebrity, that fame would trouble our little lives, and I chuckled. Who can bother with fame if he can't even imagine his stuff transfigured into a book?

In fact, she was concerned about *me,* the effect that the affirmation of a contract would have upon *me,* the change my own attitude toward writing might undergo. If there were times when she did not share in my work of ministry, which was mostly public and communal, then didn't she have the right to fear that she might not share in my work of writing, which was intensely personal and private? What would it mean to the marriage? I hid to write. Would I now have license to hide forever and completely? She would have been shut out from a great portion of my life. I would have another wife, named Writing.

"Wally, this isn't going to come between us, is it?"

For then she would be lost, in a very real sense abandoned.

This is what she was asking, a question of acute significance: Can I share in this work too? Will you share with me your more solitary work, your writing?

Marriages have broken on the not-sharing.

The husband and the wife were meant to be, in all their work, helps perfectly fit for one another—*not* nuisances to be excluded from the more elevated, more "important" work; *not* mere beneficiaries of one spouse's work (as in, "I pay for the car and the house; I support you; that ought to be enough"); *not* mere ornaments purchased by and awarded to one spouse's work, as though good work deserved a good husband or wife.

It is arrogant for anyone to assume that the marriage exists simply to support or to assist him in his own chosen life's "work." Yet many seek precisely that benefit of marriage. Many "Adams," male or female, read no more in the divine title, "a helper fit for him," than this, that their spouses are to fit themselves to their wants because of the requirements of their jobs. Because Adam is the breadwinner, because Adam has station in the world, Eve is to find her duties in Adam's needs. Eve is, in effect, to take care of Adam in order that Adam can accomplish his work elsewhere.

Adam is a doctor, a physician saving lives.

Adam is a businesswoman responsible for the disposition of awesome sums of money.

Adam is a mechanic, weary in the evenings and deserving service.

Adam sells real estate and must schedule her days according to her clients' availability.

While Eve, female or male, is that horrible mistranslation of the Hebrew text, Adam's "helpmate," the helping mate, the one who helps the other, whose duties are seen as superior.

But God said to the two together, to the combination, to the unit composed of husband and wife, "Fill the earth and subdue it; and have dominion over the fish of the sea and over the birds of the air and over every living thing that moves upon the earth." Their work, from which the world would benefit, by which they would wrest a living from the earth and all its creatures, was *their* work, a shared dominion, a shared activity.

If Adam's work, to which he has committed his time and energy and intellect and spirit, and Eve's work, which likewise demands her time and energy, her mind and spirit, remain two different works—or if one is seen subordinate to the other—then one day Adam and Eve will fall to arguing. "My work" and "your work" will interrupt and hinder one another. Or else "my work" will, for all the praise and attention given it, degrade "your work" to drudge and servitude. Finally, "my work" may become the commanding god of the household, asking all to fall down and worship it, to organize their very beings according to its requirements.

Marriages have broken on the not-sharing.

Survival-work must be the single job of both partners for the support of this single relationship. Though the various duties will be divided between the two, neither spouse can feel that his or her responsibility is an end in itself. (There's where the danger arises, when one's commitments have become ends in themselves!) Instead, the purpose of all duties shall be "for the marriage, for the good of our home." In this way no one's "work" will feed, like a monster, upon the other's "work" or upon the other's intrinsic value as a human. Then "my work" and "your work" together shall have come not to be served, but to serve. And so it all becomes "our work."

Like a sweater (like the green sweater Thanne knit for me so long ago), marriages have been strengthened by this interweaving, this sharing of the work of survival.

Now let's be practical. How will you turn individual duties into shared, marital activity? There are four guiding principles, all of which are merely common sense and ought to be performed with awareness and care:

1. Let the Division of Labor Be Willing, Conscious, and Mutual

In times past, cultures divided the labor of the household, clearly declaring what was "husband's work" and what was "wife's." There was not much room in any particular marriage for latitude or personal choice; and there were, in those days, powerful reasons for the imposed similarity of most marriages. Each family depended, for its immediate survival, upon the close association of many families. Single families could not exist in isolation; more important than any marriage was the community at large—and the community divided its greater labor between what men did together and what women did together. The community needed to trust the general support and participation of all females for certain tasks, all males for others, since the community oversaw the survival-work of everyone.

"Times past" are not so very long ago. Do you remember how at harvesting the men worked field-to-field and farm-to-farm, while the women gathered to cook and feed them as they went, to boil the jellies, to preserve the fruits and vegetables? Do you remember, at slaughtering, the natural division of labor that put the men nearest the bloody beast and put the meats in the hands of the women? Even so did our grandparents allow the expectations of the community to teach them their tasks.

But things (so suddenly) have changed today. The immediate survival of any one family does not depend upon a close association with the community. Industry has taken the basic labor out of the family's hands. As our contemporary culture has chosen to survive by mechanization, it has less right or reason to demand similarity of our various households. We do not farm together; we do not hunt, slaughter, and salt meats together; we do not, in fact, depend upon our neighbors to perform, together with us, the labors of survival. Therefore, it no longer matters to us or to the community what tasks our neighbor or her husband have chosen for themselves. Families can and do survive alone. As a result, the old distinction between "women's work" and "men's" has lost its purpose and its force.

But cultural habits run very deep in us; so parents and grandparents, and even the marrying partners themselves, maintain unconscious expectations of what shall be the wife's tasks in the marriage, and what shall be the husband's. The old pattern, the old division of labor which sent a man into the world while it kept the woman with her children, still exerts great pressure on our consciences. Is it wrong? No, it need not be an improper pattern to follow—so long as the spouses realize that they are free, now, *not so much to obey it as to choose it.*

The division of the tasks within a marriage, in order to be a "sharing," must be made willingly and consciously, each one assured that it is his and her choice, each one aware of the other's choosing.

The old pattern is not wrong; rather, it is easy because it has been so common among us. Many marriages mutely assume that the husband's greatest labor is outside the home, earning an income from society, and that the wife's most significant contribution is inside the home, keeping house and raising children. But discuss this choice! Speak it aloud; assure yourselves that you agree together. Willingly choosing this division, constantly affirming one another in the choice, husband and wife shall surely *share* in the common job of survival. Moreover, you will be flexible, making changes upon this pattern as your marriage itself changes to accommodate new necessities.

But if either partner assumes that the old cultural pattern is a law imposed upon him or her, then any divergence (in behavior or in spirit) from that law will cause trouble. The marriage, trying to conform to a code it does not fully understand (since that code's purposes have passed away) will have difficulty finding its own true character, its own unique and holy fulfillment. It will remain bound to unrealistic restrictions and so remain an undeveloped being.

A wife may feel imprisoned by the role she didn't truly choose. She may grow frustrated and then guilty at her own frustration, as though her desire for other tasks is sinful. *I'm a bad person,* she may think, *because I'm not content with motherhood. I am weak and wicked because I hate to do the dishes.* Had she chosen these duties she might still dislike them—but she would not doubt or damn herself. As it is, her discontentment will affect the marriage whole.

Or a husband may be bothered that the house is not as neat or organized as he thinks it ought to be. If the man were free, he could take upon himself some of the responsibilities for housekeeping—take them over totally as tasks of his own. But so long as a "law" constrains him (either externally or internally, in his own attitudes), his irritation will grow to private bitterness or to open abuse and complaint against his wife's "faults." And his discontentment will affect the marriage whole.

A "law" can kill. An unreasonable "law" certainly will enslave a marriage (the living relationship itself), arresting its growth. But (1) when tasks are divided in a conscious and harmonious discussion between the spouses; (2) when each spouse chooses his or her duties, thus claiming them as his or her own and acknowledging responsibility for them; (3) when each partner fully participates in the process and is obviously respected by the other ("Your opinions, your willingness, your abilities are necessary to us," such a discussion implies, "and *you* are important to me!"); and (4) when each one *hears* the other today, proving that either can hear the other as well tomorrow—then there is no law but "sharing." Both guilt and criticism have been laid aside. This marriage has shown the ability to revise the duty roster whenever necessary. Neither partner needs to feel neglected, used, demeaned, subjected, or dominated. And both partners may work with a complete and willing commitment at their tasks, even the tasks they don't particularly like, while trusting the other's contentment in *his* tasks. No woman need feel ashamed of housewifery—because the choice was hers; it belonged to her, not to her business-sisters, and was made internally, within the marriage. No husband need feel ashamed of house-husbanding—likewise, because that choice shall have been his and supersedes the patterns of the culture. Such individual contentment affects the marriage whole. For the written code (any code!) imposed upon a marriage for no good purpose, kills; but the spirit of sharing gives that marriage life.

Therefore, husband and wife, attend self-consciously to this division of labor. Talk about it, out loud and earnestly. Make your talk a special *event* early in your marriage, and then repeat the event periodically through the years.

2. Divide the Labor According to the Natural Differences of the Spouses

Remember: marriage is the union of differences, the "help" of "unlikeness." You and your spouse are not (praise God!) the same. You have different talents and abilities; different gifts of the same Spirit for the common good; different likes and desires; different physical, mental, emotional, and social attributes. These differences, however, are not altogether apparent at the beginning of the marriage. They appear in practice. So it is likely that you began life together according to the patterns of your parents or the culture around you. But as the marriage matures, discoveries are made: you know yourself better, and you know your spouse more truly. So your early roles may feel unfitting to you. That's all right. This isn't a problem, but an opportunity for marital growth.

Now you are able to revise the division of labor according to a right understanding of your characters. Now, in mutual conversation, you can (1) name and acknowledge the differences between you, and (2) celebrate those differences by assigning them the work that best suits them.

When we married, I announced to Thanne that I would handle the checkbook and the bills. As my father had, so would I. But within the first months of the marriage I made such a miserable botch of the job that Thanne, possessing a mathematical mind, took over. This was no threat to my manhood or my worth, nor a wicked criticism of my person. This was eminently practical, a glad celebration of our differences, and a righteous sharing of our survival-work. I served our marriage by admitting Thanne's superiority in this area. She served by practicing her superiority in this area. (Note that both actions, mine and hers, together constituted the sharing.) And since no law in fact compelled us to persist in mismatched roles, we could switch, and we could grow.

Now let me explain the holy consequence of this method of dividing the labor—of "sharing." When the work of the household is assigned both according to true needs and according to the true personalities of the partners, that marriage permits, encourages, and honors true *personhood* for each spouse. When you sit to discuss the division of duties, these (whether spoken or unspoken) will be the primary questions: "Who are you?" and "Who am I?" and "What does the maintenance of our household require?" Primary questions focus on *being*. They will assess and affirm your characters. Then, the secondary question will be: "What shall you be responsible for, and what shall I?" The secondary question focuses on *doing*. It authenticates your characters, allowing them reality in action. If you follow this process, *the work itself* will signify and esteem each of you individually.

As your spouse accomplishes her tasks and as you experience the benefits of them, you praise her very character—for she is actively essential to your common survival and cannot be replaced by someone else. She did not shape herself to fit the tasks; rather, you together shaped the tasks to fit her being. That makes all you do a sharing. Moreover, she will be much more motivated to do that work which suits her, which manifests her value, work which is critical to your existence—and which is no drudge, therefore.

Can we now dispense with such demeaning epithets as "the little woman" and "woman's work" and "behind every successful man there is—"? I hope so. I pray God we do. Because the division of tasks in every marriage ought finally to be specific to each marriage, dictated by the faculties and aptitudes of the partners themselves. That the survival-work be done by someone—that is the only law. That it be wisely divided between you—that is your freedom.

3. Show a Continual, Sincere Interest in Your Spouse's Work

"Sharing" the work doesn't have to mean that we actually do the work together; but neither is it enough merely to benefit from my spouse's work. I don't share the farmer's work, though I eat his corn. Why, I barely acknowledge his existence until the corn is not there to eat. I do not necessarily share Thanne's work just because her paycheck bought my shirt. But I *do* share when my spirit, my awareness, travels with her to the office and attends her through the day—attends her like the invisible angel who sees what she does, comforts and encourages her in it, and consecrates the job with love.

If I never ask about her day, or if I do not listen when she yearns to talk of it, I diminish its significance. In this case, the lack of communication communicates a very clear message after all: her work is not important enough for my attention; her work is not mine; *I* do not share in it, however much our household may depend upon it.

But she will experience triumphs and grievances at the office. Not one of her days will be without some small drama of feeling. If, during the day, she knows I will want to hear them in the evening, and if she can trustingly save them up for me, then my spirit is with her. I am a presence that sustains her all day long. We share her work. Therefore, in the evening I ask about her day.

And there are dreary days when she is unconvinced that her office work has any meaning in the world. It is boring, repetitive, ignored by her manager, and frustrated by multilevel incompetence. She is no more than a comma in an endless sentence. But if she can trust my gratefulness for what she does, and if she can anticipate my spoken praise for this, then her work has meaning after all. My spirit comes to consecrate it. I am there, sharing her most incidental duties. Therefore, in the evening I honor what she tells me. I listen.

This is the mystery of human communication: that a half-hour's sincere dialogue in the flesh can bind us in the spirit all day through. I will ask her to tell me the smallest details of her experience and her feelings—and they'll be just as important to me as they are to her. And I'll remember them for the next conversation, so that my next questions will be precise, showing a true knowledge of her days. I don't understand the language of computers as she does; I don't need to, because I understand the language of Thanne's heart. And I learned the names and personalities of her co-workers. And I know the atmosphere of the office to which she goes, and I speak from that knowledge: whether it is chilly or warm, close, uncomfortable, or free. Thanne *knows* that I know—and so I am the angel who attends her in the morning.

And I have given her gifts that fit her needs at work (since I engaged to learn those needs). I gave her a radio that comforts her with classical music. I am in that radio. I *am* the music. I abide, and I share, for this is what such presents are: presence.

But none of this happens unless one spouse self-consciously labors at the task of making the divided work a sharing, and the other spouse recognizes his intent.

4. Realize That All Your Work Ultimately Serves the Marriage

Any job that anyone performs is justified by an ultimate goal. This final purpose encourages the worker while he works; more significantly, it also shapes his behavior and his attitudes on the job. Long before the goal is accomplished, it is there in anticipation. It dwells in his mind, and so he plans; it dwells in his heart, and so it guides his actions. If a carpenter crafts a chair for a rich stranger, he may do it well; but if he crafts it for his daughter, he will do it lovingly. Much, much is different between the first and the second crafting; and much is different between the two chairs, too, though only he and his daughter may see the difference.

How, then, shall the worker "share" his labor with his spouse? By admitting that the single purpose of *all* his jobs and *all* his duties is the healthy survival of his household. Surely, other goals will encourage any given job; but this goal should justify them all. Then, whether he is at home or abroad, in the fields or in the factory, his marriage will continue to shape his behavior and his attitudes; it will be present *in his very actions*. Then his spouse indeed "shares" the work of survival.

In other words, "sharing" comes from faithfulness, which was the vow from the beginning. "I promise to be faithful to you till death" means that, except for God, "I commit myself first to you." I shall commit myself to no goal or purpose which denies you or neglects you—or contradicts my commitment to you. Sexually, I shall keep faith with you, yes. But in all other forms of relationship, and in my work, I shall keep faith with you. Ours is the contractual relationship which defines all others, which is finally served by all the others. What my job requires of me: can I do it lovingly, on your behalf? Is it a worthy offering to our marriage? Or would you be offended by it? Does it take me away from you, in spirit, in time commitments, in fact? Is everything I do at work open to your scrutiny? Is it in harmony with your image of me?

So long as the worker continues to ask these questions, even privately and apart from his spouse, his work is her work (her work is his); they share in it. His behavior persistently remembers her and allows her a presence in spirit, though none of his colleagues may be aware of it.

But if anyone should establish for himself (or herself) a life independent from his spouse, one which does not serve the marriage or which he tends to keep hidden from her, he has broken faith. He is not "sharing" the work of survival.

With sorrow I have noticed husbands remove their wedding rings when they board airplanes for appointments in distant cities. It's a tiny gesture, to be sure. (And it is only one example of the countless ways by which people can signal *un*marriage.) But these men have, at least in part, ceased sharing. Their marriages do not accompany them wherever they go. Their professions are not, for them, "marriage work," but a personal gratification. They've become two men, leading two lives; and the marriage is (however honorably they may conduct themselves) imperilled because it does not, for a little while, exist.

And I have heard men in the company of men roar at jokes that scorn women generally. Or I have heard women with other women scorn the whole male gender in bitter gossip. In either case, they broke faith with their particular spouses by denying, even for a little while and for a joke, that the marriage relationship defined all others. "This isn't for your ears, dear. Just shop talk." Or "This doesn't have anything to do with you, honey." Oh, no? If the spouse is excluded and cannot participate, then this hasn't to do with the marriage either. Something cannot be "shared." Another relationship ("the boys" or "the girls") has taken precedence.

Again, when one spouse sets up a personal and private checking account, the secrecy permitted implies a life divided from his or her spouse. Under the marriage contract, this is not the free choice of the individual, "meaning nothing." It is very often a signal of breaking faith: an alarm. There is a part of this person's life no longer to be shared with the spouse. There is a goal for this person which does not serve the marriage.

But "sharing the work of survival" means offering *all* of one's work (and all of one's conduct within that work) in service to the marriage. This is the comprehensiveness of the marriage vow. In the totality of the offering does your spouse's spirit accompany you? In its completeness is the marriage protected? For you are not sometimes married and sometimes not.

And "sharing the work of survival," therefore, means resisting every temptation toward independence, toward personal liberty, toward "doing your own thing." This takes a sober vigilance and a persistent labor in a world which elevates the individual above the community, in a society which claims that individual desires are more important than contracts, commitments, and the good of the family. How loudly the world jeers both the husband and the wife who are "subject to one another out of reverence for Christ." "Wimp!" it mocks, gesturing at its nose as though to fix a ring in it. "Henpecked!" as though the man who devotes his work to his wife were not a man. "Submissive! Oppressed! Humiliated! Tyrannized!" is the woman who devotes her work and herself to her husband. "Wifey!"—as though she were undeveloped, not fully human.

"Be—all that you can be!" sings the world, implying that one's own self is one's own standard. Its hymn of praise praises itself: "I did it my way." Its chief ethical principle is, "You can do whatever you want to do (so long as you don't hurt anyone else)"—meaning that old vows *are* old, outworn, and do lose their force with time. The hero of this world "thinks for himself," unenslaved by unrealistic, dogmatic conventions. And the free woman, the progressive woman, the woman untrammeled by archaic custom, satisfies *herself,* for she has learned that she can choose for the good of herself. Eat hamburgers because *you* deserve it! Spend more on cosmetics because *you* are worth it! Come on, come on, come on—don't let living pass you by. Be yourself: that is the highest goal, the finest purpose, the only worthwhile end to this existence . . .

Oh, the serpent still is curled around the tree of the knowledge of good and evil. Still its tongue flicks forth, and still it hisses: *You can be like God.* The fruit was never more pleasant to the eyes. Faithfulness is still endangered. And truly to *share* the work of survival—in all things, at every level with one's partner—is strenuous work, both mental and spiritual labor. It is a task indeed.

But it is a task that blesses and keeps and protects the marriage. Does the "law" kill? So would the world, which tempts the couple to divisions and independence. The spirit of sharing preserves the life of the relationship whole and holy after all.

Whenever I write, dear Thanne, whatever I write, I write for you.

THE THIRD TASK:

Talking and Listening

Glance around the restaurant. It's a Denny's on Saturday night, but it might be any place where a couple can sit to eat. There's a low hum of voices. People are talking; waitresses slide by on soft shoes; laughter bubbles up now and again; silverware chinks on dishes.

But glance around. Do you see the man and woman seated at a single table by the low, dividing wall? The couple by the plastic flowers? Watch them. They do not talk.

The waitress sets plates of food before them. He stares at his. His wife (she *is* his wife) smooths and smooths the napkin on her lap while the food is placed. The waitress smiles. The woman smiles. The man does not. They eat.

Steadily the man cuts meat. Efficiently he pokes the pieces in his mouth, his fork upside down. He chews, gazing at his plate.

It is curious that the woman should be overweight, because she takes such tiny bites. She fidgets her peas, sips water, darts her eyes around the room, picks chicken with her little finger arched, pats her mouth with the napkin, smooths it on her lap—sighs. Every bite is nibbled to death, as though she chews with her front teeth only.

He is done long before she is. So he sits sideways at the table with his thumbs hooked in his belt. Now he stares at nothing, at no one. His eyes are lost in middle distance. When he thinks of it, he blows on his coffee and drinks. But the woman—her nervous gestures have multiplied, intensified. When anyone passes them, she looks up, looks down immediately, smiles too late, then blanks her face. She is an anthill of twitchy motion. Through furious embarrassment she orders dessert. She attempts a joke about ice cream, cheese, and apple pie; the waitress smiles indulgence. The man clears his throat, gazing away, uncommitted.

When they rise to go, the man is not one whit changed from the solemn fellow who first sat down—except that we're surprised to note how short he is after all. He had looked thick and factory-hard and, therefore, seemed a big man seated. The woman, on the other hand, is exhausted, breathing heavily after much work; she checks and rechecks the table to see whether they forgot something, while her husband marches directly toward the cashier. Finally she follows. This is how they regularly walk together: she follows.

They see us. They have to pass us on the way out. It's surprising how they are almost the same size; and now that they're in motion, they look alike.

"Evenin', Reverent," the man nods, and he sucks a piece of meat through his tooth.

"Isn't it a beautiful night?" the woman overflows. "Henry and I've just been commenting on how beautiful it is," she says. "Why, the moment Henry got home from work he said, 'Matilda, we have to go out and enjoy this beautiful night. No cookin' for you tonight.'"

The night must be beautiful. Henry has already left to enjoy it before Matilda has finished her sentence.

Now I will tell you a very sad thing. This was a date, sort of. Henry and Matilda "treat" themselves to a café dinner every Saturday night. This is their entertainment. This is how they satisfy their marital urge to "be together."

Matilda does not know (because Matilda cannot admit) that they never talk together. Henry is a realist. He knows they do not talk. But he wouldn't think to mention the lack to anyone because he doesn't consider it all that important; they get along all right. They've got no problems. They're married. They survive.

Henry does not know (because Henry rejects emotional matters as "womanish") that they are, both of them, dreadfully lonely. Matilda's very skin is a tissue of feeling. All day long she suffers loneliness. She does not move from the kitchen to the bedroom without the aching of her joints and her legs and the flesh on her neck—an aching to sit down and to cry. Instead, she fidgets. Instead, she bustles about the house, cleaning it. Instead, she looks forward desperately to their Saturday nights out—because she knows that if she once sat to cry, she could not stop, and Henry would find her crying, and she doesn't know how she would feel about him then. They are married, you see.

But they are living a divorce.

You do not need to glance about the restaurant to find Alice and Bill. In fact, you can't help noticing them because there's no want of talk at their table. Listen. Hear the woman behind us? Hear that running stream of language? That's Alice. If you ask her whether they have "communication" in their marriage, she'll tell you right away they do, but she'll say it somewhat bitterly since she thinks she carries the burden of marital discourse. Her husband, she will not hesitate to mention, never listens.

"I wish," she hisses at the booth behind us, "you would just once dress for the occasion, William. For your own self-respect, if not for me. I put on a dress. I break my back to do my hair. I wear heels. So how do you think it makes me feel when my husband takes me out and he's wearing blue jeans? I feel so embarrassed—"

"They're clean—" he says.

"Oh, William! Oh, William! You are so insensitive! The pastor's sitting right over there. You *know* he's noticed. Jeans! What do you think that says to him? It says you don't care about me, that's what. If I told you once I told you a thousand times, appearances make a difference. George wears his Sunday shoes just to take Donna walking. What about that? And he holds her hand. And they act just like newlyweds. And you can't tell me you're ignorant of the nice things, because I'm not the kind of person who sulks in silence, or *waits* for her husband to come up with his own bright ideas. I'm not ashamed to ask. And I've asked, William. God knows, I've asked you for a little kindness, just a gesture or two of love—a hint! Gratitude! One bouquet as a surprise to me! In all the years we've been married, have you given me a single bouquet? What can that cost? What would it cost you to remember?"

"I put on clean pants," he says. "I said, 'Let's go out tonight, honey—'"

"To Denny's! To Denny's, William? Excuse me, but this is a motel restaurant. Almost nobody wears heels in this place. Look at this! *Look* at this—it's a plastic flower! Oh, William—" Suddenly Alice's voice skips up to falsetto and dampens with true tears. "I tell you the nice things. God knows how much I yearn for one gracious, tasteful, loving thing in our lives—for both of us. I tell you and tell you who I am and what I dream." She is weeping now. He is distressed and utterly bewildered. "But," she shudders and laments the most tragic failing she can think of: "You never listen to me. You never listen."

There is a silence, filled with sniffling. Finally: "My mascara's running. Let's go. Let's just go home."

They leave in secret without greeting us.

Now I will tell you a sad thing about their talking and their listening, a failing which is mortally tragic, mortifying their marriage. Bill's name is "Bill" because he has always, from childhood, detested the sound of "William."

Laughter explodes from the far corner of the restaurant—true, jubilant laughter. It's a foursome enjoying themselves, and when they leave the restaurant, they will be going square dancing. You can tell by the costumes, denim and flannel for the men, flounces and shoulder-puffs for the women. The Greenwalds and the Bakers belong to a club. They genuinely enjoy their Saturday nights together. Further, they *need* their Saturday nights together. Sadly, they hide themselves, they bury themselves, they cover themselves in the innocent goodness of their partying.

Esther Greenwald is the blond woman whose face burns bright red when she laughs. Quick to blush is Esther, and as you can see, she is as light and decorative as rose frosting.

But Esther spent an afternoon in my office last month, sobbing so that her shoulders shook. And when she left I could not prophesy whether it was to go home or whether she would disappear from her husband and the children altogether. "He thinks we're happy," she told me. "He's just been made a partner in the firm because he is a committed, outstanding lawyer. He comes home smiling, tired, and content. He loves the children, pastor. And he loves me. That's what makes it so horrible. He loves me. I know it. But he doesn't know that I feel like a *nobody!* Who am I?"

Here Esther broke into tears. A helpless misery blotched her neck a furious red. "I mean, where is *me?* For myself? I'm always somebody's something. I'm not just Esther. I'm the children's mother. Over and over and over again I do the same things for them—and they're too young to know, too young to praise or thank me; but, God forgive me, I wish they would. And who knows how I hate them when they spill orange juice on the floor? It's so sticky! Paul doesn't know. He's glad I mother them. But he will not let me tell him how I *feel*. I'm their mother. It all goes *from* me *to* them; nothing comes from anyone to me. Oh, Paul would be horrified if once he truly heard how angry I get. I want—pastor, don't think ill of me: I want to beat them. Oh, God!" And she lost her speech in weeping.

When she could control herself, she said, "Who am I? I'm Paul's wife. Mrs. Paul Greenwald, successful lawyer's wife. I'm a shadow. Sometimes I think I'll roll up like a window shade, invisible. Or just go away. Who would notice? Pastor, I don't even have the *words* to say how I feel. It's too terrible to speak, or maybe I don't know how. I know everything about Paul, but he doesn't know anything about me. He asks me; but if I try to tell the real truth, it scares me and I cry. So he comes to pat me, to pet me, to comfort me like a child—and I don't get it said. Or the only way I don't cry is to shout, angry. But then he looks so wounded that I pity him, and I go to pat and comfort him. 'It's okay, it's okay' we say to each other, 'everything's okay—' *But it's not okay!* I'm dying! I am suffocating in that house! But I hate myself for what I feel—and I hate Paul, who loves me. God! God, I'm so confused—"

Well, Esther went home after all. See her there? She and Paul are laughing, side by side, across from the Bakers. Esther is so sweetly pretty when she laughs.

And Charles Baker looks so confident.

Indeed. Right at this moment the athletic Charles, jogger, handball player, health nut with a bald spot, *is* confident. That's because his wife, Irma, is with him. He can see her. He knows exactly what she's doing and will know for the rest of this night, at least.

But for days during the week he's on the road, selling paper products.

And when he's absent from Irma, he worries.

Not for her safety. Rather, for her virtue.

Oh, it's a complicated matter. The athletic Charles—this crimsons him with shame—is sometimes impotent, especially after long trips apart from Irma. Therefore, he doesn't make love when he returns; and therefore, he fears that she is sexually unsatisfied.

But he will not tell her of this problem. He will not.

And because the question might be traced back to his shameful secret, neither will he ask her about her own sexual feelings.

They don't discuss sex at all.

Each is left in an isolation, desperately guessing at the silence in the other. Irma's isolation persuaded her to come to me. And that encounter took me to Charles.

Charles's isolation has filled him with a venomous suspicion regarding Irma's activities when he's on the road. It also shut him tight against me, who, he believed, was no more than a spy for Irma, or else a nosy cleric come to dig the dirt of others' lives. One phrase—"I *can't*"—revealed more to me than Charles wanted to show. "You don't understand! I *can't*— Oh, get out of here. Leave me alone! What does a pastor know of these things?"

They do not talk.

They live an increasing divorce and feel truly married only in the company of Paul and Esther Greenwald—whom they envy.

Just as Esther Greenwald envies them.

Now all is well. All is well in the Sad Cafe, because Henry and Matilda have departed mutely into their beautiful night. Alice and Bill have slipped away. The waitress has cleared and wiped both tables, finding a grim little tip on the first and none on the second.

All is well. Paul has thrown his arm around Esther—a giggling Esther—to share a joke; Charles is laughing boisterously at the joke, loudly, without embarrassment; Irma has lifted a handkerchief to her eyes. The waitress will find a fat tip here.

And we must go. What do you suppose a preacher should preach to these people in the morning? What, dear Lord, could open all the doors of loneliness in the Sad Cafe?

The third task for marriage maintenance I've entitled "Talking and Listening." I suppose I could have used the word "conversation," except that it doesn't indicate the intensity of the exchange or the depth of substance required by a healthy marriage.

Most commonly the word "communication" is used, but I'm not satisfied with that either: first because so many young couples assume this to be the single most significant characteristic for preserving marriage (it isn't: forgiveness is); second, because one partner may be satisfied that he's "communicated" simply because he told someone what *he* thought.

The better word—except that it is too clinical—is "dialogue." This makes clear that a monologue—however passionate, however precise, however satisfying it may be for one—is never enough.

Marriage exists in relationship. Relationship is healthy only in the full participation of both partners, which, when they talk together, requires four separate activities, thus:

1. One partner talks, while
2. the other partner listens. And then
3. the second partner talks, while
4. the first partner, now, listens.

Each partner must be skilled in these two related, but widely different, activities, *both* to talk *and* to listen. And each partner must be careful to practice both equally. If any one of the four parts of a complete dialogue is missing; if but one partner fails either to talk or to listen, the circle is broken. A true exchange has been interrupted (though the couple is often unaware of the failure). And a healthy marital discourse is handicapped. The marriage may find itself eating at the Sad Cafe, utterly bewildered how it came to be there.

Two human problems trouble our accomplishment of this elementary, four-part task:

1. Sin persuades us that the most important object is to talk, to *be* heard, and that the greatest frustration is that the *other* does not listen. So we raise our voices, thinking that this helps communication, and we literally shout. Or restlessly we interrupt our spouse's talk so that she can never complete a sentence. Or we repeat the same thought over and over again until, as we say, "we are blue in the face." Or we actually write down our thoughts and hand them to our spouse to read (for how could he ignore or refute the written word?). Or, pathetically, we teach our spouse to listen to us by *not* listening to her, giving her some of her own medicine (though we ourselves may not have been listening anyway, but merely going through the motions of listening, marking time until she was done).

In all my marital counseling the most common complaint is that the husband or the wife—the other—does not listen. Second in frequency is that the other does not talk. Almost never does the counselee come with the simple admission that he himself can't listen, or that she herself won't talk. If we see ourselves as the center of the relationship and gods of the household, of course we'll find failure in the other: our words, the words of god, are so critically important. Why? Because they are our own words. Sin persuades us so; so sin (*our* sin, in this instance, more than our partner's failure!) obstructs dialogue.

2. Few people are born with the native ability to talk well. Fewer still know by nature how to listen. These are difficult tasks and must be learned. Yet most people assume that the ability comes naturally, like waking or walking.

To form my desires into language (as children learn to do) is not to talk *to* another human. Self-expression alone isn't talk. It may be emotional relief; it may fulfill a personal need, may get me what I want; it may be a dazzling—or else aggressive—display of rhetoric as I grow more skillful with the language, impressing my *self* upon my world. But it isn't the talk of dialogue. Merely, it is the swelling of my spirit until I fill the room or the relationship. And I can judge that it is not dialogue by the fact that, when I'm done talking, I'm *all* done. The important part of this exchange is over. But the talk of dialogue involves the work of knowing, acknowledging the other, of shaping speech *toward* him, *for* her. It is neither done nor well done until it has been well *received* by that particular hearer. Good talk is a good giving of something, mind to mind, person to person; and as I love the other, so do I lovingly help her to take what I give. It is a careful process, exchanging the weight and the safekeeping of something significant from me to her.

Likewise, true listening is not merely to be silent awhile; silence can be non-participation. True listening does not leave the whole burden of communication to the speaker, as though I, the listener, were being carried on his back. True listening is itself a labor and shares the work of dialogue. What is carefully given, carefully I undertake to receive. I shift my stance to take its weight, and I accept responsibility for its safekeeping.

In order to be practiced, talking and listening must be learned. I described four couples in the Sad Cafe; but each couple is only a type, an example of a certain kind of communication failure. Behind those couples swells a multitude of lonely, suffering husbands and wives; and though they may tell different stories, their sorrow is the same, its causes all the same. They had not learned, or else they did not practice, dialogue—both to talk and to listen.

GOOD TALKING

The series of suggestions which follows will seem at first simplistic, so easy and obvious you might be inclined to skim the paragraphs in the confidence that you already know these things. If you know them, good! Good talk is no mystery. It is within the reach of everyone. On the other hand, what people know and what they do are seldom the same. It's very possible you do not *practice* even the simple suggestions. Therefore, I urge you to examine yourself with each suggestion, remembering specific conversations with your spouse and comparing your real behavior to these ideal standards.

But when all the suggestions are added up for you, then they may seem the opposite of simple, so many and so varied you might wonder, "Who can remember all this for a passing chat? I'll get a talker's block if I try." But everything you do is complicated by a hundred unconscious variables. The fact that you do it unconsciously and habitually is what makes it easy, after all. Even to dress in the morning requires countless small decisions, which, if we listed them all, would fill a book. We list here the decisions of good talk in the dear hope that, as you practice them, they will become the unconscious habit of your marriage. If Charles Baker had had, between himself and his wife, the wide avenue of dialogue, he might not have kept his impotence a secret; then suspicions and anguish and isolation would never have threatened their marriage.

The good talker, then, notes three elements for every conversation (the good driver notes at least as many for every city trip), and adjusts his talk according to each. Your talk will be shaped by a watchful understanding of (1) your listener, (2) yourself, (3) the actual purpose of the conversation.

1. Shape both what you say and how you say it to the person listening.

When you speak to your spouse, do you also look at her? Or do you turn your eyes elsewhere? Do you know the difference? So tiny a gesture, the flick of the eyes!—but not to look at the listener implies (especially over long years of marriage) that you take her presence and person and attention for granted, that it is the listener's duty to "wait upon you." And if you look at the listener, *where* do you look? At the forehead, as though you stood in a superior position? Vaguely, at the body or in the general direction of the listener, as though she were a thing, a telephone receiver, a necessary but not honored element to your speech?

Let your spouse be the true focus of the talk in order that the message might properly lodge in her. ("Lodge" in her; "dwell" in her; come home and live alive in her!) Know that your whole body expresses the message, and that the message is never merely information but a constant comment on your relationship. Use, wisely, *three* senses for the communication: sight and touch as well as sound.

Surely you will look your listener in the eyes; even so will you acknowledge, authenticate, and honor your spouse, encouraging her active participation in a true and dual dialogue. Besides, you declare that the doors are open that way; nothing is hidden, shameful, or forbidden between you. Isn't that the deeper purpose of all conversation—I mean especially marital conversation—that the veils are removed, that you belong wholly to one another, that you are willing to be "naked and not ashamed" before this one human in all the world?

And touch this listener. If you touch none other when you talk, touch this one. For little babies, touch is the strongest declaration (1) that they *are there,* and (2) that they are there *for you.* God gave the infants a soft and eminently touchable skin, so that we would want to touch them. But when they grow into adulthood the skin changes and we forget. Yet the need remains, even in the adult, for plain human pressure, skin to skin, and marriage not only gives the right for such intimacy but also pleads for it. Touch is a physical means of the talk itself. We *are* our bodies; our bodies are involved in the completed dialogue. But choose with care the sort of touch to use, since it will declare (3) *how* this one is there for you and what sort of talk you intend.

What do these things mean: a holding of hands? A pat on the shoulder? A finger on the other's lips? An arm around the waist? A hug? A thumb jabbed in the other's chest? A pinch? A hard, persistent gripping of the elbow? Each kind of touch means more than words. Each one, in fact, directs the words which attend it. They are the vocabulary of an elemental, universal language; yet it is marvelous to me how many people ceased touching shortly after the wedding, as though they had outgrown a childish thing. No, that's not precisely true: they cease, so often, the gentle touching but (men particularly) continue to communicate displeasure, ill will, or anger by the painful touch. But you, Good Talker—even as you know well the wide variety of spoken words and use them carefully, so will you understand the vocables of touching and not shrink from using them with your spouse.

And name this listener. I've observed that people speak and repeat the names of their pets more than they do the names of their spouses. Where dogs are concerned, they know the value of the sound alone. Where spouses are concerned, they seem ignorant that the name, the very pronunciation of it, carries gentle force and affection. There is a deep, primitive response to the mere syllables of one's own name. Thanne whispers, "Wally?" Wally?" and my whole being answers, "Here I am." Speak "Herman" in a crowd and watch how many Hermans willingly turn to look at you, a stranger. But speak your spouse's name in the crowded words of your talk, and willingly he will *be*—he will find himself present—in that talk. Speak it often, that deep might call to deep. "Dear" and "darling" and "honey" are not bad titles. But in time they are freighted with a host of other connotations. (I've seen wives drop husbands to their spiritual knees with one sarcastic "dear" shot through their teeth.) Speak her name. It's the most personal, most meaningful way we have of saying, "You."

Now, then: if you are watching your spouse while you talk; if you are touching him or her and so feeling, as well as seeing, the reactions to your talk; and if you are, by the name, inviting his or her true presence in this dialogue, then you have an excellent means also to *read how your listener is responding*. You can and will shape your talk to him, to who she is in that immediate moment. You won't speak past her. You won't cause feelings completely different from those you intended. You need not deceive yourself, thinking you have communicated just because you said one thing, when, in fact, he heard a different thing altogether.

Once, before we were married, I had a significant and, I thought, magnanimous talk with Thanne. I believed with all my heart that I was giving her a good thing. I said, "Thanne, I don't mind if you date other men." I wanted her love for me to be proven in the fires of experience—and I was announcing a sweet, infinite trust in her choosing. I said, "In fact, I think you should date others. Be free. Enjoy yourself."

So charmed was I by my magnanimity, that I didn't see her lips go thin, her eyes narrow, her body shrink. I didn't "read" her. We were walking along the shores of Lake Michigan. A rushing surf and a moon-cold sky fixed that night in my memory as most romantic.

But Thanne sent me thereafter a letter utterly void of romance. "If you meant to break it off with me," she wrote, "why didn't you just say so?"

She took my goodness most bitterly, since she had been rejected in the past. We had had a talk. Communication, dialogue, we had not.

But read your listener, his face, the total language of his listening body. Learn the signs through your years of marriage, and know that every human has a language peculiar to himself, herself. What does it mean when lips purse? When shoulders hunch? When someone beats the bread dough harder? When nostrils flare, when the smile slips, when the tongue comes forward to touch upper teeth, or the head drops to one side? Good talk always speaks *to* someone—to the one listening right now, not to your image of him (good or bad), not to who she was this morning, not to a tape recorder or a pupil, a child, a parakeet, a foreigner.

Alice in the Sad Cafe had never learned that. Though Bill was a man who didn't always fail, she saw him as nothing but a failure. She spoke to her false image of the man, to the spectre of her own futility. Alice nagged.

2. Know clearly who you are and how you seem to your listener to be, because *you* are the instrument that communicates.

In your head is one message; in the drama of your delivery, in the posture of your body, in the tone of your voice, is another. Are the two the same? And if they are not (or if you do not take the trouble to learn whether they are not), what will you say? "Oh, my husband knows me well enough"? "My wife understands me"? Really? And when did you teach your spouse to know the hidden you?

Know thyself!

The husband who begins a significant message with "By the way—" then concludes it by flying out the back door has just canceled its significance. He ought not to be chagrined that his wife forgets it. If it's important—even if it's an embarrassing topic—it wants the expression of importance.

Or the wife whose voice comes through her nose when she speaks matters most personal and serious to her, who drops her eyes and plucks at her blouse, may seem to be complaining. So the serious message was lost in a whine—but a whine was never intended. "Why does he seem impatient with me every time I need his understanding?"

Or any spouse may intensify the communication only when he or she is upset, when negative emotions are aroused. All good things are merely mumbled. Bad things come through a tightened throat, shrill and loud, attended by broad gestures. Yet that same spouse would be surprised to learn that the family has developed, over the years, the picture of a grouch.

"You're never happy."

"Yes, I am."

"You never praise anyone. Were you ever proud of me?"

"But I do praise!"

"You never really told me that you loved me."

In fact, the grouch may love sincerely, may believe that he or she has often spoken love, may indeed have mouthed the words. But he had not known how he sounded; he never shaped his *self* to the message in his head. So the best messages were obliterated by the worst.

In order to talk well, it will be necessary sometime in your marriage first to listen well—to let your spouse act as your mirror. Learn from him or her how you look to other people, then adjust your behavior so it befits the message in your mind. This is a self-conscious preparation for the task of marital talking-and-listening, a careful acquiring of the skill. It wants hard work, but it gives a blessed return. And there is none in all the world better able to help you in this than your spouse.

All my life I've been painfully shy. When I feel most bashful I seem to myself the meekest of people, withdrawn and scared and vulnerable. But Thanne avoided me during such periods, actually shrank from me as though *she* were the one scared. Then she said, "Why are you angry with me?" Angry! I, the unworthy, angry with anyone?

Right. This is what my spouse, my mirror, reflected to me: shyness looks like arrogance. Meek Wally was Wally with his eyebrows down, his face gone grim, severe, his sentences cut short, his manner hard and haughty. He seemed displeased with those closest to him.

And this is what both courtesy and skillful talk required of me: I learned instead the gestures of acceptance, even when I did not fully feel them; I shaped my expression according to Thanne's perceptions and her needs; I continually viewed myself as from a third eye above me, looking down—so that the whole self might express the message in my mind.

Are you happy? Seem so. Do you mean to praise? Enact praise. Is it a good word you wish to communicate? Then why do you glower? Is the criticism you're about to give fundamental to your relationship? Then why are you shouting so loud, and why did you just slam the door?

The first time ever I expressed my love to Thanne, I expected her to throw her arms around me and squeal for joy. Instead, she took two steps backward and wrinkled her nose, as though I'd just presented her with a dead mouse.

I had mumbled, "Well, I think I love you." Those are the exact words.

And this was her exact response: "You *think?*"

3. Be aware of the actual purpose of the conversation.

Do you truly mean what you are saying? Do you even know what you mean to say? And what do you expect from your spouse in this conversation? Some information? Agreement with your fixed opinions? A little laughter, because this is mere chit-chat? A companionable passing of time? Or sympathy for deep matters difficult to express?

Do you wish her to do some minor thing? Or to change her character? Are you saying so or merely hoping she'll get the hint? And if you desire her change, for whose sake is it, yours or hers?

In fact, who truly is meant to benefit by this conversation?

It is this sort of confusion of purposes that confuses the listener and disappoints the talker. So often the talker begins unaware of his or her own reasons for talking, whether because he is acting from impulse or whether he has deluded himself. And even when he is aware, again and again he will not make the reasons apparent to the speaker. Such conversation is a futile affair and makes communication itself seem threatening.

If the talker has not clearly assessed her motives, matters terribly important to her may come disguised in flippant statements; when they receive, then, a flip response, she may feel hurt and misunderstood. Or if she has not identified, even to herself, her purposes, then the couple may be holding two separate conversations at once, each at odds with the other.

Talker, what is the purpose of your talking?

You may *say,* "Help me with this problem I have with your mother." You may sound as if you were honestly seeking guidance, when in fact you are plain mad and *meant,* "You mother is impossible." When your husband, then, offers kindly suggestions about what you might do for the problem, you blow up, confusing him. "Ho!" you cry. "So you're on her side against me!" And your husband thereafter remembers this new principle of the marriage: *Never talk about my mother.* Talk failed because you failed to know the purpose of the talk—or to state it.

You may *say,* "Honey, you have such an innocent, unsuspicious nature. Perhaps you don't know how dangerous it is to talk to any man who passes by." You may sound as though you were sharing a bit of experienced advice, when in fact her "talking" seemed to you to be flirting, and you are simply jealous. The next time she smiles on a passing man, she won't remember what you thought you told her. "I told you," you will hiss. "I *told* you not to talk to men. Did you do it just to spite me?" Well, no. She heard well enough what you said, but had no means of knowing what you meant.

You may begin a conversation with a flurry of questions which seem to express sincere interest in your spouse's day. You may even believe that you care to know. But the questions are calculated to lead into your own day: "Well, did this heat get you down? Weren't you just exhausted? Did you accomplish much? I'll tell you what, I hardly finished the document for . . ." And soon enough the conversation that started as hers has become yours. You've satisfied your sense of marital concern (such a good husband am I!) without truly attending to your wife or satisfying her need to be, her deep yearning to talk. What were your motives anyway? Even so—seeming to think of his wife while actually overflowing with himself—did Paul Greenwald of the Sad Cafe allow his wife to wither on the vine. He asked her questions he did not intend. He didn't even notice how he neglected her answers.

And for whose sake is this conversation?

The sharp-tongued Alice, cutting and cutting William at the table, might believe her criticisms are all for his own good. She's pointing out his faults in order to improve him, because he's a good man at heart and she loves him. In fact, she's killing him unaware. She's a discontented woman whose complaining obscures the real causes of her sorrows and whose talk consoles no one but herself: its purpose is self-pity. Its purpose is to release some of her anger at someone. Its purpose is altogether unassessed; she doesn't know.

But good talk (1) is clear about its real purposes and (2) chooses purposes meant to serve the marriage. And when serving yourself by talking to your spouse can truly serve the marriage, then say so. Ask him, ask her for the attention. Be clear. There is no need in such a relationship to be devious.

Finally, regarding the purpose of the conversation, this must be emphasized: sometimes (*most* of the time in your marriage) talk is good simply for its own sake. It wants nothing greater than that two enjoy each other's company. They plan a day, a vacation, the future. They discuss the day past. Bits of information flow back and forth. Fleeting feelings are noticed, stronger feelings declared. Husband and wife observe the world together, commenting on friends, experiences, the jots and tittles of their lives. The arteries of communication are kept open by common, regular use!

Know, please, that this purpose, lightsome as it is, *is enough*. You need go nowhere when you talk, but merely *be*. Then lay no heavier burden on the interchange than that. Let there be times when the conversation is not supposed to be "deep." This is hardly (you pragmatic man!) wasted time. It is marriage. And without it the marriage starts to starve.

Somewhere in their relationship Henry and Matilda, the silent couple of the Sad Cafe, ceased such idle talk, and the arteries between them shut up tight. It is a grievous loss. Now they can talk of nothing at all.

GOOD LISTENING

At the beginning of his reign, King Solomon prayed one superior gift from God. Not wealth, not long life, but something far more valuable—he asked for "an understanding heart," which may be translated, *a hearing heart*. He asked, we say, for wisdom. But the genius of wisdom, dear husbands and wives, is the ability to open a room in one's heart for the talk—and so for the presence—of another. Wisdom is none other than the ability to listen.

And listening is an active labor, a learned skill, not a passive silence as though two were taking turns at the same game. False listening is waiting *for* the other to finish; good listening is waiting *on* the other while he or she speaks, as good servants, with intense attention, wait on their employers. It is a busy service.

A "learned skill"? No, in marriage it must again and again be a *re*learned skill, since we grow used to one another. We become each other's habit. The newness of the relationship resolves into sameness: same person, same voice, same tone of voice, the same old topics. Her talking becomes a background hum, like Musak; he repeats the same old tune (we think), the same refrain of irritations. And so we prejudice those closest to us; that is, we prejudge their talk, assuming we know what they're going to say before they say it—and do not listen. You have my ear, my dear (but not my mind, my clean attention, or room in my heart; these, for the moment, are filled with my self).

Listening, finally, requires the sacrifice of self-denial. Always talking, never listening, is a blatant self-assertion. Mostly talking and only feigning to listen ("You had your turn, it's my turn now") is hypocritical, a hidden self-assertion. But true listening lays oneself aside a while: for this moment not my opinions but yours have celebrity; not my interests but yours are ours; not my words but yours have life. Listening is giving more than mere attention to the talker, but giving life as well, so the speech truly lives for both of you, in both of you. You pay attention? You attend to the talk? Yes, but you also *tend* it as you would tend a garden: you minister unto your spouse.

1. Show the listening. Your body speaks a silent language. By how you act, when the talker is talking, you invite him or her into your heart or you shut yourself against the other.

Look at her. Acknowledge him. Whether or not the topic is trivial, the talker is not. Light glances and smiles are a significant reward, saying "I appreciate you. You *are*. You exist for me." If the topic is serious, the very posture of your body will help your spouse to support its weight and to struggle through it. Eyes to her eyes shares the matter. Nodding; murmuring, if not assent, at least the processing of what he says; frowning; leaning forward to him—these are tiny gestures but mighty encouragement and true participation in the talk.

But if you turn your back, clean your glasses, rub your eyes, cut your vision from her, what does that say? If you put on a coat, clear your throat, sigh (for heaven's sake!), tap your foot, or give any indication of impatience, you signal the judgment (even before the talk is done, in the midst of it) that he and his words are less important than something else. The atmosphere you create is often more beneficial for healthy talk than the length of time you spend listening.

Get to the point! you silently say. But what if there is no point? There doesn't have to be a point.

Language needn't always communicate some message. One of its most blessed virtues is that it creates order; it turns confusion into a sensible order. It is therapeutic, then, sometimes just to talk.

Whenever we speak in sentences, we are arranging a multitude of thoughts into a pattern, establishing relationships between one thing and another. As a noun fits with a verb, forming subject and predicate, so the detail which the noun signifies fits with the detail which the verb signifies. Now, add adjectives and prepositions and conjunctions all in their rightful places until you make a sentence that makes sense. Since each of those things stands for a bit of experience, you are adding together the pieces of your experience until it all begins to make sense. We are unaware of the process, to be sure. Yet we know how helpful and comforting it is to talk—just to talk; and this is the reason.

So, here comes your spouse, stuttering and confused by some event, or battered by the careless world, swept along by some emotion, or merely uncertain, perplexed by the day. Your active listening can encourage him to talk. Your gentle questioning can trigger her talk. And though it may not at first make sense, your continued behavior will create the atmosphere that allows the time to find that sense; you will wait, you will wait *upon* her. "Tell me," says your expression and your posture. "I want to know." Unthreatened, unpressured, then, your spouse is able to talk, even to repeat things over and over, until he or she has combed the tangled day into an order: sentences, words in their proper places, put a blizzard of impressions and experiences into proper places.

But your spouse needed an audience, a loving and active listener to focus on first: a point of departure. And your listening made his or her talk valid, acceptable, a genuine definition of things.

Even so the talking-listening marriage organizes life itself.

2. Empty your heart in order to listen. You say: "We've been married so long, I know my husband (my wife) like a book." No, I say. You never completely know the other. And the assumption that you do only hinders your true listening and so keeps you from knowing him or her.

Alice of the Sad Cafe thought she knew her husband. She was so sure of him that every time he started a sentence she finished it for him; every time he paused (which he did often, being shy by nature and intimidated in her presence) she filled in the blank. Of course, so long as she put the words into his mouth, she knew them in advance. But they were her words, not his. She was listening to her image of him, not to him. Alice had never shut off Alice (emptied herself) long enough to learn that he was not "William" at all, but Bill.

The portrait of Alice is not exaggerated. It is, I'm afraid, one of the most common and desperate maladies of marriage—to imprison the spouse in our own image of the spouse. Have you noticed that it often takes a crisis to open up our eyes, so that we marvel, "Why, I didn't know him at all! I didn't think she had it in her!" That's because, until the crisis, nothing persuaded us to listen for something new, to hear the subtle changing that humans are always undergoing. If Bill should walk out on Alice, she would be shocked not only by the act, but also by his character: "Why didn't he *tell* me?" But he did; or else, poor

Alice, your own presumptive talk disallowed it. You never listened.

And Paul Greenwald is not much different. Even though he is content whereas Alice is complaining, even though he displays an honest love for Esther, Esther is anguished, and he does not know it. He may not interrupt her talk or impatiently push her sentences aside; but their conversation is all full of his happy self. He *assumes* her happiness, too. He assumes who she is; he doesn't listen. When she tries to speak things horrible to her (her hatred of the children, how guilty!), he comforts her with platitudes because he has not heard the horror. Paul was too full of the problem-solving Paul, trusting himself by great good will to brush all trouble aside. Empty yourself, even—especially—if you fear to hear what lurks in your marriage.

Or when she *does* begin to get through to him, when he does glimpse Esther's sorrow, straightway he hangs his face with his own guilt—and for pity she can't continue. But this too is a self-centeredness, focusing all things good or bad on one's self. That self must be emptied in order to listen, in order to hear the whole of what the other is trying to communicate. Assume nothing. When the communication is most difficult for her and she struggles, we are most inclined to "help" her out by telling her what she meant to say. But we should lay ourselves, even our intrusive "help," aside and suffer the struggle *with* her.

And who listens to his spouse only to contradict her? And who must always argue the details of her husband's statements, stories, memories? These habits aren't insignificant, the curiosities of old age. They deny the talker value and a self as well.

Finally, there will certainly come times when your spouse will want and need to forgive you. But you cannot receive forgiveness if first you have not heard and admitted your sin. He or she must speak the harder thing first. Even then, empty yourself. This is humility. If you remain full of yourself, then you'll meet your spouse's necessary talk with defensiveness, not listening but arguing, disputing, denying; and if you cannot hear the sin, you will never hear the forgiveness that would bind you together again. So what, if her accusation is not perfectly accurate? So what, if there were mitigating circumstances? So what, if he is partly to blame? To shut off the listening is to shut off the dialogue altogether. Then there is no chance whatever of atonement, regardless of whose the fault—and two continue lonely.

So the listener humbly empties his or her heart in order to *be* a listener: "I am here for you. The time is yours. In this moment you have the freedom and the right to take us where we both shall go."

3. *Holy listening produces the fruit of the Spirit.*

What an opportunity for love is listening! And what shining benefits it sheds upon the marriage! Do you know that it is the active listener, and not the talker, who is more Christlike in the dialogue? In listening—by listening—the fruit of the Spirit manifests itself within your relationship (see Gal. 5:22–23).

Unselfish *love* allows the other person the central spot of the dialogue and a place in your heart, which, for the while, is emptied of yourself and truly open.

Just as the disciples received the risen Lord with joy, so it is your *joy* (and you show it!) to receive the speaker's talk, thought, and life within you.

Peace is, in Hebrew, *shalom*: wholeness, health, well-being. Not only does your listening affirm the being of the speaker, but it is the oneness, the wholeness, of your marriage.

But such listening requires of you what the Spirit itself gives you to do. You are able, dear listener, (God makes you able) to be *patient,* granting the speaker the time and the attention necessary. You are able to be *kind,* uncritical and uninterrupting, which would spoil true talk before it's done. You are able to handle the speaker's revelations, whether little or large, personal or general, happy or horrible, with *goodness,* with *faithfulness* to your spouse (faithfulness to who he or she really is), and with *gentleness,* all important qualities since these revelations are in some measure the speaker's self. If the talk is genuine, the talker is made vulnerable by it, stands disclosed, naked; but she or he is willing to do so unashamed—because you handle the fragile thing with care.

All this you do by practicing a godly *self-control.* God grants it, even to the most headstrong and compulsive husbands and wives among us. You are able.

Talking and listening, both of these performed by both of the partners, make up dialogue. It is here that the marriage lives and moves and evolves, or is, at least, aware of its evolutions. It is here that you most consciously are, dear husband and wife, a husband and a wife to one another.

And if not here—if one does not talk well, if either does not listen well—where else can you, in clarity and comprehension, be?

THIRTEEN

THE FOURTH TASK:

Making Love

---

*T*he newlyweds are alone in the motel room. He has fiddled with the lock, drawn the curtains, flushed the toilet to check the plumbing, switched the TV on and off again, stands with his hands in his pockets. She has taken an infinite time to lay their clothes in neat piles in the drawers, though they plan to leave in the morning and she'll have to repack. Busy, busy couple, up against it: sex is next. Sex is approved now, consecrated—and expected. But what, now that it is the proper business *of the marriage* (and not the mindless rush of passion, the flood that sweeps all ignorance aside), do they do? And how, now that they are about to inaugurate a practice that must last the length of a very long marriage, do they begin? Shouldn't so important a thing be right from the beginning? The private act seems suddenly so official.

So what *is* right?

Who gets the bathroom first? And what do you do in the bathroom anyway? Make yourself smell good? Gargle? Shave your scratchy chin? Put on a sexy, filmy, diaphanous gown? A thousand and one questions, but only one night . . .

He: Who turns out the lights? Or *do* you turn out the lights? Is it legal to look, to see? Or is that embarrassing?

She: Can you talk while you make love? What should you talk about? Your feelings? But what if your feelings disappoint his dreams? What if you're thinking about stuff not sexy? So maybe you should only sigh and make appropriate groans and let him guess what they mean? And what if *you* are disappointed by the experience? O Lord, what then?

He: Should you tell her where to touch you? And if you do— that is, if you *have* to—will you doubt her ability or her sincerity? Or if she's extremely skillful, surprisingly knowledgeable, will you doubt her virginity? Where did she get such experience? And if you're inept, will she secretly laugh at you?

She: Where should you kiss him? On what parts of his body? Will he be offended if you take the lead? He's got an erection already; what does that mean? You've scarcely done anything! Zip, zip, zoom! This is faster than you expected. Who owes what to whom? Do you owe it to him to let the stallion charge at his own speed, or does he owe it to you to slow down? Do you have the right to say, "Wait"? Would that frustrate him? But don't you have a right to a climax too? Would it be silly at this moment—would it even be loving—to interrupt things: "Excuse me, dear. Can we talk about this?" Would he understand? And what if suddenly you feel like crying?

He: What if you're doing all things right, so far as you know the right, and yet you suspect that something's wrong? You've kissed her. You've stroked her body in the sensual places, murmured the sensual sounds, and found in your own loins a fine, hot, pleading fire. You're swallowing a lot right now, breathing faster than you like to admit (because you want to *seem* in control of things, but things seem to have taken control of you). And you want her to be happy. You want her to be as satisfied as you. In fact, if she's not satisfied, that seems a bad reflection on you. Yet there's a horse in you that wants to run, and she's not ready! If you let it go, is that love or is that lust? And if she doesn't help you, if she doesn't respond as you hoped she would, is that shyness? Is that merely the way with women? Or is she being obstinate? And look at this: right at the peak of your desire, she is crying! She's started to cry!

So he throws himself to the side and gasps, "What's the matter?"

And she murmurs, "Nothing. Nothing." But she pulls up the sheets to cover her nakedness.

So what *is* the right after all?

And what do the words *making love* really mean?

In the best sense of the words, making love means that in the sex act the couple makes manifest their love for one another. They make known what was always there, but what is otherwise invisible or ineffable, too deep for words. It's making their love into a palpable experience. It's making a gift of love.

By "making love" I surely do not mean that one "makes" the other (forces her to) receive his love—or that one "makes" the other (turns him into) something she *can* love. It is neither a commanding nor a shaping of the other person, neither manhandling nor manipulation—not if it is the expression of love.

Nor do I mean that sex makes or produces the love which justifies and sustains the rest of the marriage. Love isn't *made* in bed, as though sex could manufacture what didn't already exist; rather, an existing love makes sex a lovely thing. Good sex won't save a marriage. Bad sex is seldom the primary cause of a marriage's failure.

And I hate the cold-blooded, loveless phrase "making it" as in "making it with her." I hate it because it is too often true, an accurate definition of the act. But "making love" and "making it" are not merely different in degree, one less intense, less committed, less affectionate than the other. They are absolutely opposed. They are different in kind and enemies of one another—one casts the other out. Because love is selfless; but making *it* is mechanical self-satisfaction, achieving orgasm or proving a personal sexuality. *It* is never a *who*, always a *what*.

When I say the words, *making love*, I do mean the word *making*. There is, in fact, at the beginning of the marriage a making, a creating, of a personal sex life. Husband and wife commit themselves to the slow and tender task of creating their own unique patterns of sexual expression.

As we said of the marital relationship in general, so we say of the sexual practice within that relationship: it is a living being on its own. It is the third entity of the marriage, together with the husband and the wife, in which both participate, from which both derive blessing, to which both give service, but which itself is defined by neither one of them alone. Sex isn't his or hers alone. It is *theirs*, the thing they have lovingly created. They do not lose individuality when they make love, as though two elements melted into one; that may be a fine romantic metaphor, but it isn't fact. Neither should one partner so dominate the other that he or she is swallowed up, stripped of personhood, so that only one remains a whole personality to which the other has conformed. No. The real and precious oneness of this couple is the sexual life they conceive together, exactly as one day they may together conceive a baby.

When a couple "makes love," the partners make a means for loving. They make, through the years, a sex life, a living sexuality.

This, then, is the fourth task of marriage maintenance.

THE QUESTION THAT HAS NO ANSWER

I could sketch a score of scenarios with various conclusions for the newlyweds who appeared at the beginning of this chapter. I could lengthen the story, showing that blissful success in the early months can mask deeper uncertainties, prejudices, and matters unresolved, so that sex later becomes for them a grim habit or a frustrated effort to recapture those first joys together. I could tell a story in which one or both of the partners come to the marriage bed with a long history of sexual experience and therefore with some definite demands and expectations—only to find that *this* relationship doesn't measure up to his or her memories of previous sex. This experience would receive the harsher judgment, then, because this is the one that must last for life.

In all my stories the same problem would recur, as it does so commonly for couples young and old, experienced and inexperienced:

In the beginning, spouses do not know each other (may hardly know the sexual tendencies of their own bodies). They do not yet know what their marital sex life will be. They do not even know what it ought to be. *What is sexually right for us?* In the beginning this question has no answer! But that's not the problem. In fact, it cannot and it should not, in the beginning, have an answer. The problem occurs when someone thinks that this ignorance is wrong, as though it were a handicap to conjugal joy, and covers up the ignorance. The problem occurs when anything whatsoever hinders that couple's mutual creation of their own personal and right sexual practices.

To keep silence before one another for any reason, for shame, for embarrassment at one's naïveté, or for the foolish notion that one doesn't talk about sex but simply does what comes naturally—that is the problem.

For either spouse to assume that he or she knows what is sexually best for them both before they have discovered *their* best in experience together—that is the problem.

To allow passions alone to lead, giving up a mutual and loving control, so that sexual desires hurtle to their own conclusions (as though sex itself were a god one doesn't argue with!)—that is the problem.

The worst problem of all, perhaps, is to bring to the marriage bed prefabricated answers about right sexual behavior, answers made up by anyone else (by society, by parents, grandparents, or friends, by the street, by a church with a moral squint) and not by the couple themselves—answers imposed upon them and denying something of their own personalities. That is a problem.

Let the spouses cheerfully and freely admit in the beginning, admit to each other, that they don't know what their sex life is going to be like, and that neither does anyone else know. This ignorance is a *good* thing, not a problem! Not a fault! For now they can begin the business of "making love," creating a sex life which benefits both of them, which is unique to their marriage alone, which shames neither with a sense of inadequacy, and to which each gives something personal and necessary.

What is sexually right for us? The answer is learned only *in* the marriage, by actually practicing sex together with a constant and dear concern for the other's experience and an open expression of one's own. Doing is discovery. Trust allows you both to act before you know. The dependability of your partner allows you to reveal your own deep feelings as you go. A humble hearing allows you to receive your partner's feelings clearly, without threat or misinterpretation. You *make* your own loving.

"What," he asks in the darkness, "do you want me to do for you?"

And she answers shamelessly, "I don't know. Try something, and I'll tell you what I think."

And so he does. And so does she. They try many things. They have more than a night for experimentation. They have as many years as God gives them life.

But instead of discovering a love-life for themselves, far too many couples allow themselves to be influenced by external standards of sexuality. Trying to conform to some foreign law, they handicap their own sexual expression and suffer unnecessary frustration. If they are timid, no one may ever know the deprivations of their bedroom. But if they are bold and willing, I may find them in front of me—in my pastoral study. . .

THE COUPLE CONFUSED BY THE STERNER CHURCH

The woman sitting before me has a slender nose, eyebrows perfectly balanced and even, high molded cheekbones, a slim body dressed in brown decorum—and a problem so difficult to state that she twists her fingers in silence. She has come alone and looks a little lonely.

"I'm sorry," she says. "I just don't know how to say it."

"Take your time," I say.

She smiles a small apologetic smile. "He," she says—she's referring to her absent husband. The problem is in their marriage. "Whenever we, ah, make love," she says, dropping her eyes, hazel eyes as quick as a fox's, ready to run. But this woman sits straight, with her knees and heels together; she makes a nearly perfect column, an Athenian column, from the base of her spine to the small bones in her neck.

As though she has just made up her mind, she says the sentence smoothly: "Whenever we make love, he laughs." She looks up. Her eyes question me.

"At you?" I ask. "He laughs at you?"

"No. Oh, no." Now she is concerned that I don't misunderstand. "No, he laughs for joy."

This is what she thinks the problem is: that her husband's pleasure at entering her causes a low, murmuring laughter in his throat. As his pleasure increases, so does the laugh—until sometimes at climax his hilarity fills the room. He laughs like a boy at a new joke; the tears run down his cheeks and he kisses her.

"Does the noise distract you?" I ask.

"I don't think so," says the woman. We're talking about her feelings now, so she drops her eyes again and twists her fingers. "I," she whispers, blushing: "I sort of giggle with him. He's having so much—" Her poor face blazes with embarrassment; her voice falls to a distant whisper, "—so much *fun,* you know. But that isn't right, is it? Isn't he being, I don't know, disrespectful, like laughing in church? And then, when I laugh too, I feel so—guilty."

The poor, dear woman, blessed with joy! The problem is not her husband's laughter. The problem is her own lackluster notions of what sex ought to be. Where did she get the dogma that sexual behavior is so serious and ceremonial as to be solemn? She has permitted an external code—a law from outside their relationship—to dictate the right actions and the acceptable attitudes of their private marriage bed. *What is the right thing to do?* She came to the marriage with answers already in place. Where did these answers come from?

A Falsely Moral Horror at Sexuality

Fearing sin, the church has not always been clear about what *is* sin. When the church is not clear, neither are its people. If it speaks of sex chiefly in prohibitions; if it shows more intensity over sexual misbehavior than exaltation of sexual *good* behavior; if it fulminates against a dangerously loose society, the subliminal message to its people is that sex is more wrong than right—something both to restrain in one's self and to fear in others.

The Western church has a long history of suspecting human physical desires. In many places it still heaps indiscriminate judgment upon anything compulsive, suggesting that bodily urges are guilty for these two reasons: that they are bodily and that they are urges. Piety (but a false piety!) forgets it has a body at all. And religious vigor in roping the sexual desires of the faithful does not always seem different from its vigilance against that roaring lion, the devil; and so the message is that the devil may, my child, be dwelling in you: Beware!

So there are devout wives and husbands who are frightened of sexual passion in any form. Anything not immediately necessary to the swift completion of the act (like a little laughter) is suspect. If it's unusual, it could be abnormal. If it's abnormal, it could be wrong. If it's wrong, it is definitely obscene and a sin.

So there are husbands and wives whose sexual drive is, by nature, very strong, but whose "moral" sense is equally as strong. These feel a nearly intolerable guilt; and since sexual expression always involves them in a private, monumental struggle, they can be neither open nor tender with their spouses. The love is twisted within them. Guilt taints everything. And though their spouses may have tried to comfort them, these people, driven and haunted by their sexuality, conceal the great "evil" within. They will not talk for fear of losing their partners' respect, and sometimes, not respecting themselves, cannot talk. They do not trust their spouses to understand the hidden sin, the secret struggle. This moral "law" has more power over them than the marriage or the one law, love.

And so there are couples of strong religious conviction whose sexual behavior has neither variety nor ease. The first way in which they practiced sex becomes the only way, because experimentation requires too much attention to the act and to pleasure alone—and to think only of personal pleasure seems self-indulgent. Even to discuss sex for its own sake feels like reading dirty books. They do, then, only what they must, and after some years of the repetition they do less and less of that.

All of these—ignorant of their freedom, hog-tied to a false, extraneous law—never can make their own means of loving. They allow a squinting religion to unsex them, and they live narrowly, ever on the edge of guilt.

Shuck this law! It is not of God. (It comes, in fact, from a heretical tendency of the early church toward Gnosticism, which divided all creation and every human being into spirit and matter, soul and flesh. Spiritual things, it elevated. Material things and the body, it abased.)

What *is* of God is the boisterous, unqualified judgment: Good! *Good,* said God, of all creation, including the bodies of the man and the woman who were naked and not ashamed. *Good,* too, were their desires for one another, desires so strong that they superseded even the ties between parent and child: "Therefore shall a man leave his father and his mother, and shall cleave unto his wife: and they shall be one flesh." *Cleaving* implies not only a spiritual union, but also huggings and kissings and pressings into one another, the making one of two fleshes. It is most outrageously "bodily." Your sexuality is a gift from God for your own delight. It is not in itself a guilty thing. It is good— and you are free.

THE COUPLE INTIMIDATED
BY TALK-SHOW SEX

A man now sits before me, in the same chair, desperately in love with the wife beside him and grieving for her. He's on the edge of his seat, bowed, with his elbows on his knees and his hands folded between them. Every once in a while his right hand flies to his wife; he pats her arm, then snatches the hand back to fold it again in the other.

His wife gazes expectantly at me as though convinced I'll give them the answer they came for. They both eat the same foods. They are both comfortably overweight.

"Excuse me for saying it out loud, Marie," Marie's husband speaks to the floor. "We got to talk about it." Marie nods and smiles at me. She quite agrees. She isn't at all as racked as her husband. "What it is, pastor," the big man tells his shoes, "is that Marie here don't have—what-choo-call-'em? Orgasms. She don't have orgasms the way a woman should." He sighs, having said the thing, and pats Marie's arm.

What a kind and brave and simple man, I think: loving enough to sympathize with his wife, even to know her experience, and at the same time bold enough to act upon the problem—and trusting enough to reveal it to me. But that "trusting" might be the deeper problem after all—if he trusts the wrong counselors.

"Marie," I ask, "forgive me a silly question, but do you know what an orgasm is?"

She smiles a sweet forgiveness upon me, purely comfortable with the question. "Sure," she says. "I get 'em sometimes. They sorter sneak up on me, y'know, like a surprise. It's other times he's worried about. I don't get 'em all the times."

Finally the big man looks up at me with appeal in his eyes, as if to say, *See? What can we do about this?*

"And when you don't have an orgasm," I ask, "that bothers you? It leaves you frustrated? Tense? Unfinished?"

"I don't know 'bout flustrated," says Marie, screwing up her face to recall the accurate truth. "What I do is, I go straight to sleep."

"Oh, pastor, it's a bunch of problems," her husband bursts out. "Her sleepin' is just a single for-instance. We're findin' out that our sex ain't what it's s'pposed to be."

And what did they suppose it ought to be?

Please don't blame this couple for their earnest concern. They represent a multitude of common folk who merely grieve in secret. They are special only in this, that they talked to me—and in this, that they talked together. But they are like countless, countless others who fear that their sexual behavior is bland, boring, and even blameworthy for its lack of excitement.

They watched the "Phil Donahue Show" and were filled with anxiety, because they learned that a woman is supposed to come to climax fully as often as a man; that they should be making love often and creatively, not once a week on Sundays, sometimes skipping a Sunday when one felt tired, and not always in the same position, always according to the same pattern. So routine is their own sex that they feel like failures; they have, they think, missed out on their birthright of human sexual enchantment.

But they have come to me. How many individuals suffer guilt or anger or the anguish that they themselves or their partners do not measure up to the standards which the sexual revolution has published to the world? How many are embittered because what was their common, unremarkable sexual practice suddenly seems dreary and reprehensible, a criminal denial of ecstacy?

I say to the woman Marie: "Do you want to have an orgasm every time? I mean, do *you* want it?"

"I can't say's *I* do," she says, then glances to her husband. "I'm happy for him to be happy. I always felt kinda glad for him to be in me, just that. And for the little surprises that come." Now she looks back at me. "But he's startin' to be nervous when I ain't had one. So I guess I gotta say, yes. I want 'em."

She smiles a puzzled smile. He pats her arm.

Their real problem is trust, after all. They've begun to trust in a standard not their own—a law from outside their relationship—which dictates to them right actions and the acceptable results of their private sexual activities. *What is the right thing to do?* Someone else is answering this question for them.

The Sexual Standards of Contemporary Society

Here is a sad irony: prophets of the sexual revolution announce that they have set free the people of repressed libidos. They preach, "All things are lawful for you," nothing condemns you for anything sexual. And then they publish exactly (in detail, in figures taken from public polls, in clinical data, and in graphic description) *what* things are now lawful. But as they publish this information, they also proclaim it. They preach it. They praise it by their very attention to it. And so they change it. It is no longer mere data but has become the standard of good sex. It is the criterion by which a couple's sexuality can be judged healthy or unhealthy, successful and complete, or miserable and unsatisfying.

The irony: announcing freedom, they have imposed a whole new law upon the people.

The news that women can have orgasms soon becomes the judgment that if women don't have orgasms they are unfulfilled. And that translates into the decree: Women must have orgasms. If you don't, something somehow somewhere is wrong.

The polls (which are nothing more than the average sexuality of the society) estimate that people like to make love three times a week. But soon this faceless average feels like a standard, and those who make love less than that (the anxious couple in my office) feel that their sex is indeed *less* than it ought to be. Something is lacking; something is wrong.

Marvelously—sadly—virginity itself becomes a shameful thing, simply because so many have so happily given it away. And the individuals who don't experience a sex drive equal to the world's exacting standards are not free to be themselves, but are sick: a sort of anorexia of the gonads.

This law, this subtle coercion of a sexually intense society, creeps into any couple's bedroom and does exactly what it con-

demns a grim religious piety of doing: it commands certain behaviors and condemns others. It shames them and keeps them
from "making" their own "love."

No matter whether it comes from Masters and Johnson, from
Playboy, from the persistently sexual depiction of love on television, from talk in the office, or from the street—it can make
those partners miserable who think they should, but cannot,
conform. What they are by nature, that is good. But they are
persuaded it is bad.

So there are husbands and wives who, failing to achieve
orgasm, feel that they have failed their marriage, failed at life.
Men occasionally impotent can be terrorized by this law; their
manhood itself is called into question; and fear certainly will not
help them find their potency again. Women sometimes satisfied
with all sorts of sexual touching apart from orgasm may become
convinced that there is fault in this. If it's his fault, they grow
angry. If it's their own fault, they grow guilty. Then the anger or
the guilt certainly will frustrate any sexuality, but it wasn't a
sexual frustration in the first place. It was a *social* frustration!

So there are individuals who fantasize experiences simply impossible for them or their particular relationship. No, Ernest
Hemingway, the mountains almost never move. Sex never was
more powerful than earth, but was meant to have its place—its
good place, to be sure, but its reasonably limited place—within
the whole of a relationship. Yet, the fantasy becomes the goal of
these individuals; and the goal becomes a standard; and when
nothing matches the standard, they feel cheated. Instead of seeking what may be, they damn their spouses for what is not—or
they attempt sexual acts, maneuvers, aids, advices which are in
fact unnatural. Unnatural, I mean, to their natures, the natures
of their spouses and their relationships. Then everything has
gone wrong: they are no longer servants of one another, but
servants of a false god, a fantasy, an experience that does not
and cannot exist. They are merely using their partners, reducing
the spouse to a body only. Therefore, the things they do (though
others may do them most naturally) *are* obscene, because they
kill the spirit of the spouse even while they cannot satisfy the
desperate, personal longing. There is no love made here.

Shuck this law, too! Society has no right in your bedroom. Its
vision of sex is no more valuable to you than, say, its vision of
love (which is always self-serving) or its vision of God (which is
always blinded by human pride). What society happens to do at
any given time is neither right nor a law; only you can make it so
by believing that you must obey it. Your homage to it gives it

power. But then you have surrendered your *self* to a mere statistic and to a herd that does not love you, does not know you, will not forgive you when you fail its furious standards. The law kills.

If you empowered this law in your bedroom, then you can as well disarm it. In fact, you are free—to find yourselves in one another, and to find out *who* that other is for yourselves, and so to find the sexuality that admits you both. You are unique; your relationship is like none other. Let your lovemaking celebrate that.

THE COUPLE WHOSE SEX DIVIDES THEM

Opposite me sits a pastor's wife. She has come from another congregation, another town altogether, because she cannot speak her pain in the place where it would jeopardize her husband's ministry or reputation. But she must, finally, speak the pain to someone. She is crying. She is alone.

"He hurts me," she says. "He just plain hurts me, every night, night after night. He hurts me, and he doesn't know."

I know the man. I know him to be dedicated, selfless where his congregation is concerned, faithful. He's small of stature, a pale, unsmiling face with a lean blade of a nose, the flesh drawn so tight over the bridge of his nose that it is white. His manner in public is quiet, unassuming. He's humble in company of other pastors, in company of men generally, I think. He gives no outward sign of sexual prowess, of sexual desire even, or of aggression.

Nevertheless, for ten years of marriage and for all the nights of that marriage, except when his wife is having her period, he has performed his sex upon her.

"Have you told him?" I ask.

She is weeping and can't talk for a while. The tears come both from the remembered pain—the physical and the emotional pain—and from the present torment of accusing her husband aloud. Please know that she loves him, and he does her. In this one matter they are divided.

"I've tried," she says. "I have tried to tell him."

"What does he say?"

"Sometimes nothing. Sometimes—when I used to ask him not to make love—that it was—my duty. Once at supper, out of the clear blue, he said, 'I'm a man. I can't help it.' But then his voice went very quiet and he said, 'If I can't do it, what sort of man would I be?' But he said that only once. I remember it because he said it so strangely, and I wanted to hug him then, but—well, we don't hug much. I mean, we're not children any more, patting and tickling. We quit that long ago."

At night, in the dark of their bedroom, this man would present his wife with his erection. But he never spoke. Silently he mounted her—while she, too, held her peace. And then he drove himself so hard into her that it hurt. She was, she said, continually sore. Even in the act he allowed himself no sound, and she repressed her own; and when he was done, he shrank suddenly. He took himself from her, turned to the side, and fell asleep.

There was a law in this household and in this marriage bed which governed the sexuality of this man. But it was not *their* law—except insofar as it was imposed upon the woman. I cannot at this distance judge, but this I know: it was a code of behavior to which the man alone was beholden. It was his, not theirs. And whether it arose out of his individual needs (the need to prove his masculinity, as he defined masculinity) or whether it had been imposed upon him (psychologically) as much as it was imposed upon his wife (physically and emotionally), doesn't much matter. They had not "made love," had not made together a mutual means of loving; therefore, however "right" this man may have been according to some external law, within this relationship he was wretchedly wrong. He abused the woman he loved. His sex was no less than physical abuse.

What is the right thing to do? Why, he had never asked her.

Individual Expectations about Sex

This must be said: the sexual practices of a marriage must be created by *both* partners in dear regard for one another and in clear disclosure, each to the other, of personal needs and tendencies. Both! The only law for "making" your means of "love" is that you be servants of one another.

But again and again marriages are threatened by another law: the law of one spouse's self. That is, a husband or a wife assumes that he or she knows what is right, what is best, what is the point of lovemaking, or what he wants, and imposes this upon the other. This law of the self is perhaps more universally killing than any other.

It doesn't always take the brutal form described above. That may be an extreme case. But it does always judge sex according to one's own standards. It says, "*I* am the purpose of our sex. Serve me. If I am satisfied, it is good. If I am not, it is bad."

Where does this wicked (and all too common) law come from?

In practice, it often comes from premarital experience with sexuality. When two people who are uncommitted to each other practice sex, despite all their protestations, the easiest object of the encounter is self-satisfaction. They are not bound to sacrifice their personal desires to the other's need. They are not "bound" together at all. If the sex is unsatisfactory, that alone can accuse the relationship and break it off. Sex, without the covenant, can be the ruling standard.

Now, whenever anyone practices sex, he learns a certain sexual behavior. Consciously or unconsciously, he discovers what "works" for him, and he repeats those actions until they become his pattern—a law, if you will, defining what is right for him. But if the purpose of his activity has been to satisfy himself, then this behavioral pattern will focus mostly *on* himself; it will not leave room for the presence of another whole human being. His own nature shapes it, not the nature of a particular relationship.

When this sexually experienced person one day marries, then, he brings with him a ready-made law. His behavior is *already* established. He comes with unconsidered expectations to which he will want his wife (or she her husband) to conform. He will say, "This is the way it's done," without realizing that this is only the way that *he* has done it—without admitting that this way has always been for his own benefit and denies his wife (or their relationship) a complete participation. Or he may kindly say, "Let me teach you," but the words mean, "I will command you." It will seem to him, who has known satisfaction in the past, a most frustrating thing both to *un*learn what he learned, to sacrifice his pleasure as well as his patterns, and slowly, slowly to discover all over again a whole new way for making love.

But unless he shucks this personal law, it will be deadly to his spouse. Sex between them will continue to devalue her, to be a forced affair (as it was between the pastor and his wife), will not allow love, and will never affirm a marriage of the two. In the end, he too will find it futile, because a dominating sexuality does not satisfy the more spiritual need to *be* loved, or the holier need to give wholeness unto the beloved.

In order to make love, to create the right means for loving, you've got to start at the beginning, *all* laws, *all* expectations and experiences and fantasies laid aside, each of you perfectly new, both of you free. Then anything may be lawful, so long as you are servants of one another.

Again, where does this law of the self come from?

Why, from our sinfulness. Finally, it doesn't matter whether we fooled around or not before we married. To one degree or another, we all like to think that sex is for ourselves, that we are to be served, and that we have a right to pleasure. We are by nature selfish; but here in bed this self-centeredness becomes intense. The law *I want* cuts humans dead in bed; it more than uses, it abuses, bodies; it is plain bestial. Simply, it hurts the other person. Sex has then become sin, and no "right," no explanation or excuse can justify that. No one has a right to pleasure at another's expense. That law is a lie—and though few are audacious enough to speak it aloud, most of us do sometimes believe it. We believe it by the trick of denying that our pleasure *is* at another's expense; yet I tell you this, that in marriage *all* pleasures either exclude or include the other. There is no third alternative. And if we have not consciously and kindly included our spouse, then we have taken that pleasure at his or her expense. That is simple fact. This law kills.

To shuck this sinful law (that I am the more important in our lovemaking), then, means to humble one's very self. What is *shuck?* It means to strip away. To take off, as one takes off one's clothing. We strip something of ourselves away in order to serve our spouses. We *both* lay aside the personal desires, both searching for the other's.

In the beginning of the marriage (and periodically throughout it, as things change) the best, most loving purpose of sex is not anyone's individual satisfaction. But your sexual behavior is like a baby, the third being between you. It needs your mutual care. In the beginning the task of sexual activity is the sex life itself: creating it, making the means of loving, discovering its own specific personality, and nurturing its growth. And then there will be moments of the sweetest pleasure for each of you; but because neither of you demanded the pleasure, these moments will come surprisingly, undeserved, as sheer grace from God. Do you see? The very nature of pleasure changes: it is no longer a thing taken. It is given. And therefore, it is most dear.

THE COUPLE WHOSE SEX HAS A PRICE

Once again, a man sits, sunken in the chair that's seen so much.

"I wish," he says, "that she wouldn't play with me. She plays with my emotions."

More than unhappy, he is nervous—but not because he's talking to me. He is generally an edgy man, swift to suspect the

careless phrase. His eyes dart about the room, as though checking the walls to see whether they've inched closer to him, as
though commanding the suffocating walls to stay away.

"She keeps changing the rules," he says, "without telling me.
Or maybe she's telling me things *by* changing the rules. I can't
count on anything."

"What rules?" I ask.

"I don't know how to say it," he says. "Last night we were
making love and everything was fine. I mean, she started it, you
know. She started it by touching me and sighing through her
nose, as she can do. And I always wait awhile—well, because I
am suspicious, I guess. But she seemed to really get into it, and so
I got into it, too. Only, at the last minute she stops. She goes
completely cold, and I'm left hanging. I say, 'What's the matter?'
She says, 'If you don't know, I can't tell you.' This always rips
me up. I get mad. I say, 'Look! I'm not a mind reader. You *tell*
me what's wrong.' And she says, cool as you please, 'If you can't
remember our anniversary, then I can't get it on with you. Good
night.' But sometimes she gets it on with me just fine. Sometimes
it shocks me how she wakes me in the morning *just* to get it on."

"Did you forget her anniversary?"

"Well, yeah," says the nervous ferret of a man. "I guess that's
my fault, sure. But that was last week! She sort of lay in wait for
me a whole week. And when is she going to let me make love to
her again? I don't know. I don't know. I guess I've got to do
something good first. But even then it's her moods that make the
difference. Happy or sad, angry or proud, good days or bad
days—it all comes out in our sex. She says I should touch her
more, just casually, during the day; it builds her up to it, she
says. But then I shouldn't paw her, should just leave her alone;
she'll come round on her own. I should tell her nice things when
we make love. But then there comes the morning when I
shouldn't talk so much, just get it done. Or I shouldn't talk to
break her concentration. Hoo-eee! God in heaven would toss up
his hands. The woman's a puzzle."

What is the right thing to do? In this case the answers are
changing all the time, and one spouse truly cannot know, because the law imposed upon his sexual behavior is the law of
whimsy. Right and wrong are established always according to
one partner's personal (even extrasexual) demands; yet, these
capricious laws do judge him. Try as he might, then, he can
never quite measure up. He is always found wanting and is
meant to be ashamed. Sex here has not been made a means for

expressing love, but a judicial—a punishing and rewarding—tool for manipulation.

The Use of Sex to Bargain or Manipulate

You are, in your sexuality, free. Keep it that way. Free of a false religious oppression, free of the world's exaggerated claims, free of either spouse's selfishness—and free, too, of the junk of the marriage which does not belong to lovemaking.

But if they are not careful, spouses some years married tend to make their sexual relationship *conditional*, qualified by other concerns in their relationship. Petty power plays are made in bed, not love. The petty rules of their daily lives are imposed upon their sexual activity. And what then? Then sex becomes strategy. It's no longer free to find its own good nature, but is shaped in the image of an argument, an unfinished argument, a fight—a sin. There are elements of the marriage itself that have no business in the sexual bed. They will desecrate sex.

Far from sacrificing herself, the wife described above sacrificed their sex life for the sake of her pouts! By her sexual behavior she communicated to him feelings that had nothing to do with sex; moreover, those feelings dictated what sort of sexual behavior *he* was to be permitted.

She is not unlike the spouse who wins an argument in bed, or the wife who, in bed, seeks vengeance for the argument she did not win. Power plays. Nor is that husband any different who, feeling inferior to the verbal assaults of his wife, proves his superiority upon her body and in bed. Sex is not a conference table, not a summit, not a court of law, not a scourge for offenders. Neither is it money nor a commodity to be bought and sold: "Be nice to me, and I'll take you on a vacation." These things debase it.

There are other means in a healthy marriage for resolving relational disputes, for persuasion, for barter and decision-making. Forcing these issues upon your sexual experience is like taking a small-claims case to the Supreme Court. It will render a decision, surely, but the consequences are too drastic for little differences of opinion. It can kill the loving. The more two people freight their sex life with unessential, nonsexual matters, the less they can manifest a sincere love by it. Used in that way—*mis*used—a spouse will become sex-shy, skittish and suspicious, more and more reserved and less able to trust the pure truth of a loving expression. Husbands and wives, it is too grievous a loss to discredit your lovemaking for the sake of personal power, to prove a point, or merely to announce some trouble you're suffering elsewhere in the marriage—or to whine.

Lovemaking is for this, to make love. Shuck, then, all the minor concerns with your clothes. Or use common sense. If you simply cannot get some extraneous issue off your mind, then keep your clothes on after all. Talk. And listen to each other. Practice forgiveness, the tool that God has given you, as an event apart from the sex so that the unforgiven sin, the un-acknowledged sin, doesn't profane this other gift of God. You wash before you touch clean food; then wash before you touch each other; dirty hearts can infect the open, vulnerable, trusting, undefended blood of your sexuality. Attend, with all the means God gives you, to your differences *first;* and then attend to your union.

There is one law only a couple need obey when they develop sexually, when they discover how often they'll make love, what positions they'll use, where and when they do it, how much noise to make, what parts of the body are engaged, what the foreplay is to be, how long to linger together afterward. And that law is summed in the single word (in the fullness of its meaning): love.

Or, as the apostle Paul says it: "For you were called to free-dom, brethren; only do not use your freedom as an opportunity for the flesh, but through love *be servants of one another.* For the whole law is fulfilled in one word, 'You shall love your neighbor as yourself.'"

Servants of one another, servants to no other code of behavior whatsoever. From all things else, you are free!

BE NAKED AND NOT ASHAMED

In the beginning, make love. Make your own private and par-ticular means for expressing love, sexually, together.

And now that most of you are some years past the beginning, now that you have come to a comfort with each other (now that you know so much more about who your spouse is, who *you* are in this marriage, what vast freedom you have for the sexual bed), make love all over again. Again and again, as your situation and yourselves do change, discover the sex that befits you.

Look: you practice sex one way when you are alone in the household, before children are born. But children make a dif-ference, and your sexual habits reflect that difference. Then the very growing of the children revises the times (and the energies) you have for one another, and your sex life gets nudged into smaller corners. Sometimes it seems a most fugitive critter, hidden away in the woods of your responsibilities and the schedules and the teen-agers and the tiredness. But one day you are alone again together; yet by that day your own bodies have changed, and your desires have been refined. You can't go back to the exact same practices you had before you bore the children—can you?

Changes in your lifestyles force changes in your sexuality. Shall that sex life merely react to all the changes—get moved about like a piece of furniture, bumped and battered, *used,* to be sure, but yet be taken for granted, until it ends up in the attic? ("Honey, what's happened to us? Didn't we used to enjoy a toss in the hay? Why, I remember once we made love on the kitchen floor, halfway through lunch—")

No—but keep making, *remaking,* the means of a loving, sexual expression, always refitting to your new circumstances.

The mystery, the joy, and the value of this fourth marital task, lovemaking, is that once done it need never be completely *done,* finished forever. It can be done again and again, always with brave new results.

And how do you do it, actually? (By now you know I don't mean, "How does a couple have sex?" Their actions are for them to decide. Rather, I mean, "How do they *decide* how they will have sex?" How do they go about finding their finest, most expressive, most personal sexual behavior?)

The attitude necessary for such a discovery we've already discussed. It is *trust*—the same trust which you earn of your spouse by the first task, *truthfulness and dependability.* Trust allows him, encourages her, to be naked before you and not ashamed. Naked physically: no part of the body is hidden since no curve of it, no organ or flesh of it will be hurt or troubled by embarrassment. Naked emotionally and spiritually: no part of the personality, no feeling, no memory or fear or internal delight need be hidden either, since *nothing* of your spouse will be hurt or abused or embarrassed. Trust allows him, encourages her, to present a whole self before you. And honesty in you, likewise, hides nothing of your whole self from your spouse.

Desire draws the two total selves together. Your hands do not have to be commanded to move; they move on their own. Flesh finds flesh quite easily and happily. Huggings happen. Breasts and chest come together. And you are free! Nothing whatever, except the law of service, forbids anything you might do. Neither shame nor guilt restricts you. All the fruit of Eden is yours and before you.

But some of that fruit is more to your taste (*your* taste, the preference of *both* of you) than others. How long will you linger, just touching? What kinds of caresses, on what parts of the body, *with* what parts of the body, are most delightful and generous? What positions increase excitement, sustain desire? How do you know? How do you choose?

You have already trained yourselves to name the best actions of your sexual expression—to name them, to know them, to celebrate and to save them. You have learned (or you are learning) the third marital task, *talking and listening*. Now you use it to a fine effect.

Before and after, and even in the very heat of, sexual activity, you will listen to your spouse. You will never be so busy with your self, the driving of your own desire, that you cannot hear him, feel her, talking to you. Listen! His breathing whispers, *Good! Good! Keep doing that*. Or the slightest stiffening of her lips says, *Not that. Try something else*. You listen with your skin, if there are no words. The naked, trusting body itself is talking all the time, sending out an endless stream of messages. But you know your spouse. You know the subtle gestures that communicate. For the sake of your mutual sexuality, use that personal knowledge here, never assuming the sex to be for yourself alone, nor ever letting it become so habitual it can't say something new to you. Listen!

And talk. Why would you not praise her, thank him, for a gift well given? Or is the gift so unimportant that it merits no mention? Praising will preserve it, that it become a part of your sexuality. (It's when we think we deserved the thing we got that we say nothing about it. Pride shuts our mouths. But a healthy humility teaches even the taciturn male and the shyest female to speak out loud their gladness.)

Talk unashamedly. There is no law to keep you silent about your bodies, about the sexual motions in them, the dampenings, the erections, all the sensations that come before a climax, the climax itself. Why wouldn't you translate these pleasures into sound and words, just as you do the other pleasures of your life? One of the holiest joys of lovemaking is the *spiritual* entrance into another human being—to know what someone else of the other sex feels like on the inside. Our flesh divides us; we can be lonely inside our bodies and exiled from the deepest feelings of other people. But an expressive lovemaking truly draws us inside each other. Your spouse (if you talk!) can know your body *and* your heart.

Talk truthfully, without a hint of guilt or else of criticism, even about sexual difficulties. Where there is fault, there can be forgiveness, and forgiveness permits a beginning again. Where there is no fault (sex can fail for reasons perfectly blameless), there can be helpful, open, and constructive talk. Be sure you know the difference between fault and no-fault! (How often our personal frustration makes us take things personally—when in fact there was no sin done against us at all.)

But in either case, talk as partners who are discussing the third being between you—as parents would discuss a child in need of special care. Then all your talk will be positive, a building up and not a tearing down. It isn't a baby, of course; it's your sex life. But speaking this way, you will be able to handle even heavy things (impotence, frigidity, genital pain, unexpected feelings of anger) without focusing guilt on one or shame on the other—which would divide and silence you after all, and would perpetuate the problem between you. Parents talk very well to share the work of healing a sick child, because together they love that child. Spouses likewise can talk openly, and share their talents, their perceptions, opinions, and their actions to heal a troubled sex life—because *together* they possess that life. Of course: talk. Doesn't the sexuality of a marriage mature precisely in the overcoming of problems? Don't you know it better and better each time you solve a new perplexity?

Talk and listen at all times for the sexual signals that come in the course of a day, so that time and place and readiness and frequency are learned.

Then the thing you create for yourselves will have something of both of you—like a baby whose face shows characteristics of both your faces—but will be the possession of neither one of you. It will be yours, no one else's, unique unto you. And (*Playboy* or the preacher notwithstanding) it will be right!

And then what? Why, then the baby, the means of loving whom you have made, grows up, grows strong and stable and able to carry the both of you together. It blesses you with confidence, both in bed and in each other, both now and in the years to come.

The years will steal the beauty from your body; yet your body still will function beautifully—in the sexuality of your marriage. What does it matter if the muscles soften and the breasts sag and the climax diminishes to a gentle twitch? Someone (so will say your stable sex life), someone likes to touch you, and does. Someone receives your aging flesh without offense but with delight. Someone is "turned on" by you—and that will be no small praise, after all, no mean accomplishment, to rouse the sexual desire of another even when you don't meet the standards of a youthful society. You will be beautiful. This isn't a figure of speech or a comment on your personality, but a physical fact. You will be beautiful. And this will be the proof, that someone still is making love with you.

FOURTEEN

AVOIDING ADULTERY

William Blake wrote a poem that haunts the reader. Its imagery is simple, universal, and full of dread. It sings of a sweet thing blasted. It sings of a glad thing cankered:

> O Rose, thou art sick!
> The invisible worm
> That flies in the night,
> In the howling storm,
>
> Has found out thy bed
> Of crimson joy,
> And his dark secret love
> Does thy life destroy.

What is that rose—besides the summer blossom on the trellis at my back door? Blake doesn't say. But the sharp urgency of his compassion and the words that make it as living and sentient as he, elevate the rose: she is more than a flower. She is a being in Blake's comprehension, vital, graceful, dear to him, whose dying wrings from him grief and a cry.

What is the rose? She may be any good thing, both blessed and delicate, mortal when misused, and killed by the wrong kind of loving. She is a symbol.

In this book let that rose be a striking symbol for the third being of a marriage, the living relationship between a husband and a wife. The relationship which is trust, nourished by truthfulness and dependability, which is itself the sharing of all work, which lives in the talking and listening of the spouses; which is made manifest flesh (one flesh!) by their lovemaking; which is good and graceful, glad and dear—that relationship, that is the rose.

It is both blessed and delicate. The sad news is that it can be destroyed. It can die.

And what, then, is "the invisible worm that flies in the night," straight to the heart of the rose to canker it? Let that, too, be a symbol for a spiritual, impalpable, but real existence. It is the attitude of self-centeredness, the conviction of either spouse that he or she is the god of the relationship, whose desires are its priorities. His will has authority. Her "good" is best for both.

It is dark and secret, this love, because under a seeming love for the spouse it really loves itself. And the bitter news is—the worm feeds on an innocent trust until it is gone. Selfishness can kill.

Healthy lovemaking between a husband and a wife is a sort of incarnation of the rose-relationship—physical evidence that this third being is hale and hearty, living and whole.

Adultery is physical evidence of the worm-self. The worm existed before the adultery took place. The attitude of selfishness was there already, however invisible it might have been to either partner. But when the married person acts to satisfy the self, in flesh, in fact, apart from the spouse, upon another body, then the worm is no longer invisible but incarnate. Extramarital sex is manifest, dramatic, palpable proof that one's self is one's god.

And even if that act remains a dark secret from the spouse, nevertheless, the worm has curled in the heart of the rose. Self-love is there as a parasite in the marriage relationship.

AVOIDING ADULTERIES

Perhaps it is clear to you already that the strongest protection a marriage can have against adultery is in the *attitude* of the partners toward the marriage and toward each other. No one—absolutely no one, male or female—who has vowed faithfulness to another human deserves sexual satisfaction outside the marriage bond. Yet self-centered adulterers have justified their sin by the premise that sexual satisfaction is somehow their right—because God made them this way and they can't help it; because the world makes so much of sexual experience; because they don't receive enough "loving" from their spouses.

The Right Attitude

But in fact, the marriage vow subordinates one's individual satisfactions in all areas to one's marital partner—declaring publicly that sex is less important than one's spouse, less important than the health of the relationship. Sexual satisfaction is no longer a right, but a *blessing*, a gift of the relationship *to* its partners. This attitude, then—that the health of the relationship is infinitely more important than one's own desires, and that the sweet fulfillment of one's desires is an undeserved bounty within that relationship—not only closes the door to adulteries, but abolishes the door and the thought altogether.

He who worships anything of himself is a candidate for extramarital sex. His marriage is vulnerable. His desires have become his privileges. So long as he is his own god, he feels himself free to obey nothing and no one *but* himself.

But he who takes seriously his declared commitment to the rose, the mutual relationship with his spouse, will guard the marriage even against the assaults of his own desires. His attitude sensitizes him, making him careful, wary, and aware. He will be able to identify as threats those desires that are purely personal and merely self-satisfying. He will recognize them already when they're weak and small, before they grow monstrous and demanding; and then he will not nurse them to size, but, while he can, cut them off and quench them.

When a desire is born in us, we have a choice. When it exists still in its infancy, we have a choice. We can carefully refuse it existence altogether, since it *needs* our complicity to exist. We can dread it from the very beginning, naming it straightway as a parasite that intends no good for us. Or else we can attend to it, think about it, fantasize it into greater existence—feed it! We can feed our sexual thoughts with pictures, books, videos, and a wandering eye at work. But if we do the latter, if we give it attention in our souls, soon we will be giving it our souls. We've lost free will and the opportunity to choose. The desire itself overpowers us, commanding action, demanding satisfaction. The only choice left, since we've been enslaved by a passion, is how we might justify the sin. By then the "invisible worm" has fattened to a viper.

How important, then, that the attitude of each partner be a self-conscious DEW (Distant Early Warning) line within the soul, internally alert against his or her dark and secret self-loving. This, even before opportunity presents itself, is the first strong protection against the destructive acts of adultery.

The Moment of Maybe

Adultery is never a sudden, spontaneous, and totally unexpected act. It is always preceded by a longer drama, at the beginning of which you are not helpless. The drama may be spiritual, as I've just described it, a struggling between two attitudes regarding your marriage. When the right attitude does not prevail, the drama can end in what seems an unplanned one-night stand, furtive sex with a prostitute, sudden passion with an acquaintance. "It didn't mean anything to me," you may say. But it does. It means much. It reveals your deeper priorities in this marriage. It uncovers the drama that had been hidden in you for some time.

Or else the drama may have been acted out between you and the one with whom you committed adultery. Even in this case, you were not, at the beginning, helpless.

Early on in an extramarital friendship, there often comes a moment of "maybe." Even when that friendship is altogether innocent, your friend may send the signal, or you may sense the feeling, of further possibility. It occurs in a glance more meaningful than mere friends exchange. It arises from a touch, a hug, a brushing of flesh that tingled rather more than you expected— and you remember the sensation. A mutual understanding seems to establish itself between you, unspoken. Perhaps you succeeded together with a difficult project at work, and you celebrated the triumph; but a greater closeness crept into the celebration. Perhaps one of you supported the other in a crisis; but the dependency became more personal, more valuable than the crisis truly warranted. This is the moment of "maybe."

In that moment nothing more is communicated than this: *our friendship could turn into something else.* Neither of you need say, or even think, what that "something else" might be. The friendship is still quite innocent. Both of you still maintain control. Nothing has been said or promised or done. It all remains a mere "maybe." Nevertheless, it is precisely here that the drama toward adultery begins. Whether it also ends here, or whether it continues hereafter, is a terribly critical question. For a door has opened up.

If, in this moment, you do nothing at all, then you enter the door. If you make no decision (privately but consciously) to close the door and carefully to restrict this relationship, the drama continues. For though a promise has not been made in the moment of "maybe," it hasn't been denied either. And though you may not yet love each other, neither have you said no to love. You permit, by making no decision at all, the "maybe." And "maybe" takes on a life of its own.

Well, let's see what we will see, you think, excited by mystery and possibilities. *We're only friends, after all,* you rationalize to preserve this moment of pleasure, *and I can draw the line.* But this is deceptive. In spite of the fact that nothing yet is passionate or out of control, you have empowered the "maybe," granting it permission to mature; you've surrendered something of your independence. You have, by silence, approved it. Hereafter, every small exchange with your friend will *be* a promise of things to come; and somewhere in the progress of this drama, promises will subtly turn into commitments. To renege hereafter will be to break commitments. Helplessly, then, you will say, "How can I hurt him now?" "How could I break her hurt?" *How,* you will think, *did we become so entangled?*

How? By not kindly indicating No at the moment of "maybe." For at that moment No is as possible and still as kind as Yes. At that moment both answers are equally available, and neither answer would wound, since no commitments have been made. It is, therefore, your responsibility to perceive these moments when they come. And it is definitely in your power to close the door then, right then, by a wise defining of yourself and of this friendship *as* a friendship, nothing more now, nothing more in the future. For who you are includes your spouse. Your very being is bound up in that one. And every time you chat with or buss or hug another, it is two who do.

Let no one seriously insist of his adultery, "I couldn't help it. I don't know what came over me." Whether it was a spiritual drama reflected, finally, in his selfish attitude toward marriage, or whether it was a romantic drama enacted with her paramour, there was a moment when he could very well have helped it, when she could have closed the door. No adultery is sudden. Every adultery has its lingering history. Only the willfully blind are taken by surprise.

A Natural Warning Signal

Do you fear that you are unable to recognize a "maybe" moment when it comes? Is it your concern that you are unaware of your own internal attitudes? Well, here is the one good purpose of your spouse's jealousy: to act as the warning you may lack. A reasonable, controlled jealousy has its purpose; it is the marriage clamoring "danger."

"I was only being kind to her," I said to Thanne early in our marriage, protesting my innocence. "She needed someone. She was crying. She was hurting, and surely you didn't expect me to abandon her—"

I said these things at midnight, having come home later than I promised. Thanne had met me at the door, still awake and visibly upset. We were only one year married; I was still in school; and I was discovering sides of this woman which I had not suspected.

Thanne shocked me with what seemed ludicrous accusations. Had I been with—that woman?

Well, yes. But she was my friend, a colleague at work.

Did I know what time it was?

Well, yes. But we'd only sat in her office talking. What's wrong with talking?

"She's using you."

Oh, Thanne, no. You don't understand how troubled she is. I offered her sympathy.

"She's using you!" Thanne snapped.

I thought her a hard wife then, suspicious, ill-willed and weak in confidence.

But the rest of her charge was this: "She's burrowing into your life, and you don't even see it!" She was angry that I would be so easily flattered and so gullible.

In the days that followed, sensitized by Thanne's sharp feelings (rubbed a little raw, in fact), I watched my friend through different eyes. Then I saw that she was asking more than sympathy of me, that all her tenderer communication was *not* restricted to the matter of her suffering, and that it was more than my counsel which she cherished. It was me.

"You are so understanding," she had said to me; that was safe and specific. But it became, "You are so wise"; and praise jumped the boundary of friendly support. When she began to say, "You are so strong," with eyes that said, *And I depend on you,* Thanne's jealousy jangled in my ear. I learned the "maybe" moment not by nature but by drastic instruction.

In fact, Thanne is not given to irrational jealousies. I should have remembered that from the beginning; for jealousies may be rational (when they are not exaggerated) and necessary indeed. They sound the warning at the "maybe" moments. Moderate jealousy is an alarm bell to be heeded—and only those who are self-centered in their love think all jealousy purely suspicious and evil.

Since then I've learned through *Thanne's* eyes to see the "maybe" moments. And even so do I recommend to you that you see all your friends through the eyes of your spouse; those eyes see clearly, unblinded by vanity. Moreover, it's wise that all your friends should know your spouse; and your spouse, your friends. (If you have any friends you're inclined to keep from your spouse, immediately ask yourself why. Know your truer motives! What you keep from him or her, you keep from the marriage—and you are conducting a friendship, then, as an unmarried person.) If your spouse knows your friends, a natural restraint is imposed on all your action, because he or she is there in spirit, even when physically absent. More practically, you can enlist the aid of your spouse to overcome the "maybe" moments even at the early stages. If all things are open between you, this spouse will be able to act not out of threat or an unrealistic jealousy, but out of trust—helping indeed, and not blaming you.

When marriage partners believe their relationship to be more important than their individual desires, when they establish a DEW line within their souls, when they say No to moments of maybe should the DEW line fail, they will be protected from the worm of adultery.

But what if you and your partner have never developed such defenses? What if one of you has allowed this worm to blight the rose of your relationship? Once the deed is done, what happens then? How do the adulterer and the spouse deal with adultery after it has occurred?

TO THE ADULTERER

It is a hard adulterer who does not feel that something in the marriage has been thrown into violent disorder. He may not call it a sin. Nevertheless, he's living with the sense of violation. He may not call it his; but a wrong has defiled the relationship which wants some sort of righting.

What, then, does the adulterer commonly, foolishly do with the deed?

Covers it. Separates it as much as possible from his marital relationship as though one had nothing to do with the other. Ignores the effects it might have, spiritually or physically, upon his marriage—denies that it can have any effect whatsoever.

But in hiding the deed, he hides something of himself from the marriage, something of his real being—an adultery, either brief or lasting, is always evidence of an attitude, the quality of the adulterer's soul. He hides *his* personal tendencies, *his* view of this marriage, *his* needs or weaknesses, *his* character. The marriage cannot be whole when something so essential has been amputated from it. Lies lurk in all the communications of this husband and wife, permitted (like the "invisible worm that flies in the night") to grow unrestrained, according to lawless design, feeding in secret upon the good substance of the rose. His spouse will not understand the anemia which their marriage is experiencing; she will imagine other causes and try to heal those. But all her labor will be frustrated because it will have been misdirected.

What else does the adulterer do with his deed?

Explains it away to himself. Argues his right to it, or his essential innocence in it, or his spouse's deeper fault in the matter. Assures himself he's not alone and eases his mind by applying to sociological statistics: the majority of the married population experiences extramarital relationships. Or he discounts old morals in order to comfort himself with new ones: "It can't be wrong if it feels so right." "She doesn't understand me; she doesn't love me as she should, as I deserve, after all I've done for her." One may absolve *oneself* with a thousand reasons, in a thousand ways.

But justifying such an act changes the spiritual rules of this marriage covenant and gives credence to principles of behavior which were not mutually agreed upon. Then there are two standards of ethics in this marriage, one for the adulterer (by which he has exonerated himself) and one for his spouse (which he still expects her to obey). In effect, then, *two* covenants are in existence—and *two* different ordinances for marriage.

Who can assume true union to continue hereafter? It simply can't. Mutuality shrinks until they are married only in a few things, but unmarried in most other things. They may be married where the children are concerned, but unmarried in the children's absence; married according to their basic, external schedules (when they will have dinner, leave home for work, keep appointments with their friends) but unmarried in their hearts (speaking nothing significant in the privacy of their bedroom, remaining insensitive to one another's feelings).

What else does the adulterer foolishly do?

Suffers the memory truly, deeply, but in solitude—a misery her own, a cramp of conscience she must bear without the help or healing of another. She hurts mutely with the guilt of the thing because she fears that speaking it can only redouble the hurt.

And maybe she makes furious resolutions for herself, never again to be so careless, so sexed, or so sinful. She appeals to God. Either she stands back, humiliated, from the goodness of her spouse, or else she lavishes upon him a nearly desperate love. But so long as she remains unforgiven, or else unfinished in the experiential process of forgiveness, her love and her communication to her spouse are strained, unnatural, confusing to him. She is not free—free to *be,* or be whole in this relationship. Therefore, neither is her spouse free—free to be, as God desired, a "help perfectly fit" for the one he cannot know.

But what, for healing, wisely, can the adulterer do?

Why, confess the sin.

To the spouse? Perhaps. Perhaps not.

THE FOUR PARTS OF CONFESSION

The adulterer's attitude toward confession determines its successful outcome. He or she must determine to adopt two important attitudes: "I will deny nothing" and "I will judge the deed rightly. I will call it by its true name."

1. Recount Everything

Nothing of the adulterous deed can be denied or suppressed. The adulterer is not free of the deed until it is altogether understood—not just the overt actions of it, but the attitudes and the conditions, the feelings, the whole drama that led up to it. To name it is to objectify it and to take some control over it. When you are required to speak the thing aloud, in all its facts and causes, to another human ear, a confessor, you can no longer deceive yourself or skip significant, spiritual details. Speaking it aloud in accurate words finally eliminates the lie—at least this once.

2. Admit Fault

The deed, now that it is uncovered and known, must also be judged according to the marriage covenant, if that covenant is to continue as the guardian of your relationship. All false justifications fail here, or truth itself remains in doubt.

Confessing the deed means calling it a sin, your sin, your own fault. This is the admission that something greater than you governs this marriage, something you trespassed but which you still do honor. Not only is adultery a sin, but this adultery was your deed and is *your* sin. You grieved the marriage covenant, breaking faith with it. You grieved God.

This is the most painful part of the confession, if it is sincere. But it is good! It declares God still to be your God, and it reinstates the marriage bond also as your own.

And that you should call the adultery a "sin" is also exceedingly hopeful. You can repent of a sin; sins can be washed away. But if you insist that the adultery was merely fated, or if you explain it as a quality of your personality—that is hopeless. Personalities are frightfully difficult to change.

On the other hand, the sincere admission, "I sinned. Lord, be merciful to me, a sinner," invites the power of God into the situation, who can abolish sin and change sinners. No—it is not your spouse who can change you for the better, saving you from future adulteries. Don't lay that dreadful burden upon her! (But you will, if you make of this deed anything less than your own sin, if you justify it still, if you find its causes in your marriage or in her coldness.) Nor do you truly give it to God if you *blame* him for it (saying, "He made me this way," or "He put opportunity in my path"). By naming the sin as yours, you prepare yourself for the cleansing of forgiveness.

3. Speak It to Another

To confess in your soul before God may be the beginning of goodness; but there you don't experience God's hearing you. The words become more real when someone of flesh and blood—someone who will have obvious feelings about what you say—hears and reacts to those words. It is this *hearing* which authenticates them, which places the secret deed clearly in the open and in the community where you dwell. When it is no longer hidden in your heart, then it can be dealt with.

But choose your confessor carefully. Surely he or she must know and be committed to the same ethics you hope will prevail in your marriage. Surely that one will love the same God you love. And surely she or he will be convinced of the forgiveness which God has to offer—for it is the *speaking* of forgiveness which finally routs the sin and can transfigure the sinner.

Choose one, too, who loves you and your spouse together, so that the hearing will be done with true compassion, not merely with hard legalism. Choose someone who loves you *and* your spouse, so that he or she is not inclined to take sides but is able to see your marriage whole, undivided, and yearns for that wholeness to continue.

But choose someone you can't deceive, who loves honesty as much as he or she loves you—for this listening person is the presence that shall require more or less honesty from you. His very listening is something of your guide; how he listens will encourage you to greater, more dreadful truth, or else to prevarications and distortions.

I don't think you'll want someone unacquainted with the world or else too worldly. On the one hand, she shouldn't be horrified by your revelations, or her word of forgiveness will sound hollow, ineffectual in your ears, and you may leave guiltier than when you came. On the other hand, he should call sin by its rightful name and not shrug off the evil of your deed. Otherwise, he may see no need at all for acute expressions of forgiveness, and you may leave full of the same excuses with which you comforted yourself before.

And of course, this confessor will be no gossip, thrilled to hear a juicy intrigue, but one well able to keep confidences.

Should this confessor be your spouse?

Well, if he or she has any notion already of your deed, yes. The drama is not yet done until it is done for all—for your spouse as well, who needs to know your repentance and, by God, must finally (though this may take awhile) complete it by his or her expressed forgiveness.

But if your spouse truly knows nothing of the deed—not anything—and if you are truly penitent, truly infused with the forgiving Spirit of God to change you, then let your confessor be someone else. It isn't necessary, then, to make your spouse suffer your sin all over again; for the sin would, in fact, live again in the experience of your spouse's mind and in the spiritual space between you. Nevertheless, you must be ready at any time in the future, should your spouse discover the past deed, to confess it all over again to him or her and not deny it or belittle it. But then you can bring your confessor with you to your spouse to act as a witness of your true sorrow and your devout prayer to God for change. That witness will not take away your spouse's hurt or your own, but he will make hope and healing possible.

4. Listen and Believe

Finally, the last act of a complete confession is that *you* listen, while your confessor speaks God's forgiveness to your sincere sorrow. This, too, must be spoken out loud and must, when it is heard, be believed. This is the administration of the power of God. It makes that power present, personal, perceptible, and real. It isn't a mere ceremony, representative of something else. When faithfully we use the words of God, the very Word of God is active among us. In that moment the promises of God come true, and the Spirit snatches from our hearts the tangle of our sin, both its causes and its consequences. *You* must hear this, not as a general declaration, but as an immediate and personal operation of that Holy Spirit in and for *you*. That's why the word needs to come in a personal human voice—from a confessor who believes the words spoken to you. The speaking of forgiveness authenticates it, makes it here and now and active. Your whole being—your restless body, your tragic face, your sagging heart, your burning memory, your downcast and uncertain eyes—can respond to a human voice, a human touch. As your body was involved in the sin (guided by your attitude), so let it be involved in the confession (admitting your attitude), so let it receive forgiveness (revising your attitude).

Listen to the words. Believe them. Be set free.

TO THE SPOUSE

But when you discover that your *spouse* has committed adultery against your marriage—what then?

I repeat what I've urged throughout this book: forgiveness is the tool which maintains the marriage against the shocks of sin. You may want to reread chapter 7 on practicing forgiveness. But this sin needs special attention; it is a direct attack upon the marriage bond itself. It is the worm in the crimson bed of the rose, and it can kill.

Forgiving Adulteries

Because adultery strikes at the core of the marital relationship (no matter how casual the adulterer is about his sin, how meaningless he says the sex to be), forgiveness is hardly the first response you have to its discovery. In fact, it shouldn't be, not if you're swept up in the storm of emotions caused by this treachery. Forgiveness then would be false or ineffectual. The emotions should not be suppressed, denied, or sublimated, but rather admitted, understood, channelled, and so brought to a proper conclusion. Until you know yourself and your feelings, you are reacting, not acting; you are not in charge of yourself. Until you are in charge of yourself and *choose* to forgive, your forgiveness will be rote, a mere mimic or an uncommitted attempt to "do the right thing." A hollow forgiveness will fail. This forgiveness must be accomplished with courage and a severe honesty and an endurance which will not be sidetracked by anything, by your spouse's self-justification or by her counteraccusations or by her sweet, unrealistic assurances. This forgiveness must drive to truth, to true repentance and change. This forgiveness is a surgery. You don't want to begin with a faint heart or a shaking hand.

Therefore, know first what you are feeling when you react to the adultery.

(I may exaggerate the following emotions slightly—but only slightly. Since this society is not much outraged by adulteries, it has contempt for those who are outraged, as though we were being naive and childish. And because of this general scorn, we are embarrassed by the depth of our emotion and do not publish it. Privately, we hurt terribly; publicly, we present sophisticated faces to the world. It is this private turmoil that I do not exaggerate, the internal storm which is much more common than television admits. If you feel in the anguish at your spouse's adultery that you are going crazy, you are not alone. And you are not going crazy.)

Anger. When something dear to you (especially a living thing for which you are responsible, upon which you depend, the marriage relationship) is threatened, attacked, and wounded, you react with a fiercely protective anger. Compulsively, your emotions like adrenaline prepare to strike back. You seek the enemy. In a flash, your spouse *is* the enemy—but the anger is intensified by the fact that you had thought your spouse an ally. So his sin is betrayal. He was Judas at your table, in your bed, smiling upon your vulnerable love. She was Delilah causing you to trust in her. All the good things you had shared are trash. All the marriage is suspect. It is the totality of its destruction that makes this sin so monstrous, and anger comes in waves, swelling each time you think of one more thing for which you cannot trust your spouse. "This is the gift he gave me at our last anniversary. Was this, too, a lie?"

Hatred. Against your own wisdom and your own desires, you may find yourself imagining the details of her adultery: the room, the bed, the words she might have murmured, the positions he might have used. You wonder whether they are the same as you two used in intimacy. You see, and you can't believe what you are seeing. You say to yourself, "I won't! I don't want to think about it," and you truly don't want to, but you do nonetheless. Anger is focused like a laser on the specific actions of your spouse. Disbelieving/believing: "How *could* you?" And when the reality of the deed is finally urged upon you, when it no

longer seems impossible or improbable but a historical fact performed by *this* person, this wife, this husband of yours, then
general anger sharpens into personal hatred. (You hadn't known
you could feel such an emotion for the one you loved, whom you
still do love.)

Anger may be diffuse; it doesn't need an object. But hatred
always has a particular object, one who is hated. Now that one is
your spouse. Now she can do nothing for you without exciting a
deeper hostility. She can do nothing for you at all. Now his very
presence, his body, his smell, his bulk in bed—and especially any
gestures of kindness or love, his smile, his touch—are offensive
to you. You do not choose; you cannot help but shrink from
him.

Guilt. But in direct contradiction to hatred is the anger which
is turned inward upon yourself—guilt. It is the madness of these
emotions that, though they are opposite, you may feel them
both. Yet it is natural to seek causes for the adultery, to ask
"Why?" And it is not unnatural to find the reasons in an unsatisfying marriage, in some fault of your own sexuality—even if
you cannot figure out what you did or did not do. As hatred will
want to punish the other, so guilt is sure that the self should
suffer. And a questioning of yourself is the beginning of that
suffering, a piece-by-piece destruction of your value, your confidence, your performance.

"What did I do wrong? What could I have done better? Was I
so selfish that I couldn't see? What is the matter with me?" The
questions are all clearer, more intense than any answers. Sadly,
then, guilt will be not only willing but grateful to hear some
concrete accusation from the adulterous spouse. But this spouse
is the enemy and unreliable! Should you listen (as one moment
you long to do)? Or should you absolutely reject anything that
one says (as the next moment you cannot help but do)? Even so
do guilt and hatred contend within you, bewildering your relationship with your spouse and ruining your own self-concept.

Pain. In the whirlwind of such emotion, however healthy you
may be, you feel physical pain. Constantly you find yourself rub-
bing something: your temples because of a headache, your stomach as though with indigestion, your eyes for lack of sleep. The
body itself reacts, sympathizing with the spirit. And then come
ridiculous moments when you actually want to laugh at yourself,
to giggle aloud at the silly picture you must make. Are you going
crazy? But those moments pass, because the physical pain is real

after all. The shortness of breath is not imagined. And this is the reason for your bodily distress:

Humiliation. Your spouse's adultery—however much he or she may protest that it had nothing to do with you—is a very personal insult after all. It is as humiliating as a public repudiation, a slap in your face, because it has declared that you—your body and your spirit, your most intimate gift to him or her—are dismissable, uncherished, unworthy of preservation. For a moment you were nothing, *no* thing, to her. You were rejected, specifically exiled from her life, and replaced. That's both personal and humiliating. And if that adultery indeed "didn't mean anything to me," as the spouse may suggest, then the lovemaking of your own marriage was sold for a mess of pottage. Its value is meaningless if it can be betrayed for a meaningless moment of sexual pleasure. That is personal. That is humiliating.

And since all sex (sex sacred and sex sinful) includes the body while it comments upon the soul, of course your body will suffer a real pain. And the pain is grave, because this spouse had been your mirror before, the one human by whom you best knew yourself. His or her reflection of you had been taken as the true you. Are you truly, then, nothing? Are you, body and soul, replaceable?

Confusion. Until now, the trust you invested in your spouse had been foundational—one stable factor in an existence essentially uncertain. You could endure changes in the other areas of your life precisely because this one fidelity did not change. When this trust, then, is broken, your whole world is affected and seems to tip.

Strangely, a sort of fog settles over all things, and you may feel like a child again, afraid even of the dark, doubtful of *anyone's* word or promise, terribly lonely. A child, I say—but one without parents, one who is lost. It irritates you how easily you cry over small things, how difficult it is to make even minor decisions, how the distress at home leaks into every part of your life. "Why did I come into this room? What did I come here to get?" Or you are persuaded that all women are what your wife has become, that all men do what your husband has done to you. "None is righteous. No, not one." In the world, among people, you stumble in confusion. So what do you do? Well, you move through your days by habit, doing what you always did simply because you can conceive of nothing else.

The emotions I've described will be different for everyone, some feeling them less than others, some experiencing only the anger and no guilt, some hurting with the humiliation only. But this is true: to the degree that the marriage was valued and necessary for one's peace of mind, to that same degree adultery will seem a violation. And then something of these six emotions will be suffered.

What shall you do with these feelings? Certainly you will not suppress them, or they will linger in secret, feeding on you and on the marriage, waiting for the day when they may lunge from hiding (perhaps at some insignificant annoyance), astonishing everyone by their violence and strength.

Rather, release them twice, once for yourself and once for your spouse.

Express your feelings for yourself. Find a friend. Find someone identical to the confessor described earlier in this chapter, one who faithfully serves God, one who loves both you and your spouse, who will not merely take your side and match your anger against the adulterer. You do not need your feelings redoubled; you need them to be listened to by a kind, objective human. You need to express the dangerous excess of emotion where it will not do hurt, but where the speaking of it can both relieve you and help you to understand the complication of your feelings. Dump it with your friend. All of it, with as much drama as it requires. Go several times to your friend, if that's necessary (likely it will be, since you will pass through several stages).

Then, as the emotions cool in the disclosure, listen to yourself. In conversation with your friend (always with the object of returning *prepared* to the marriage again, to forgive your spouse wisely and well, not cheaply, unconvincingly, or sentimentally), identify the kinds and the causes of your feelings. Know yourself, who you are now. Find in the patience and the enduring love of your friend your own worth, so that more and more you reject the judgment which your spouse's sin had placed upon you, and more and more you strengthen yourself for the acts of forgiveness to come.

Now, then: when you understand the effect of your spouse's act upon the marriage; when you understand the causes and the nature of your feelings and have therefore taken control of them; when you are persuaded of your own value and convinced of the goodness of preserving your marriage, *now,* then, begin the important process of forgiving that spouse. This sin must have its end in healing. Forgiveness, openly experienced by the both of you, is the single tool truly to knit you one again. Forgiveness alone can abolish an evil—not hide it, not make room for it, not explain it away or justify it, but annihilate it—and replace it with a new thing, a good thing.

Express your feelings for your spouse. For the second time, you will release the feelings your spouse's adultery caused in you. This time you are in control, so the release will not be explosive and haphazard. You will speak clearly the effect of his sin *for your spouse's sake.* You will tell her (without rancor!) what her deed has done to you.

The purpose is bare and simple. The adulterer must know and confess his fault *as* a fault. Only when he perceives his sin can he perceive forgiveness. Only when she admits the full consequences of her act can forgiveness root up the full tangle of those consequences. And only with a sincere repentance can the Spirit work change in the sinner. Therefore, yes: at step four in the process of forgiveness you will need to speak the full effect of the adultery. You'll need to accept nothing from your spouse—not rationalizations, not defensiveness, not mere promises for better behavior, not gestures of love (kissing and making up)—except repentance. In that repentance alone rests the hope of conversion.

Do you see why you need to be both prepared and strong for this process? You must have the eyes to see, and the will to deny every dodge your spouse may use, except repentance. Of all things, repentance will be for him the most difficult state to come to. So you will struggle against his human tendencies for his soul's, and your marriage's, sake. He will wonder why, if you love him, you do not forgive him sooner; but you will know that premature forgiveness would be nothing but empty words and a return to sinful attitudes. Without repentance, the forgiveness *is* nothing.

Some time may pass, then, between your speaking of the sin and your spouse's purely penitential confession that it is a sin, her own sin, his own adultery. For a while you may have to withhold the words of forgiveness, and the gestures of reconciliation. Please love enough to last that time. It won't be wasted time. It may be necessary for your spouse to believe that "all is lost" between you. Forgiveness is most powerful when it is most undeserved and unexpected. Therefore, the sinner must realize that all his efforts—anything except repentance—are worth nothing. This he learns: he has given up the right, by his sin, to save himself in your eyes.

But when he knows he cannot prove himself, and when her sin has become a prison around her and she knows she will never get out on her own, *then* forgiveness can be received as forgiveness. Speak it then (though you had felt it all along). Speak it with complete love and an unqualified commitment. Then it is grace indeed, because he clearly did not earn it or deserve it—but it came nonetheless! Then, right then, forgiveness can transfigure the sinner to humble love again. Despair, the penitential sorrow, had removed him from the center of his existence; it had killed the godlike attitude in her; it had proven that he or she, in fact, deserved nothing. This despair destroys "the invisible worm that flies at night." But forgiveness gives you back the rose again in gladness. Forgiveness is the resurrection of the marriage.

Once, when you discovered your spouse's adultery, you questioned privately and sadly, "Can we ever be the same again?" Your spouse asked the same when he realized, early or late, that this adultery was his fault. And when you asked it, each of you despaired. "No, not ever the same again."

But when couples bravely choose the difficult course of honest declaration of hurt, a loving watchfulness for repentance, a sincere confession, and an earnest forgiveness—why, then marvelously the answer is, "Yes! We can be the same again, making love as ever we did before." And the renewed vigor of their sex life shall itself be evidence of the grace of God: a miracle.

FIFTEEN

THE FIFTH TASK:

Healing

---

*F*or years I've supervised the annual tours of the choir of our congregation: forty people in a speeding bus, forty good voices from a small parish in inner-city Evansville, Indiana, children and adults together—a ranging family. Except for the salting of a few white Wangerins, we were altogether black in the early days, and we were *all* together faithful. We perceived it our ministry to breach the racial barriers within the broader Christian church, and we accomplished that ministry by singing in the deep South, by singing in white congregations, and by accepting the hospitality of white families who offered us their homes, their food, and their beds. For many of these families we were the first blacks to sleep beneath their roofs.

The second tour we planned took us through Memphis and New Orleans and Galveston, then sent us north through Texas.

It was in Dallas that I wept.

The tour alone is an exhausting proposition. My watchfulness for the health and the happiness of our people drained me daily. The fact that they slept with strangers kept me from sleeping soundly myself—and on that particular tour the weather was chill and wet.

But on that particular tour a different sort of problem oppressed me, a human element which I couldn't understand until I met it face to face.

In Galveston my host said, "You're going to sing in Dallas."

I said, "Yes, yes," making conversation. "And I think we'll get the chance to look at Southfork—see if it's as white as television makes it."

"But you're going to sing at Paul Rasp's church," said my host, earnestly.

"That's the itinerary."

"Do you know him?"

"No. I only talked to him once, on the phone. I've never met the man."

My host sipped his coffee, gazing at me earnestly. "It's a pity," he said.

In a suburb of Houston another host, a breezy man with a cherry face, said, "Listen, how in heaven's name did you ever get Rasp to agree? I mean, how did you persuade him that your choir should sing in his church?"

"It was a fluke," I said. "A pastor in Alabama knows him and made the contact for me."

The florid man shook his head. "I mean," he said, "why would the fellow have you come? Does he know who you are? Maybe God's changed him, but I haven't seen the evidence."

"Who are we?" I asked, "What do you mean?"

"You know, he built that church. I mean, he built that fancy building, and it's got his feelings in it, even in the carpet." The pink man cocked an eye at me. "Does Rasp know who you are?"

"Well, I don't know," I said. "I sent him information—"

"Did you send him a picture?"

"A picture? Yes, a publicity shot—"

"When?"

"Two, three weeks before we left."

"Ah-*ha*!"

When we rumbled north out of Houston, Cheryl Lawrence and I talked in the front of the bus. She's the choir's director, my partner. Thanne sat in on the conversation with us, her head bowed in silence.

"I don't feel good about this," I said to Cheryl.

Her eyes widened. She knew exactly what I was talking about. "You, too?" she said. There is an alarm in the human flesh, just below the skin, that tingles a warning and shrinks the scalp when one approaches situations of danger. Cheryl's face was tight, suffering alarm.

"Do you have any idea what we're getting into?" I asked.

"Do you?" she said.

I said, "I talked with this Reverend Rasp once. He scheduled us immediately, because I told him we'd be in Dallas on Ash Wednesday. He said they were having services that night anyway—and that we'd fit right in. That's all. It was so easy. I had a good feeling then—"

Cheryl said, "I never talked to anyone but the secretary. She made the arrangements." She thought about that awhile. "Pastor," she said, "what'll we tell the choir?"

The choir filled the bus behind us, playing Uno, laughing, sleeping, chatting together in their seats, rifling their bags for food, blithe and innocent of the dangers, trusting us.

"What do we truly know about this church?" I asked.

"Nothing," Cheryl said.

"Then we'll tell them nothing," I said.

Rasp's church was in downtown Dallas, right in the middle of that city's glass-and-steel prosperity. It was itself a handsome complex of buildings, self-confident stone, green grass, and canopied walkways. It seemed to me that I could smell the mossy perfume of wealth. These people breathed their own air.

The choir smacked hands together when we turned into this place. "Comin' up in the world," they said with delight, staring out the windows. Someone hummed the theme from TV's "Dallas." You don't arrive at grandeur without a soundtrack. "Comin' *up*!"

We were met by one figure in the parking lot, a short man with boy's skin and thinning hair who did not smile but maintained a nearly monstrous decorum. This was not Rasp, that was evident. He shook our hands, Cheryl's and mine—one shake each—identified himself as the intern, then requested that we follow him to his office. He didn't walk like an intern, a seminary student taking a year's experience on-the-job before graduating. He walked like a Cardinal, careful not to step on the hem of his invisible, flowing robes. Oh, he was a severe, officious little boy.

But he spoke for Rasp.

In his office, behind his desk, he made a steeple of his index fingers and said, "You have twenty minutes." He closed his mouth to let this decree sink in.

Cheryl and I looked at one another. Twenty minutes for what? To explain ourselves to him? To account for our right to be sitting in his office?

The intern said, "These are the facts: we have our own service tonight, and that takes priority. Reverend Rasp will preach. Our own choir is scheduled to sing. We've a rather long Scripture reading. We can afford you no more than twenty minutes for your presentation. We're being generous."

"But it lasts an hour and a quarter," I argued. His face remained bland. "How can we shear the material to a fourth of itself?"

Cheryl was quiet in this alien place.

I controlled my voice in order to negotiate. "Why didn't you tell us this before?"

The intern began to drop his eyes. Smudges of a blush entered his cheeks.

But then the very atmosphere of the room changed, and he raised his eyes with new authority. "Twenty," he said, popping the two *t*'s in that word, "minutes."

Reverend Rasp himself had floated into the room behind us, a tall, lean presence, a silence unannounced, unspeaking. The intern drew strength from the hovering phantom, and we were diminished to the role of children. "Sing a few pieces," said the boy Cardinal. "Cancel any talk you might have planned. Be brief. Twenty minutes."

During our audience, the rest of the choir had acted according to custom, carrying luggage to the dressing rooms and instruments into the church sanctuary. They had gathered there to wait for Cheryl and a short rehearsal, both happy and unaware.

They had to wait awhile longer. When we were dismissed, Cheryl and I went outside through the fellowship hall, talking, trying to save something of our strafed presentation.

I was furious. "These Christians!" I fumed. "These self-righteous, self-satisfied, self-confident, assassinating—Christians! These racists!"

It was evident that not a scrap of publicity had preceded our coming. This congregation did not even know that we were to sing for them that night. We were a reproach to Rasp's ministry, a crimson, black embarrassment to him, and he meant to make as little of us as he possibly could. With cold contempt he had consigned us to a helpless ineffectuality, to the role of rude children who are only barely tolerated. It was an enormous church; but we had been told that we'd sit in the balcony. *Blacks to the back of the bus*—just like the old days.

It was a thin-lipped smile that Cheryl and I had received from the women setting supper tables in the fellowship hall. Darting eyes seemed to watch our hands as though we might snatch silverware. This mild presumption of their goodness to our grubbiness, even their Christian goodness in condescending to serve the grubby, is so humiliating. The choir was my family! I knew the treasure of its heart. I loved and was loved by its people. Dear God, they did not deserve the subtle, prejudicial attack.

"Rasp is the poor," I said to Cheryl. "Rasp is the needy, not us."

So I planned to preach after all, despite the ban on my tongue. I would mount Rasp's own pulpit (I was shaking with this thought, shaking with anger and fear together), and I would speak forthrightly where these religious leaders had been veiled and indirect. I would name the racism and proclaim Christ's particular love for the outcast. So be it!

Cheryl selected five songs and left to rehearse the choir. I secluded myself in the church library (this church had a whole room for its library) and began to create thought and themes and sentences by which to weave the songs together and to prophesy unto a white and wealthy congregation.

It was four-thirty. We had two hours to make up a new program, eat, dress, and prepare to sing. My stomach had shrunk around the hammer of my anger. I kept swallowing while I paced because I was afraid of the thing I had to do.

And still the Reverend Rasp had not deigned to say a word to me.

But the Reverend Rasp *did* have words to say to the choir.

At five-fifteen, Herman Thomas found the room where I was working. He knocked once, walked in, collapsed into a chair, and burst into tears.

Herman was no child. He was a college graduate, newly active and successful in a business position, kind, able, self-possessed—and sensitive. These were nearly violent tears he wept; he shook with weeping them. But the violence had been done *to* him.

"Let's go," he said. "Let's just get out of here. Why should we sing for them? I feel like they don't want us here. No, they don't want us here. There's no reason to stay—"

Rasp had floated into the church while the choir was rehearsing. His presence alone was a pall on joy, and the choir grew nervous. They became intruders. He made the bass player feel a fool for not knowing where electrical outlets were. When someone reached to touch the altar, Rasp leveled an icy, caustic, long, and absolutely heartless rebuke against that child, against the choir whole, against us. And then all tensions snapped like piano wire. Several lead soloists discovered that their voices were too raw to sing. And Herman came to me.

"Can we sing for hate?" wept Herman. "No, I don't think so. We can't. We shouldn't. We shouldn't have to."

What I did next was not my own decision, and what I said was not my wisdom. It was the picture of the weeping Herman—the pain that prejudice deals out—which triggered a completely new thing in me, filling me with a holy certainty.

I knelt in front of him, my eyes even with his, my hand gripping his knee, and I preached, lowly, urgently, a different sermon than I had intended.

"Of all the places where we have ever sung," I said, "we most need to sing here. Herman, we cannot leave. Not with God's blessing. We're here for a reason. These people flatly do not know the love of Jesus." I spoke intensely, as though I had inside information. I talked and talked, and in talking I found how I would talk from Rasp's pulpit: not condemnation, but mercy. "It's up to us to teach them the love of Jesus," I said. "We have to sing. We have to *be* that love before them, do you understand? I'm going to center our whole presentation on one song, Herman: 'For God So Loved the World.' You have to sing that song."

By the grace of God, Herman believed me. His tears dried up, and his jaw set, and he went out.

But I was left kneeling alone in the room, tense and unprepared, hardly started on the work I now had to do—and so scared.

And then Thanne came in, carrying a plate of supper for me.

I saw her familiar face in this alien place. I saw her kindness in the midst of enmity and criticism—and *I* burst into tears.

I stood and put my arms around her and hung with all my weight on her thin shoulders and sobbed so hard I couldn't speak. I was weaker than Herman. Neither did Thanne speak. But this precisely is the point of my story: I *could* cling to her, and she didn't *have* to speak.

For five minutes we stood wordless together, saying nothing, doing nothing, accomplishing miracles. This wife of mine had through the years assured her husband—for whom tears were an embarrassing difficulty—that tears were a fine, acceptable release, that she did not love him the less for them, that they were no shame at all. This wife had so patiently done the marriage task of comforting that she had created in me the *expectation* of comfort. She had caused to surround us the very atmosphere of "home," so that however far we traveled, however strange the territory, I was "home" as long as I was with her.

It was in the city of Dallas that I wept. But that says nothing significant. Rather, it was within the "home" of our marriage that I was given the right to weep; here I could safely reveal my fears, my exhaustion, my brokenness: I could be true. And from the spirit of our marriage I could be assured that I would receive comfort and healing and strength again. I could heal. I could be empowered.

Thanne didn't have to tell me anything new. She offered no solutions. I had already learned with Herman what I needed to know. Thanne merely came to me, and that was enough. Her being encouraged me.

Though no one else knew, that day of our encounter, the rest of its events blossomed from my healing and Thanne's holy nourishment. With a greater freedom of mind, with greater ease, I prepared the words I'd speak from Rasp's high pulpit. After dinner I gathered the whole choir together and told them with steady conviction the same things I had told Herman. The choir watched me, listened, grew solemn, and believed. They had a divine commission to this church in Dallas. No, this was nothing frivolous. They were to be witnesses. Soloists found their voices again.

And when we were installed high and out of sight in the balcony of the vaulted sanctuary, Herman Thomas nudged me, nodding seriously. He pointed to certain scratchings on the seat of the wooden pew between us. The scratchings had been made, perhaps, by a bored worshipper long ago; but I knew by his nod that Herman felt they carried an immediate, pertinent message. They spelled out, *I don't know this.* Herman smiled. "I" was the church to whom we meant to sing; "this" was the news we meant to bring.

Reverend Rasp was preaching his Ash Wednesday sermon. I listened to the drumming rhetoric and felt pity for the scratcher of messages upon pews. How *could* they know love if this was what they were fed? Rasp announced that his Lenten sermons would answer certain questions posed from the cross. First sermon, first question: "Do we need forgiveness?" Answer, in terms accusatory: "Yes!" Then over and over again he repeated the phrase of a hymn until we were almost beaten down. "Pour contempt on all your pride!"

Our turn came.

I whispered to the whole choir, "Love them. Love them. Look them in the eyes, and sing your love to them—"

In perfect solitude, the beautiful Gina, soprano, walked down the long aisle singing a cappella, "For God so loved the world, that he gave his only begotten son—that whoever believes in him, should have everlasting life—"

Her cousin, Tim Moore, sweet deep tenor, took up the second verse from the rear of the church, and they sang the song as a duet, drawing closer and closer together. They sang in killing harmonies: "That whoever believes in him should never die, should never die, should never, never die—" The last note came loud and high, a celestial invitation; and the male voices responded, progressing down the aisle and singing with foundational steadfastness: "For God didn't send his son into the world to condemn the world, but that the world through him might be saved." Up tempo! Speed the beat. Raise a holy excitement. The bass and the drummer charged the whole place with energy while the men mounted the steps and formed a solid curtain, while the women swept down the aisle, and the entire choir exploded in a driving, delightful reprise: "For God so loved the world, that he gave his only begotten son—"

The building trembled. Oh, the curious heads of this Dallas congregation swiveled at this unexpected music, unexpected people jamming their chancel, unexpected blackness—this unexpected visitation! In the very front pew, Reverend Rasp in his robes, and his officious intern in his, sat side by side staring straight ahead, denying responsibility for the breach of Lutheran conduct.

The song swelled to the ceiling beams, then settled in silence.

I spoke. I climbed the pulpit in order to be seen because I was hidden, otherwise, by the choir, which never left its standing position in the chancel. I spoke five minutes, then sat down again while the choir sang again. And so we traded off between singing and speaking five times, five songs, five brief words from me. I could never see the congregation while the choir was singing. I only saw their faces between songs. It was like watching change in a stop-action film.

Our choir did not clap or sway, as they did in every other place. They delivered the music straight up, careful not to intimidate the tight white people in front of them. But they sang dearly, earnestly, so innocently, and full of a gentle love. The congregation changed. Every time I rose to speak, the people were looser than before. Soon Dallas was leaning forward the better to hear. Dallas tipped its face trustfully up to us and smiled. And some of the women were free to cry, and soft was the air of the sanctuary.

Love them. Love them. Look them in their eyes and sing your love to them.

The last song we sang was a fast one and could have been boisterous. We would walk out singing it. Usually Tim, who sang its verses solo, would invite the congregation to clap along with us. But on this evening, in this place, he invited no such response. With blessed assurance the choir sang, "Soon and very soon, we are going to meet the King"—and then began to file out of the chancel. The curtain between me and the Dallas faces slowly separated. "No more crying there; we are going to meet the King." I was the last to go, the tail of the recessional.

But when I descended the steps of the chancel, I came upon a miracle, a wonder: the entire Dallas body of that church was standing—and clapping. "Soon and very soon!" All on their own they had found the rhythm of that song. They clapped in spontaneous rhythm, grinning, and beginning to sing themselves, "We are going to meet the King." And there were tears running down their cheeks. And some reached into the aisle to touch me. "No more crying there, we are going to meet the King." The choir kept walking, down the aisle, out the back door of the church. But the congregation, applauding, fell in step behind us and followed—out the church, along a sidewalk, to the dressing rooms where they wept and hugged black shoulders and begged us to understand, to believe, "How much we needed you."

This is a true story in every detail—and in this: when Cheryl later returned to the darkened church to gather her music, she saw the Reverend Rasp walking down the long and empty aisle, unaware of her. She saw him, and she heard him. He was humming to himself. And the tune that he was humming was: "Soon and very soon—"

The name we give to the fifth continuing task of the marriage is meant to be very broad: "Healing." It recognizes that the spouse will suffer, and that intrinsic in your promise to be faithful is your promise to heal his suffering, always to be her first physician—to "keep" your spouse in sickness as well as you keep him in health. Healing, too, is essential to marriage work.

But the name is broad because suffering is not restricted to bodily ailments alone. Your spouse will suffer both physically and emotionally, will suffer both diseases and dis-ease. The world will surely batter his self-esteem, and he may grow uncertain regarding himself. Her duties outside the house and inside of it will surely try her fortitude, drain her energy, and leave her weary. Sadness wants healing as much as a flu. Fearfulness wants comforting as much as convalescence after surgery. Grief and bewilderment need careful ministrations as much as does diabetes, or incontinence, or high blood pressure, or any of the hundred handicaps that come with old age. And to care for your spouse in this way requires more than a medicine chest. You are married. Healing is not a profession but a way of life. Your spouse is not your patient but your flesh. Healing, then, is a task for your heart as well as your head and your hand. And it cannot wait for some dis-ease to strike before it acts; it prepares for all dis-eases even before they come.

This task is performed at all times, with all your being, by three miraculous acts: nursing, building a house of mercy, and sympathizing.

NURSING

The most obvious fulfillment of this marital responsibility is to nurse the ailing spouse, directly to serve her in her sicknesses. Do we need to be reminded of this, or persuaded that we willingly obliged ourselves to be a live-in nurse when willingly we married him? Perhaps we do. Because at marriage we couldn't imagine the sicknesses to come or how they might complicate our own lives, forcing us to do the work of two while one lay down and did the work of none. We have a foolish human tendency to blame the sick one for the sickness—especially when the sickness is emotional and we can't see clear symptoms of attack. "It's all in your head" is an easy accusation when *our* head continues busy and active though *our* body nearly drops for exhaustion.

But the unique mercy of marital nursing is this: you are able actively to serve your spouse *without immediate reward,* with no compensation at all, since sickness is precisely the inability to return one kindness for another. You are more than doctoring your spouse; you are loving her: love helps the helpless; love needs no payment, not even gratitude, but is motivated by itself. And love is your most potent medicine for healing.

Husbands, you make love to your dehydrated wife when you make a soup to provide her liquids, and when you take over her chores without congratulating yourself on your own goodness. Better yet, you prepare to make love to her by learning how to do those chores when she is healthy! What good are you if you do her work poorly, or if you keep entering the sickroom to ask her where she keeps the salt or the bills or the budget? And when you take her temperature, or when you bring her aspirin, you are *being* husband to her. This is husbanding.

Wives, the healing is in your hands when you bathe your help-less husband, washing his buttocks, wiping the waste away with dignity. How you touch him—that you touch him—assures him that you love him even while he is ashamed of himself. The can-do man can do nothing; but your nursing says that he is something after all. You are making love to him; you are re-making *him* by your love. This is marriage work.

It doesn't matter how skilled you are in healing therapies; no one is more able to nurse the whole person of your spouse than you. No one else can mix exactly this element of loving in his other medicines. No one—however long their professional education—has learned to interpret your wife's groanings in the night as you can, because you have learned her language by committed experience. You have for years depended on understanding her language. You can diagnose her soul.

Spouses are always their spouses' first and most abiding physicians. The paid professionals come and go. They have their reward. But your spouse is your life.

BUILDING A HOUSE OF MERCY

Who will take my tears when I most need to cry them?
Thanne will.

How do I know this? Do I have to cry first, in order to find out? Do I have to suffer a blatant, punishing racism first? Do I have to hazard human evil *alone* in order to discover that I'm not alone? Do I have to despair before I can hope?

No. I knew before I cried that I could cry. That very knowledge allowed me my tears and was the vaster comfort to me. In order to open myself to healing, first I trusted that Thanne would heal me. And I trusted because Thanne had spent time and energy over the years to build around us an atmosphere of mercy, a house of healing—a spiritual home, wherever we happen to be.

The task of healing doesn't wait until one is sick before it reacts. It requires, too, the work of assuring your spouse that you will not fail her in a sudden need, that you will be merciful when she breaks, that you will be a healer precisely when he is most weak. The task includes long preparation.

But some wives nag their husbands mercilessly. Their tongues are quicker and sharper than their husband's tongues. They criticize the things he does as though he never does them well enough. They correct his speech, his dress, his manners, as though he were an incompetent boy. They blame him for the things he does not do. They seldom praise him, supposing that he gets enough praise elsewhere or never thinking that he might truly need a wife's praise. When they do begrudge him a word of praise, it is not free, but lost in qualifiers. "You are so nice to other people. Why can't you be more nice to me?" "I guess you did a good job. But next time remember to comb your hair." Some wives find it difficult, impossible, or simply unnecessary to speak spontaneous words of love. Or they take for granted that their husbands know they love them. "I've stayed with him all these years. That ought to mean something to him."

Far from building a house of mercy for their spouses, these wives are tearing down any hope for healing in the husband (no matter how willing they may in fact be to nurse him when he needs it). They have utterly neglected the work of preparation. Consequently, when the husband does suffer dis-ease, he will likely hide this weakness from his wife—for she's shown him what she does with weaknesses: she nags them. At the time of greatest need he will most withdraw from her, and maybe he'll heal, and maybe he won't. But she will say, "It's not my fault. He never talks to me. How can I help him if he won't tell me what he's suffering?"

On the other hand, some husbands make jokes of their wives. "The wife. The little woman." Their humor at home is sarcastic. If their wives' feelings surface, whether joy or sorrow, these husbands don't participate in such demonstrations but belittle their wives for a lack of self-control—as though it were childish to be emotional and they, these men, have put away childish things. They are superior, realistic, men of the world, whereas their wives are idealistic, unrealistic, "touchy." They may, in fact, be threatened by an expression of feelings; but they lump all women together: "sentimental, hysterical." They truly relax only among other men, because they "don't understand women." They consider that they've fulfilled their duties to their wives by supporting them economically, with a secure house, food in the refrigerator, a nice car. And they don't cheat, and they don't drink, and they don't gamble.

But neither do they praise their spouses in terms of honest equality. Praise is more a pat on the head. ("Hey, I tell her she cooks good!") And it seldom crosses their minds to make spontaneous gestures of love for the sake of loving only—touch for touching's sake, hugs for hugging's sake. Rude men, they hardly know how to say "I love you" without couching it in some ulterior purpose. So the love seems always less important than the thing they want. ("Hey, I'm not that kind of guy, all right? I'm a practical sort—keep my feelings to myself. I can't go moon-eyed just to prove I like her. I give her a good house, don't I?")

A house of sticks and brick, yes. But a house of mercy, no. These husbands, too, are neglecting an essential (and absolutely practical) construction in their marriage; they are not building a spiritual home for the healing of their wives. They are, in fact, announcing a personal unwillingness to act as a healer, with a sort of horror of sickness and helplessness. Weakness will have no place in their world. They should not be surprised, then, if even a long marriage never feels quite complete, since the dependency of healing was denied a place in it. Nor should they suffer jealousy if their wives prepare beds of healing for themselves in other relationships—in friendships with sister-women, in profound relationships with the children (from which the father/husband feels exiled), in the blessed comfort of their church communities.

But for me there was a hospital. Wordlessly I could reveal a certain sickness to Thanne, right honestly and fearlessly. And wordlessly, upon the whole history of our good relationship, she could heal it. Tears were my relief, the holding one another was my worth, and the marriage was our strength together—to accomplish whatever was necessary in a Dallas congregation, in the world. We had taught one another in the healthier times—when teaching was possible—what these small, most potent gestures signify. Healing begins before healing is needed.

SYMPATHIZING

I say, the healing happened "wordlessly." In order to heal me, Thanne didn't have to say anything. She had merely to be—and to be with me. Her sympathy was enough.

One of the reasons we (men and women alike) neglect and even deny the task of healing is that we feel finally helpless before it. We're not almighty; troubles and diseases will arise greater than our resources to solve them. Nursing the little sicknesses for a little while is well and good; but we know that some problems simply cannot be solved, some maladies cannot be cured (or we, at least, will be baffled by them and impotent), some emotional distresses, some grievings, some of the fears of our spouses would simply overwhelm us if we tried to struggle with them. So we turn away from the hurt and ignore the need. "Don't tell me about it. What can I do?" We set a hard face against the hurting spouse—or else we rush that spouse to every other professional in the community, whimpering about our powerlessness, matching her sickness with our own. And if there is no help anywhere (in the end comes death) we are filled with impotent rage or with despair.

All this comes because our concept of healing itself is wrong, and, therefore, we are blinded to one significant thing that we can do, however little skill we think we have.

We can sympathize.

Ours is a pragmatic, utilitarian society. It supposes (and the foolish among us agree) that the single method for healing a problem is to solve that problem. Every riddle must have its answer. Every sickness must have the medicine that will cure it. There is no comfort for suffering except to do away with the cause and so the suffering. Failing these things, we fear we've failed altogether.

But healing is in fact more than a mere cure; and sometimes it doesn't involve a cure at all; sometimes it comes with the admission that there is no cure. Thanne healed me in a church library wordlessly; she didn't even pretend to offer solutions. But she didn't shrink from the task simply because she couldn't *solve* my problem. She used another method for healing: sympathy.

Sympathy is made up of two Greek words: *syn,* a preposition meaning "with"; and *pathos,* a noun meaning that which is endured or experienced, a "feeling," a "suffering." To sympathize, then, is to experience with someone her own experiences; to feel with someone his own feelings; to suffer with someone the sufferings he or she knows in that same moment. It is, in the deepest sense, to abolish internal loneliness by entering into the experience of the one whom you love.

How will you do that if you listen only for the facts of her problem in order to solve it? First the problem itself must be *lived,* and that requires of you a hearing heart, not a calculating brain. Sympathy allows your spouse's pain to become your own as you imagine yourself not only to be in her situation, but also to be within her personality, within her. (Certainly you might act and feel differently if the dis-ease were yours; but right now you are called upon not to be yourself, but to be her.)

Long, long you've learned to interpret the expressions on her face; sympathy feels the same expressions as if they were in your own face; the same internal moods she feels within herself. Sympathy imagines the motions and the gestures of her body to be your own; so you mimic her being inside your own; and so the communication between you two, though it may be wordless, goes much deeper than words. You "feel with" your spouse. You *are with* your spouse completely in this suffering. But you enter her confusion and brokenness with your healthy, steadfast, reassuring strength. Though she may herself never be healthy (if this is, perhaps, a lasting handicap or a terminal illness), you are healthy for her. *You* are her health. That is comfort. That is a healing not of, but in spite of, her disease.

If you are truly "feeling with" her, then your health will not belittle her or be such a contrast to her sickness that she feels the worse. Yet she must know this sympathy in order to believe in it. So you will communicate it to her. If you talk (as Thanne did not), you won't give her suggestions on how to improve, or solutions; these aren't sympathy because they imply your superiority. No, if you talk you'll tell her in your own words what she is suffering, and then she'll know that her feelings dwell in you and you in her. Better than talk, you'll use the more basic language of intimacy. You will touch her. She will feel both your presence and the quality of that presence. It will be a giving touch, not a taking touch; you'll touch her for her sake, not your own.

It will be a touch that names her, and proves your awareness of *her* presence, her goodness and worth. She will feel herself in the touch, exactly where you touch her. (This is the marvel of the human touch, that two are made present in one sensation.) When you touch her cheek with your fingers, she knows both your loving fingers *and* her cheek—which is dear to you. And since, by sympathy, you know her feelings now, you will also know which touch best comforts without demeaning her. Shall you hold hands? Stroke her hair? Brush her tears away? Embrace her and surround her with an unashamed, affirming, stabilizing strength? Or perhaps you do no more than make a pot of tea and serve her.

Even so do you heal your spouse. It is an unspeakable blessing to discover that someone else understands; it relieves both isolation and the pain of shut-up emotions; the sufferer is set free from his sufferings in order to experience some control over those sufferings. And he is healed of—what? Of enslavement to the dis-ease. Of the debilitating *power* of pain. The sickness no longer masters his whole person (and if solutions are available, now they can be sought and found). Instead, the person may be whole in spite of the sickness.

Even so, Thanne's silent sympathy didn't change the enmity of racism or anything I had to do; rather, it was the strength that freed me from my lonely fears *about* what I had to do and so changed my relationship *to* that racism. It no longer mastered me by making me helplessly angry; now I could choose how to act in regard to it. Thanne hugged me; I cried. All the world remained the same—except that Thanne had entered my suffering by sympathy, had touched my grief from me, and so had allowed me to see the same old world new. She made a half heart whole and a faint heart strong. That is healing.

Don't be confused by a search for solutions and cures, when the best that you can do for the suffering spouse is merely to *be,* and to be *with* him, making a wholeness of you two. That is healing.

THE HOLY SPIRIT, THE COMFORTER

One more element makes your healing possible, even in the face of impossible troubles and insoluble sufferings.

God the Creator established marriage and yearns to be the God of yours. God the Redeemer is the source of forgiveness between you and your spouse and the love you two may image to the world. Likewise, God the Holy Spirit may be the breath of healing one of you may breathe upon the other. The healing you bring to your spouse originates outside you in the power of God. Why would you be timorous and hesitate to serve your suffering wife? How could you deny your husband such a benefaction?

In the night before he died, according to John, Jesus promised that he would not leave his disciples all alone. "I will not," he said, "leave you comfortless," without a source of comfort. "I will not," he said, "leave you desolate," abandoned. "I will not," he said, "leave you as *orphans,*" cut off from the relationships that could heal them. He would send them the Holy Spirit, the Spirit of Truth, a "paraclete." This paraclete would be their relationship with Jesus; moreover, the paraclete would work in their relationships with one another. They could scarcely be orphans with such a power among them.

But what does the Greek word *paraclete* imply? How rich is this promise of Jesus?

A paraclete is "one called alongside to help," like an advocate or a defense attorney—or (perhaps the closest to John's thought) a witness in support of someone, a character witness.

It is "one who intercedes, entreats," an intercessor, a mediator. More broadly, it is a friend and helper.

A paraclete is "one who comforts," a consoler.

It is the exhortation and the encouragement one companion gives another.

In every sense, it is the active, powerful presence of the Spirit of Jesus, both in and for his disciples after he had departed from their seeing. It is the power that becomes available to them when they gather in the name of Jesus, the power that enables them to perform the work of their Lord. And you, when faithfully you approach your suffering spouse to heal her of her pain—this is the power available to you! Do you understand this wonder? In your attempts to heal this beloved one, the Holy Spirit finds opportunity to keep the promise of Jesus—and indeed, to heal.

In you the paraclete draws alongside your wife to help her, to defend her, to cry in her defense against all the evils that would bedevil her.

Through you the Holy Spirit becomes your husband's friend and helper, his comforter, soft with consolations.

Did you think the healing was altogether up to you? Is that why you drew back? Ah, poor little child! Your fumbling ministrations are the Holy Spirit's chance to witness to someone the imminent presence of the Lord Jesus Christ. *In you your spouse sees Jesus!*

So, sympathize. But know that your sympathy for your spouse is not merely the mutual support of two helpless human beings. Its source is as deep as divinity: it is the very consolation of the Christ, leading both of you in the way of truth. It has the value of eternal Truth. *Syn-pathos,* one's "suffering with" another, grows holy and healing in this, that it is Christ's "suffering with" your spouse. The source of sympathy is the cross, and none knows suffering better than the crucified, and none has ever turned suffering to such a good for others. His stripes healed us! So, touch your husband. Touch with confidence, not faithless but believing. It is Jesus who touches him, gathering him like a chick beneath its mother's wings. And whether your husband's sickness leaves him or not, that touch can master it with comfort. So, hug your wife. Don't be ashamed of your helplessness or afraid that your hug is too mean a medicine. Hug her with an unhesitating love, full of the health of faith: one more powerful than you is hugging her. For you who fear the name of God, the sun of righteousness is rising, with healing in his wings. She shall be well.

And finally, this is what I think: Someone more than Thanne was comforting me when I cried. I think the Comforter himself consoled me, the Spirit of Truth—and so it was no less than the torch of Truth that I bore before the prejudicial ice of a Dallas congregation. The Spirit in Thanne was the Spirit that took up dwelling between us, was the same Spirit that commanded my warm love and sweetened the choir's song—until that congregation melted hate to holy tears. This was the Holy Spirit, my Helper and the promise of the Christ. From him came the teaching that served a host of wealthy whites. But him I saw first in a brief, healing moment with my wife—and in private.

·SIXTEEN·

HEALING THE ABUSER

T he previous chapter certainly implies that the spouse you love can't also be the spouse you hurt. Healing forbids hurting. From the hand that hit can't come the oil of healing. Each excludes the other, and the blessing of the whole fifth task is denied the husband or the wife who has become your victim.

I suppose we could make the implication blatant and speak the truth bare, as though to children: don't hit. It is wrong and can never be made right. Don't slap or punch or beat or kick the one whom you have married; don't pinch for pain or pull his hair or in any manner strike her. Don't hit. This is abhorrent to God. Nothing can excuse such behavior, not your frazzled nerves, not your spouse's disobedience, not your parents' example, not even your own beatings when you were a child—nothing. No man was ever given the right to "smack my wife into line," to "knock some sense into her head"; he seized it for himself (no matter how much his buddies support the action) and is more to be blamed because he descended lower than the animals to find it. Even the beasts do not attack their own; they strike what they mean to eat, or what eats them. Hitting comes from human aggression when humans are most separated from God. It comes of our wickedness. It is nothing else than a sin, which, if you can't control it, has become a sickness.

We could speak the truth as nakedly as this, and perhaps one or two who had been taught wrongly might repent their behavior and cease the sin of abuse.

But the sad fact of our society is that marital abuse is, more often than not, uncontrollable. The abuser, as much as he desires to dominate, is in fact a slave to passions and patterns stronger than he is. He is weak after all, unable to choose for himself. He suffers a sickness. Therefore, we direct this chapter to the spouse who *seems* the weaker.

In a marriage that experiences abuse, both of you are enslaved by a certain repetitive pattern of behavior, a behavior which is both compulsive and destructive—he directly to it, and you to him. If he cannot disentangle himself from it, then it will not change so long as you continue to permit it. You do, you know, "permit" it, however you suffer the situation. But you are the more objective of the two; you can more easily see the devil on your spouse's back; therefore, you are the freer to take independent action and to force change. The redeeming of the marriage enthralled to the demon of aggression-and-submission is the responsibility of the one who submits, who may choose, finally, no longer to submit. It's up to you. But the terrible anxiety of such an emancipation is that to free yourself from the demon means, for a while, also to separate yourself from your spouse—whom, marvelously, you continue to love. I know that I tell you no easy thing.

But we are not speaking of abuse alone. No compulsive/destructive behavior can be tolerated in a marriage or should be protected within the walls of silence, within the family. *All* compulsive/destructive behavior is a parasite that feeds upon the marriage, drawing sustenance directly from the relationship which allows it, until the marriage and its partners are eaten up inside themselves, are shells, mere masks that hide the parasite within.

Physical abuse, yes. But alcoholism too is a pattern of behavior which enslaves a whole marriage, and not just the alcoholic. Addiction to any drug is parasitic, to cocaine as well as to Valium. Sexual abuse also falls within this category, even though the abuser assumes that any sex is his right by benefit of matrimony. That behavior, which is (1) compulsive, uncontrolled, but rather controlling its host, and which is (2) destructive, hurting the spouse, oppressing the spouse, destroying the good health of the relationship, will not one day leave its prey for goodness's sake. It won't just go away. It must be willfully, consciously, carefully, patiently, lovingly named and rebuked and extirpated, cut away as in a surgery.

It's up to you, the permitter, the victim.

This, too, is a healing, but of a different sort than the affirming consolations which we spoke of in the previous chapter. It is meant to heal the marriage whole by freeing the abuser from his sickness.

This is forgiveness, but of a harder kind than the forgiveness we outlined earlier in the book, because this may require that you reject the one you love in order to redeem him, that for a while you "let him be to you a Gentile and a tax collector," a heathen and a publican, an alien and an outcast.

This healing may have to hurt both of you. This forgiveness may scald. But it can burn clean and yield a healthy marriage after all.

The Diagnosis

Before anything else, test whether your spouse's behavior is indeed compulsive. (We'll focus here on physical abuse and speak specifically of the husband's abuse of the wife; but all compulsive/destructive behavior should be considered in this way and we know of cases where the wife has been the abuser.)

When once he strikes you, he will shortly afterward explain why he did it. Listen this once, with all your heart, to that explanation. (If he doesn't offer one—though that's unlikely—ask for one.) Any blow intended to hurt you is a signal that simply cannot be ignored. If in his explanation you find anything you can do to change the causes of his action, do it. If he protests that the fault was in you (if you do indeed have a caustic, cutting tongue, if you demean him, if in fact you fail in duties the two of you had agreed upon), then change yourself. Curb your tongue. Affirm him, and fulfill your duties. At this point, please don't let your feelings of pride or self-pity compromise the genuine commitment of your change. This is the sacrifice of your love.

More practically, it is absolutely necessary that you test truly and completely the truth of his explanation: a half-hearted, grudging attempt to change yourself will not allow you to assess the causes of his behavior since he can still argue that the causes persist in you. Take that argument away from him. You are preparing to show him the falseness and the absurdity of his excuses.

On the other hand, if, after you have in fact made sincere and strenuous efforts to change, he hits you a second time, a third time; and if his reasons then are different, though the anger and the blow are clearly the same (or if his explanation is not substantially different from what it was the first time—usually it is a variation of what springs quickest to his mind), then you will know what he cannot admit: he can't control himself. The reasons are a mere dodge, worth nothing.

In the case of a compulsion it is not enough just to speak his sin to him, to seek repentance, and to forgive him. You are dealing with something subtler than a simple sin. This is a sickness. So he can be truly, abjectly sorry for what he's done, without truly repenting—without truly changing. Then both of you will suffer the deceit of the sickness; abusers are often flooded with guilt, and then tomorrow flooded with rage again. His seeming repentance and your heartfelt forgiveness will only become part of the greater cycle that will end again and again in abuse. So your forgiveness, in this case, shall have become his permission.

It's important that you begin to act a different kind of healing, that you act right away, not lingering in the hope that he will (as he promises so convincingly) change. That hope grows dimmer with the years, until you don't remember any more when it was that you stopped hoping. Compulsive behavior does not get better on its own. Like cancer, it only gets worse. Accept that grim reality sooner than later; act immediately. The chances for your husband's and your marriage's recovery are vastly improved, as they say, by "early detection."

Prepare Yourself for the Surgical Operation

Do two things:

First, talk to someone. Do not be ashamed for yourself or your husband. Your talking is not gossip or betrayal, but will ultimately be to his benefit. And silence merely permits his sickness to increase. Would you keep silent if the sickness *were* a cancer?

Talk to someone who may have authority over both of you: a wise member of the family who will not react with a disabling anger; a pastor who is able to understand the difference between compulsive/destructive behavior and simple sinning, who will not read you your duty to submit to your husband; a professional counselor; women in a support group who have suffered the same abuse, but who do not merely feed one another's outrage. You need the talk in order to rise above reaction and emotion, so that you might view the situation realistically. In private you'll only build up guilt and rage, and move bewildered through your days. Alone, you will finally live by compulsive habit no less than your husband.

And you need an ally, both to encourage you in what you have to do, to keep your strategy clear before you, and to support you before your husband when the confrontation shall come. This confrontation is why the ally should have an authority your husband acknowledges, why a family member or a familiar pastor has a special advantage for you. Your husband may recognize the depth of his problem when it isn't you alone, whining in self-pity, who objects to what he does.

Second, as clearly as you can—but with the help of knowledgeable people—assess the *real* causes of your husband's abusive behavior. Does a present stressful situation drive him to act according to past patterns and models? Is this situation unique, about to pass away, never to come again? Or will any stress trigger abuse? Was he himself abused as a child? Did he watch his father abuse his mother? Is he aware of the effect of these experiences upon his own personality and of the humiliating self-image this presents? These are the sources of the sickness that need somehow to be excised from him, cut out, and cast away.

As you learn the true causes, you will be relieving yourself of a crippling guilt. To know and to believe that you are not at fault frees you from your husband's dominance, at least psychologically, and from the enslaving patterns of the sickness. Then a period may come when you must express anger at having been falsely accused and having suffered pain you did not deserve. That anger may shock you by its own violence, but that's exactly the reason it wants expression. Of that, too, you must be, and you can be, free. That, too, will fill your ally's ear until the two of you have bounded it in boundaries. All this enables you wisely and with self-control finally to perform your husband's surgery.

But as you learn the real causes of your husband's behavior, so do you discover the very things he struggles mightily to deny. They are the self which would humiliate him unspeakably, which he buries under his false reasons for abuse. They are a self of horrible memory and of craven weakness (but he wishes to appear strong). This is what must be cut out and cast away. But the surgery requires precisely that he confront this *self,* to turn and see the devil on his back. And though it should be a professional counselor who actually completes the surgery, you participate, and you are the one who initiates the process. You undertake a difficult task.

You may be sure that your husband will fight such a confrontation, even from the beginning. The more you press the matter, the more wily or desperate will be his defense; his games become more cunning, his counterattack more blunt. But you are free of his sickness, now, not to be confused, bought off, or again subjected and stopped. And one more thing enables you: now you know (though he still doesn't) that his real enemy is the self he despises. He will fight your effort to reveal that self as though you were the enemy. He will even believe you to *be* the enemy; and if you were not free, you might be inclined to agree, making enemies, not spouses, of both of you. But you are prepared. In spite of his accusations, you may continue to pity him and love him and hurt the monstrous self in him in order to heal the good.

The Stages of the Operation

In Matthew 18 Jesus has outlined successive steps by which to confront a sinner with his own sin. These steps work, too, to confront the abuser with his sickness or any compulsive person with the personal weakness he denies. Step by step, the purpose is to make the sinner know his sin. But this is more than intellectual knowledge: he should himself experience the sin, should suffer its consequences until the suffering persuades him that this sin is intolerable to life. As it kills others, so does he suffer its killing effects.

And these are the steps you now follow. The goal is that your husband change; his behavior is intolerable to the marriage. The more specific goal is that he admit the compulsion *as* destructive and as no one's responsibility but his own, and that he willingly accept the professional therapy that can complete his healing.

But in order to reach that goal, you must be willing from the beginning to follow all the steps, right down to the last one, which makes him to you an alien and an outcast. Are you prepared to cut your husband so? To hurt him whom you love? If not, even your first steps will be taken without conviction. Are you truly prepared to present him with such an ultimatum? If not, he will doubt any effort you make at healing and can remain unchanged. Yet, this isolation must somehow become his experience, or he will never truly recognize the consequences of his present behavior. Finally, are you prepared to hurt him not in vengeance but in pure love, even though he will not see the love in it? This cannot be punishment. Its whole purpose must be healing.

1. So, then. Go to him. "Tell him his fault," as Jesus says, "between you and him alone." Do not accept his explanations any longer, or let him think they carry any weight with you. Do

not enter into dialogue with him. The single goal you seek is that he should not hit you any more; and the proof shall be in his action, when he begins to deal with the true causes of his abuse. He stops drinking, if that was the cause, or doing drugs. He admits himself to counseling. But as for hitting, you have made this clear: there will be no hitting in this marriage. Not at all. Not even a grumpy punch. At this first step the rule is established for the whole marriage hereafter: the marriage will not tolerate hitting. Be that simple. You will separate yourself from him. He will be to you an outcast. This is an ultimatum.

Will this change him? You have begun to lay the responsibility on him, now, removing it from yourself or from any other false cause. Will he truly repent for that? Well, he might; and if he does, then good. You have gained a husband.

But it is likelier (and you must be ready for this so that you don't despair) that he will not change. It is a sickness in him, and deep. What has been changed is the situation and your relationship together. By laying down a rule of your own, you have ceased to be a permissive partner in that sickness. You will act, you've told him, according to your rule, not according to his will. This is a significant difference, setting up the second step.

2. The very next time he hits or acts destructively (this process contains no free chances; your reaction must be immediate upon his act) confront him again, but this time "take one or two others along with you, that every word may be confirmed by the evidence of two or three witnesses." So says Jesus.

The matter is, to some degree, made public now. The rules he breaks are proven universal, and the presence of the others indicates that. This is no longer the private choice of your particular marriage, where a husband may think himself king of his castle, permitted to make up his own rules. He is transgressing laws other people recognize. His sin grieves not only his wife, but all of society.

But the witnesses come with you in order to confirm your words before your husband. One of these witnesses ought to be the authority both of you respect (whom you went to immediately with the problem). It is no longer a foolish woman's hysterical opinion; it is supported by other authorities. *His* is the fault; *he,* the abuser, must change. And if he does not, others now will see to it that the marriage does not tolerate the violence. The proposition is strengthened; more than one will react if he hits again. More than one will be watching.

And if, in this second confrontation, your husband makes promises to change (as he may have before), now there are witnesses also to *his* words, to remember that promise. If he forgets the promise, they won't. And their evidence, their remembering, will give teeth to the ultimatum that as long as the abuser remains unchanged *he makes of himself* an alien and an outcast. Isolation will be the result not of your mean spirit, but of his sin.

Will this change him? He may have himself, this time, admitted responsibility; and he may truly be moved by the introduction of an outside authority into your private situation: the world is watching. Has he also truly repented then? Well, maybe; and if he has, good! You have gained a husband. The sooner you begin this process (before behavior is fixed in the marriage) the better are his chances for healing now.

But it is still possible he will not change. He may not seek counseling with a genuine and humble commitment (there are many false starts at this stage); may not quit drinking or doing drugs for more than a little while; has not been altogether persuaded of his more horrible *self;* will continue to deny it. If he thinks he has the strength to change himself, he is still deceived, however much he desires the change. His strength will come only in admission of absolute weakness.

Yet, again the situation has changed; for now the danger of his behavior has been turned back upon himself. His repeated abuse will have the consequence of exiling him from wife and friends and society.

3. If he still refuses to listen, if his actions still prove him unchanged, he has but one more opportunity before your ultimatum becomes his reality: "Tell it," Jesus says, "to the church" (Matt. 18:17). In this way a divine confirmation is given to your words. The abuser breaks not only the laws of society; he is not merely a public reproach; and it is not only from the community that he exiles himself. He also offends the law of God, and he must be told this. Therefore, someone comes to speak it to him with the church's authority. God himself is grieved by this abusive behavior. God is neither unaware of it nor indifferent to it: the abuser is a cosmic reproach. And he threatens himself with a triple isolation—from his spouse and family, from his community, from his church, and from his God. Beyond that no further word can be spoken, for the last isolation of those three is hell.

4. At any step before this one, the man may change. The motive he had for changing was always the certainty that you would separate yourself from him if he did not, making him to you an alien and an outcast. Now the final step is here. Part of

you will be ready for it, if the drama has lasted this long. Part of you will never be ready. But it's here.

"If he refuses to listen even to the church," says Jesus—if the divine word also has no force for him, if even now he cannot fully confront himself, confessing complete weakness and finding help for healing, if he repeats the destructive behavior yet a third time—"let him be to you as a heathen and a publican," a stranger unrelated to you, an outcast contemptible. One or the other of you must leave the house; and it were more righteous and more beneficial that he should leave.

Is this the end of the marriage? With all your heart you pray not. It is an event in the process of the healing, the strongest possible argument you have to persuade him of sickness and need.

Is this punishment? Is this vengeance for the hitting? No! He may at first interpret it so, but it is not. When he is genuinely healed, the husband may return. But *this* is done in order to turn the behavior back upon himself, to make him experience the utter abandonment his compulsive/destructive behavior shall infallibly bring him to in the end. His or her life will end like this. He ought to feel it now, while yet someone loves him enough to recognize true change, or else he'll suffer it hereafter when no one will care to notice any change in him. His or her eternal life could likewise end like this. The marriage is on the very brink of ending like this. Indeed, he may believe for a while that it *has* ended like this. The pain of such an ending, no longer a threat, no longer a concept, but the very experience of lonely desolation, may finally persuade the confrontation with himself and the confession of weakness: "As horrible as this experience is, even so horrible am I. This is my doing. This is *me*. How can I save myself if this is all that I can do? I am helpless. I am weak."

And what of you, during the period of separation? Well, there is relief in you because the immediate suffering has been removed. You don't flinch every few minutes. You don't throw up your hands for protection. You don't read the expressions on your husband's face, trying to decipher whether you can relax this night, unafraid, or whether you should creep silently about the house or go visit your sister. You sleep, and that is sweet.

But paradoxically, you are also filled with a sort of terror that he *won't* change after all. It is marvelous that love can endure so much, yet it does. You love him still. The absence is in its own way as intolerable to you as was the abuse. And so you pray. He's in God's hands now; but you appeal to God as though it were all still your responsibility. You pray that your husband's present suffering would teach him (like the Prodigal in the pigpen) that he is altogether dependent upon the help, the healing, and the love of others. You pray that his loneliness would cause him (like the Prodigal) to "come to himself" and, in an absolutely accurate vision of that *self,* to confess, "I am no longer worthy to be my father's son," my wife's husband, or God's child. Morning and night you pray that your husband would, in that admitted weakness, throw himself upon another's mercy, expecting little or nothing; that he would take himself to counseling, to a detoxification center and support for substance abusers, to Alcoholics Anonymous, to a true and abject confession, to help and to newness again.

And so you wait, watching out the windows daily for his return. You wait to do what you have never ceased doing, but what he could not recognize before: to love him, to forgive him now that he may understand the pure grace of forgiveness, to put shoes on his feet and your own wedding ring around his finger, and to throw a party. For this one surely was dead. But if he comes home weak, he is alive again, and very strong indeed. For God himself takes up dwelling in the pride that was hollowed by humility.

For this, precisely, you stand and wait.

·SEVENTEEN·

THE SIXTH TASK:

Gifting and Volunteering

---

*H*adrian died betimes—both the Roman emperor in his day, and our yellow VW convertible bug in its. The car was hit broadside on Highway 30 west of Fort Wayne, and all my possessions from the apartment in Oxford, Ohio, spilled onto the road. I was traveling home for the summer. I was done with graduate school. I was coming, Thanne, to marry you.

So passed the car in which I'd courted you, the little fellow whose top went down to give us the sky, the sharp October air, and memories: yellow Hadrian, who crept through darkness on a county road toward the Lantern, the floating light of a farmer crying for his children—remember? Intrepid Hadrian, who bore me north through a falling snow, from Chicago to Milwaukee, from ignorance to destiny while I suffered the question of whether to ask you to marry me—remember? Faithful Hadrian, my first horse, a plain, unpretty courser, died before the wedding. But I survived.

And other things survive those times.

I still have the green sweater you knitted for me when you were thin and the nail of your index finger was corrugated. The sweater still is bulky warm. It will ever be the first gift you gave me.

You saved dimes in those days. They fit perfectly through the neck of a large glass vase. They were all you could afford to set aside when you were a student and working and poor. Why were you saving them? To save them. But for what? You didn't know. Because they fit the vase. Oh, Thanne of the chipmunk's smile, whose ways were inscrutable to me! Even before I began to court you your hoard of dimes made a jingling pile; they were your character, your curious, conservative, practical, nonsensible self—saving dimes to save them. No reason. "Do I have to have a reason?"

But when we married, you had converted all your dimes into a single thing, a brushed brass cup with the heads of lions on the side and a handle like a wing. This cup you gave me as a wedding gift. Dear Thanne! The Cup of Dimes survives. The Cup of your Curious Personality is with me still. And inscribed on it, as clear as ever, are the words from our wedding text: "In quietness and confidence shall be your strength."

And you survive, you giver of perfect gifts. And many of your manners do: you still will sit with your legs drawn up to the body, your arms around your shins, your chin on a kneecap, smiling. How I watch you, Thanne!

And I survive—much because of you. Do you know that my soul has fed upon your gifts?

And our marriage survives. That, too. Eighteen years we have been married, twice nine, thrice six, a trinity of trinities of years, a holy figure.

Ah, Thanne, how much I love you still.

We call the giving of gifts and the volunteering of yourself to your spouse a task, the sixth task of marriage, something that must be done. And we're right to do so.

But it's a paradoxical task. From the receiver's point of view, from your spouse's point of view, the value of a gift is exactly this, that it *didn't* have to come. You didn't *have* to give it. Nothing forced you; you did it of your own free will. It was not expected. In fact, a gift is always more than could have been expected. This gratuitous element of the act is its very nature and its virtue for the marriage. Nothing more genuinely gives *you* to your spouse than the gift no law commanded, but which your free will chose to give.

The marriage hungers for such a nourishing food; and though it might not miss the gifts when they don't come, the marriage grows lean without them. It isn't as robust as it might have been.

The blood of it—the love of it—has become thin and watery, less rich, less evident, less expressed. That's why the giving of gifts and the volunteering of yourself are a necessary task after all.

But because this task is the free one, the gratis-task, too many wives and far too many husbands neglect it altogether, unaware that their marriage, though it may be complete, is poor—that their marriage, though it may be healthy, is pale, colorless, and wan.

A DEFINITION

In practice the task of gifting and volunteering will always seem a contradiction, because it ought to be fulfilled, yet it fulfills no law whatsoever.

—Neither the marriage vow nor the holy ordinances of God command it; righteousness may come from obedience to universal statutes, but gifts do not. And a voluntary act is precisely one which was *not* commanded.

—It is not some duty agreed upon by the two of you; you are bound to do duties; gifts are free.

—It is not a courtesy required by the culture or the community, for then you would be serving a greater authority and not your spouse particularly.

—It is not done to "reward" your spouse for something he has done or something she has given you; for that implies a compensation, and the thing which was earned or deserved cannot be a gift. Gifts are for free.

—Likewise it is not done so that you might receive a reward in return; for then it is but the price paid to purchase something. Be clear about this: giving doesn't seek so much as thanks for itself. It is utterly free.

Your giving of gifts and your active volunteering of yourself must be above and beyond all routine, all exchanges, all expected courtesies, all duties, all the commandments to which you are beholden. This task is pure grace, motivated by no other reason than your love for your spouse. No, not even gratitude for the love that your spouse has shown you motivates you. It is born out of itself alone. It is the incarnating of your own love.

It is the dearest, clearest way to say, all wordlessly, "I love you."

I LOVE YOU

This alone is the sum of the act and its substance, and it has no other purpose than this. If it is a true gift, the communication of love is uncompromised by any other consideration. The love is pure. Yet the act is full of a complicated meaning.

You say, "*I* love you," because the action was taken totally on your own initiative. No hints from your spouse, no pressure of society persuaded you to give the gift, no fearful need ("If I don't remember her birthday she'll jump all over me"). You alone initiated the act. Therefore, you perform it with a certain purity—and *you* are truly present in it.

You say, "I *love* you," because the act is its own reason for being. You truly want nothing back for having given something away. Moreover, it *did* cost you something to give it, whether time or energy or uncommonly close attention to your spouse's tastes, or the care that remembers special dates, or money and labor. It costs you. A true, if tiny, sacrifice was accomplished. And you bought yourself nothing for the cost. You made that part of your own being—the cost of this gift—hers or his alone. Your complete attachment to your spouse, which is affection and care and thought and a fullness of feeling, too, is present in the gift.

You say, "I love *you*," because you shaped the gift particularly to your spouse—to his character, to her delights, to his habits, to her dearer memories. You made the gift truly his possession. It finally lodged with no one else. Better than that, you made the gift not just hers, but *her,* the reflection of who she is. It contained her, and finally no one else could lodge in it but her. And behold: the *I* of this transaction has become the *you* of it.

When, in this manner, you say to your spouse "I love you," you have lifted the two of you above all that is common, legal, routine, and expected in your existence. You have, as it were, redeemed the dreary day and caused a *newness* to embrace you for a while, because this act came of nothing old, was caused by nothing evident except the love. You've made *her* new; you have revived *him;* you have resurrected your relationship.

This is what grace does. It comes as a surprise; it lingers in the rare atmosphere of unqualified love, since love itself is breathed by it, and love by it is made manifest. This expression of love is "ecstacy" in the Greek meaning of that word: to "stand outside" the ordinary, outside predetermined marital contracts, outside the systematic and the expected. Gifting and volunteering are acts uncommon. Sweetly, they break routine.

I remember you, Thanne. The memories survive and the benediction of them.

I remember how you came to me in my cemetery loneliness, though you didn't have to.

Five years into our marriage I had returned to graduate school to complete residency for the doctorate. I was on the faculty of the University of Evansville in those days, and the higher degree seemed necessary for my career. So I traveled to Oxford, Ohio, again; but because I had a family this time, a wife and children lost elsewhere in the bowels of America, I felt lost. This time I suffered a criminal homesickness.

I lived in a single rented room, a wooden table for a desk, two chairs, a chifforobe, two lamps, and a bed that wallowed on its springs. No car. You had greater reason for the car. I walked, then, between my room and my classes and the library. I walked through another autumn, and I remember that the trees burned with a cold, red fire. Elms were lighted with a yellow that gave no light. Berries on certain bushes were like spits of flame, the frozen flashes of firecrackers. And I remember that all this color killed me. The very beauty of it made me want to cry. It was silent, indifferent to me who walked the campus without you. It was creation already dead, still dressed—bones made pretty by raiment alone. I studied well enough in that cemetery season of southern Ohio. But I always carried in my chest the dead brick of homesickness.

And then two things happened:

The trees relieved themselves of their leaves. They became skeletons scratching at the grey sky, and the ground was hidden in tweed. The paths on campus were buried. I shuffled a dry water when I walked. My nose and my fingers grew cold, the one gone pink, the others white. It felt like winter long before the winter came.

And the other thing was this: even before the winter came, you did.

One Saturday afternoon I stood on a bleak corner watching the traffic of High Street, my hands in my jacket pockets. The day was loveless, but I was smiling. I grinned at farmers in their pick-ups, making them suspicious. My cheeks bunched under my eyes with the smiling. I remember hearing roaring from the football stadium. That's where the student body had gathered, but the sound was distant . . .

Then I saw our car. And your face so familiar behind the windshield, earnestly driving. And the kids, staring out at things, still not seeing me.

Oh, Thanne! How your coming loved me in an instant—the sight alone!

I laughed out loud and stomped my foot for gladness. You were peering about, looking for street signs. Any second now you'd see me. Thanne! That moment when I spied on you in the foreign town of Oxford was exquisite; something broke and bled sweetly in my chest, and I grinned so hard I cracked my cheeks.

How long did it take to drive from Evansville to Oxford? Five hours? You drove five hours with three children at your ear so that we could spend a weekend together. And Mary was an infant, Matthew was a bouncing ball, Joseph a perpetual talking machine. You prepared for that trip, packed suitcases and kids into a little car, managed maps and roads and food, a stick shift, the safety and the entertainment of a family, spent half the day traveling, found Oxford, and came—to me, for no one else's sake but mine alone. And I witnessed the tag end of all that labor: I saw you frowning though the windshield, trying to find the sign and the street to my apartment.

Then you noticed me, and your face smiled. You curled your fingers in brief greeting, reached for the gearshift, said something to the children—who began at once to jump and point at me. You turned the corner where I stood and motored past me to the apartment, still serious about the business of driving. I ran after you with all my heart.

Why did you come? You didn't have to come. I yearned, but I did not beg, your coming. Nothing I could ever do would repay the labor it cost you to come. Even today the memory of your coming is vivid and precious. Do you know how often it has sustained me in later lonelinesses? I could never deserve such kindness.

But why did you come? It was an extravagant, preposterous gesture, driving all that way for two days, only to pack and to drive back to Evansville again. It was altogether impractical, thou practical Thanne—except that you loved me.

Why did you come? Because you loved me. By the very impracticality of the project, I knew you loved me. It had accomplished nothing else but that. But more than knowing the love, I received it. This was the stuff of loving, visible before me, hard all around me. You parked the car; you yanked the emergency brake and stepped out, children tumbling after you like wolf cubs. You turned to me, sighing, smiling with one tooth like a chipmunk. And then, Ruthanne, you lowered your head and we hugged in grey November. Unreasonable! There was no pragmatic reason for us to be hugging in autumn jackets, in a sea of fallen leaves, in Oxford, in Ohio, on an insignificant Saturday.

But we were. I surrounded your small ribs with a mighty, squashing joy, and I simply could not stop myself from smiling.

Do you remember the moment?

Winter did come before I finished my studies and moved home again; the first snow fell on an evening early in December, silently, kindly . . .

Did I ever tell you, Thanne, how kind was the season to me after you had left? I walked through the woods outside of Oxford and saw that the trees were not skeletons after all. No, they seemed to me rather a sort of hair, fur on the body of the living earth—which put me very close to her. I walked, that snowing night, within her coat, comforted by an intimacy which would not allow me loneliness. Neither was anything dead around me. Only sleeping. And the snowfall seemed a coverlet tucked around the sleep. Everything would wake again and stir and smile—when I came home to you.

All this was thirteen years ago. Do you remember?

GIFTING—NOTHING BUT LOVE

Birthday gifts, anniversary gifts, Christmas gifts, and the like: do they fulfill the definition of this sixth task? Do they redeem the times and love your spouse to newness? Yes—if they are true gifts.

—But underwear because he needs underwear, though it clothe him, will not make him new. It can be accounted for; it may be eminently practical. It may not, therefore, be purely a gift.

—And earrings because she wanted them and asked for them, if she also expected them, will not surprise her with newness. They can be accounted for: they may satisfy her desires, and that's a very good reason to give them to her. But it doesn't make them a gift.

—And a car because you thought the family needed the finer, more powerful, and redder conveyance, though she may be glad in your gladness and laugh in your excitement, is too much yours to be solely for her. It may cause you both some cheerful moments. But it can be accounted for by some reason besides your loving of her: the family may need better transportation, or you may love—cars. It isn't, truly, a gift.

—Or anything given because the day *requires* a gift may obey some law besides your love alone. Surely you won't forget those days. But the focus must be on your spouse, not the day, in order to accomplish the task of "gifting."

Neither do presents meant to apologize "gift" your spouse; they ask something in return: reconciliation. And certainly those presents, which mean to buy your spouse's love, do not "gift" him or her. Even if it is only love, they seek something for yourself.

But a single rosebud (can we be "romantic" here? Yes, indeed, we ought to be), given uncharacteristically by a husband oblivious to the sweetness or the sentiment of flowers, such a rosebud in a clumsy hand can melt his wife by the love expressed. This is a gift. He shaped it to her, not to his own instincts; and he may be puzzled by the power of the thing; but he will certainly recognize the gladness in her.

And a birthday present which shows long forethought, an acute sensitivity to the tastes of one's spouse, and a sincere self-denial in its making or its purchase, that is a gift: "I" and "love" and "you"—all three.

Those presents, too, which satisfy a personal need that your spouse did not recognize in himself (but you did), or else a need that your spouse could not admit or would not satisfy on his own (but you could and you would)—these are the gifts of "gifting." Your husband needed to rest, but his conscience wouldn't allow him to rest without guilt; any rest he took for himself would feel to him like failure, as though he were inferior or weak. But since he needed rest, you arranged for him the vacation he never anticipated, and you consoled his soul in taking it. You sanctioned his sabbath. You gave him the moral permission for a while to do this necessary nothing, to rest. And though he might never thank you (because you so persuaded him of the rightness of resting), yet that is a gift.

And surely you know the value of presents given even when the season doesn't call for them, when it is not Christmas or someone's birthday. Just as holidays make room for gifts, so gifts make holy days of common days by the surprise of their appearing. True gifts are always an advent.

VOLUNTEERING—LOVE ENACTED

Volunteering makes a present of your *self,* in what you do— but didn't have to do and weren't asked to do—on your spouse's behalf. It breaks the marriage contract in a blessed way, not by neglecting your responsibilities but by superabundance, by crossing into your spouse's responsibilities and carrying them. It breaks the marriage covenant, I say, to replace its legalism with simple love. Rights and privileges are overshadowed by grace.

True "volunteering," then, obeys no law, seeks no return, pays no debts, plans no praise for yourself, nor proves your goodness—but purely, purely is meant to demonstrate by your time, your energy, and your action no more than this: "I love you." It is what you *do,* unbidden, unexpectedly.

Without this, the marriage survives, and no one blames you for the omission. No one can ever push you to volunteer your services, or else they would be neither voluntary nor the evidence of love. But without this, the marriage doesn't learn to smile as it might.

Be careful: it isn't "volunteering" finally to do what your wife has been asking you to do—finally to clean the garage some Saturday afternoon.

—Neither have you volunteered anything to *her* if you clean the garage with the intent of "feeling good about yourself," even if she hadn't asked you to do the job.

—"Volunteering" is not the good help you give your husband if it is given grudgingly, because then he'll feel he owes you something for it, or else he pays by his own emotional distress. Worse, love is not revealed in grumbling.

—"Volunteering" is not a job begun but left unfinished. What good have you accomplished if someone has to follow after you? Do you think "it's the thought that counts"? Hardly. "Volunteering" is action, and the action must relieve your spouse completely, or else it isn't "I love *you.*"

—Neither does true "volunteering" ease a spouse once or twice, then rest forever on these little proofs of goodness. ("Hey! I used to change the baby's diapers, didn't I?" "I mowed your lawn when you were sick, remember?") "Volunteering" truly accomplishes its task when it becomes a persistent characteristic of the marriage, when it is itself a quality of the relationship. Whatever duties you do for your spouse *remain* his or hers. They don't become yours (or you've merely revised the marriage contract). It isn't expected that, having done them a few times, you'll do them now forever. But that you help in many areas, and that helpfulness is your virtue on account of your love for your spouse, this is "volunteering."

It also honors the sort of work your spouse is obliged to do if you choose cheerfully to do it for him or her. Let me explain: in certain marriages men (or women) consider some jobs "beneath them." They avoid that work not because they can't do it, but because it would embarrass them to do it. Some men will never scrub the kitchen floor; whether they mean to or not, they scorn it as "women's work." Implicitly these men scorn both the labor and the laborer. They make of their wives their drudges. Then all the spoken praise in the world cannot disprove the low estimate they have of her life's work—and of her life and of her. On the other hand, if they are proud to try any of her jobs, all of her jobs, without being asked and with a glad good will; if they do the job well; if they scrub the kitchen floor with as much satisfaction as (let's say) they write books, then they honor the work and the worker together. "Volunteering" abolishes distinctions and degrees of value. No, *love* does that, but "volunteering" manifests the love. All work is valuable in the home where no work is held in contempt, and where love is not kept in hiding.

Finally, "volunteering" focuses not so much on what the household requires, as on what your spouse is required to do. You won't wait until he's helpless before you help him, until he's exhausted or behind some schedule; then you would only be taking up slack in the household, and your help could be accounted for by something besides your love alone. And surely you won't imply, by your helping her, that your wife is inept or ignorant or lazy, that if anything's going to get done in the household you have to do it. "Volunteering" speaks the opposite of criticism (which the marriage can do without); it speaks love (which the marriage needs). No, you didn't have to do this. Nothing in all the world argued that you should. But you did.

Who cooks regularly? Let the other sometimes cook.

Who does the laundry? Who drives the children around? Who scrapes and paints the house? Who maintains the car? Makes the beds? Rakes leaves? Cleans up after parties? Throws parties for the children? Stands in lines at banks, the license bureau, the post office? Let the other sometimes choose to do these things—willingly, gladly, with unassailable dignity.

And so shall that other say in deeds: "I" and "love" and "you"—all three.

I remember you, Thanne, in flashes, in frozen images all throughout these eighteen years. It's as though I have snapshots of you on the wall beside me. The times are fixed by the love that shone in them, caught them, and kept them in my memory.

You are standing in the huge garden we raised in the country, your face turned toward me. You're wearing shorts and a halter and a granny apron. The apron is caught up by the corners in each of your hands, and you are leaning slightly backward because the apron is lumpy-full of a load of tomatoes. It is a summer's abundance. You are smiling at me, calling, I think, some casual word. I don't remember the word. Rather, I remember this, that your thin body, so willingly bearing so swollen a load, pierced me with a sudden, nearly painful love. I thought, "I was the one who desired the garden. But you are the one who picks tomatoes, and you know how to preserve them."

And then there are two memories, side by side:

I am standing at the kitchen door, holding the publisher's letter that promises to print my book. You've just stopped me to ask an earnest question. Your face is upturned, your eyes dead on mine. "Wally," you say, touching the letter, meaning the book, "this isn't going to come between us, is it?" I am surprised by the intensity of the question and deny that anything should come between us. "Well," you say, not fully convinced, not wholly persuaded by this occupation of mine, "you're an author now." Did you have second thoughts about my desire to write?

Well, but the second memory is of the interior of our house when I happen to be home, once, and you are not. You've rearranged the furniture, and I stand gazing at the change you've made. I'm shaking my head. I'm shaking my head over you, astonished by your kindness. This house has two bedrooms; one is the children's, one is ours, and these are the only two rooms with doors and privacy. But here, in what used to be the sitting room, is all our bedroom furniture—and what used to be our bedroom has become a study, in which I am invited to write. Thanne! You've given up your bedroom. How can I answer that kind of love? I can't. I can only bow my head and stand in its light. And write.

The more I look at these memories, the more I realize that their radiance is unearthly, though you are no more than an earthly woman. It's a nimbus, Thanne, a divinity. It's a sort of cloud of glory that shines around my remembering and our marriage.

You are standing in the doorway of my study, so shy, so small and shy. I have turned from the typewriter to see you. For a full minute we look at each other in silence. Then you walk to where I sit. You touch my shoulder. "Wally," you say, "will you hug me?" I rise and I do hug you with all my might, because you have just brought me the pure and radiant gift of forgiveness. What can I do with such a gift? Receive it. Take it, and no more.

Again: you are driving me home from St. Louis, where I've just had an emergency appendectomy; and it isn't so much that you came immediately to be with me and to bring me home. It's the utter gentleness with which you do it. You, Thanne, make a gift of gentleness, the assurance that there is nothing else in all

*the world you should be doing now but driving me home. Your
spirit says, "You will be well." And what is that to me? Why, it is
the gift of faith to me. I will indeed be well. In all my parts and in
my spirit and before the God whose care you witness unto me, I
will be well.*

*Again: in my memory we are sitting on the living room sofa,
one friend with us, an African named Farai Gambiza. Between
us is a document and a question. The document is from a small,
inner-city church. The question is whether I will be its pastor.
The salary offered would be something of a difficulty for a family of six; and besides, I've bounced by now through a whole
circus of professions, and this last would require that I go away
to school—again. In my memory of the occasion, we are sitting.
I am listening. You are speaking. And I, by the grace of God, am
learning.*

GRACE

The sixth task, gifting and volunteering, introduces, maintains, and images divine grace in the marital relationship. Can
there be a better reason to perform it than this?

The Lord God established *two* covenants with the people, but
the second was the more merciful of the two and the lovelier.

At Mount Sinai God first set up a conditional covenant, a contract wherein he promised to keep Israel and to be their God so
long as they obeyed his laws and remained loyal—faithful—to
him. God's faithfulness to his promises depended upon the people's faithfulness to God; the people's faithfulness would be re-
warded by God's. It was an exchange, both legal and reasonable,
a perpetual transaction in which each party gave to get, earned
what was received.

In many respects, marriage vows are like this first covenant.
Much of the marriage relationship is an exchange, faithfulness
for faithfulness, giving and getting mixed together. It is reasonable and legal, a contract. What the spouse gives and does within
and for the marriage can be traced back to clear sources—to his
promises, to his responsibilities and obligations in the relationship, to the benefits he expects to realize, or else to his partner's worth, work, and *her* investment in the relationship. Under
this sort of contract, by this most common marital status,
nothing comes from nothing. Everything has its price and logical
purpose.

But God's first covenant with the people failed. More precisely, the people failed the covenant, breaking it, disobeying,

chasing after other gods, killing its spirit in external, hypocritical service. God could, then, have himself kept the terms of the contract and abandoned them; he had that right, even according to human principles. Instead, the dear God revealed another characteristic besides a righteous adherence to laws. He manifested mercy, a perfect love; he canceled the old covenant with another one, altogether different, altogether new, in which the obligations were altogether one-sided, altogether *his*. He chose to love people unworthy of his love; he chose to be the God of the undeserving. "While we were yet helpless," says Paul, "at the right time Christ died for the ungodly. . . . God shows his love for us in that while we were yet sinners Christ died for us." The new covenant was offered in the blood of Jesus Christ.

No longer is there a giving for a getting; we give absolutely nothing to get this love. No longer is it an exchange, faithfulness for faithfulness; God was faithful to the faith*less*, to sinners. No longer is the act of God reasonable or even legal; rather, it is the abandonment of law itself. It is gratuitous, a perfectly free giving on his part, to save the "weak," "ungodly" transgressors of the covenant: instead of holding them to terms, he dismissed the terms from them.

This new relationship is one in which something indeed comes from nothing, since we the people neither deserved nor could earn what we received from God, and since the divine gift cannot be traced back even to the first promises of God. It can be traced back to nothing rational, nothing radical—nothing but his love. This relationship is called *Grace*.

Likewise, in the marriage there may be a new covenant.

Gifting your spouse, volunteering *whether he deserves it or not,* for no reason whatsoever, for no payment in exchange, fufilling thereby no law, no courtesy, no obligation, but doing it gratuitously, perfectly freely, for his sake alone, regardless of his work, his worth, or his investment in the relationship; giving him something for nothing—this is *Grace*. This displaces the marriage contract again and again with newness. And this images in action the divine face of the Lord Jesus Christ. As Jesus loved, so do you show the same love to your spouse.

Whereas the contract is (and will continue to be, so long as you live in this fallen world) conditional, your gifting and your volunteering is unconditional. It depends on nothing but love itself. And if this in any way means being "faithful till death," it means being faithful *to God* within the marriage, to God's manner, his mercy, and his new covenant—but for the sake of your spouse. Do you see the richness of this marriage work, this task?

It invites the loving God to come and dwell between you, and it is he who empowers you to do so unworldly and irrational an act as to give for nothing in return, to set yourself aside for your partner's sake, to die a little that she might live a little more.

When God loved the unlovable, he made us lovely after all.

Why will you give rosebuds to your wife? Because she is already lovely? No, not always—but to make her so. The one who is loved, she is the lovely one.

Dear Thanne:

It hasn't been lost on me. This is the message of all my remembering—that none of it has gone unrecognized.

No thanks can balance the abundance or the purity of it. No writing can account for the mystery or the strength of it these eighteen years. Who knows what causes it? But I have lived in its virtue; my life has been revived again and again by its merciful coming, unbidden, undeserved—and I have learned to name it after all. The gifts that you have given me, they've taught me its name. Its name is Love. You love me.

What would we have done if you hadn't found ways to let me know? Oh, we would have survived well enough. But we wouldn't have been so rich.

We would have made a marriage of it, I am sure. But I wouldn't have seen the living face of my Lord Jesus Christ so clearly or so closely.

Thanne, I love you. I love you, too.